To Our Dear Friend Michael:

Happiest of Birthdays —

Love,
Kevin Davis

5/25/77
San Francisco

*Lucy & Ricky
& Fred & Ethel*

Lucy & Ricky & Fred & Ethel

THE STORY OF
I Love Lucy

BART ANDREWS

E. P. DUTTON & CO., INC. | NEW YORK

Library of Congress Cataloging in Publication Data

Andrews, Bart.
Lucy and Ricky and Fred and Ethel: the story of "I Love Lucy."

1. I Love Lucy.   I. Title   II. Title: I Love Lucy.
PN1992.77.I253A5   791.45′7   76-22170

ISBN: 0-525-14990-2

Published simultaneously in Canada
by Clarke, Irwin & Company Limited, Toronto and Vancouver

To my mother and father.
For over thirty years of fine tuning,
I thank you, with love.

ACKNOWLEDGMENTS

This book, obviously, could not have happened without the extraordinary influence of Lucille Ball, Desi Arnaz, Vivian Vance, and the late, great William Frawley. Equally significant have been the incredible contributions made to the TV sitcom form by Jess Oppenheimer, Madelyn Pugh Martin Davis, and Bob Carroll, Jr.— the three creators of *I Love Lucy* who were clearly the unsung heroes in this holocaust of hilarity. To them all, I owe my greatest, most heartfelt debt of gratitude.

I must thank the entire staff of Viacom for its cooperation and assistance, above and beyond the call of duty, particularly Carolyn McAteer and Todd R. Gaulocher of the New York office.

Also the nice people at *TV Guide*, especially Barbara Bowers in New York and Jeannie Kalla in Los Angeles, whose addiction to *I Love Lucy* is almost as severe as her fetish for *All My Children*.

Thanks also to all those persons who granted interviews in connection with the research for this volume, especially Marc Daniels, Bill Asher, Eliot Daniel, and Elois Jenssen, to name just a few; nods to Mary McCartney, William V. Dunn, Annelen Hughes, Judy and Jerry Ervin, Bill Blackbeard, Gloria Foster, and Christopher Sergel, Jr., for their assorted favors and kindnesses; a special vote of appreciation to William Ballin of American Export Lines for helping me track down Allison S. Graham, the company's former publicity director; to Maurine Christopher, the talented radio/TV editor of *Advertising Age;* to Carmine Santullo at Sullivan Productions, Inc.; and to Donald M. DeLuccio, president of the "We *Still* Love Lucy Fan Club," for helping to keep the *Lucy* legend alive.

I can't possibly overlook the likes of a few special *I Love Lucy* fans: Ira Steingroot, the team of Peter J. Black and Rory Schwartz (their combined memories would put any elephant to shame), and, especially, Rick Carl for his truly matchless, sincere, and thoughtful efforts.

Finally, I wish to express my deep appreciation to my patient, talented, and resourceful editor, Bill Whitehead, whom I hereby forgive for not owning a TV set; and, of course, Brad Dunning, my dedicated assistant—without him, I never would have made it through this assignment in one piece.

BART ANDREWS

Los Angeles, California
July 1, 1976

Lucy & Ricky
& Fred & Ethel

1

Twenty-five years ago at a posh dinner party in New York's elegant Gramercy Park district, a prominent public relations specialist was overheard to say, "We've just bought a little thing being made out on the Coast . . . a situation comedy with Lucille Ball and her husband—whatsizname. I don't know if it will amount to anything."

That "little thing" turned out to be the most popular, most watched, most talked about television program of the 1950s: *I Love Lucy.* And "whatsizname"—Desi Arnaz, of course—soon became TV's most successful entrepreneur of mirth, the brains behind not only Miss Ball's million-dollar laugh machine, but also fifty or sixty other prime-time series like *The Untouchables, Our Miss Brooks, December Bride,* etc., etc., etc.—enough film to stretch all the way from Hollywood to Nigeria, where, incidentally, *I Love Lucy* is still running.

The Desilu empire, dissolved officially in 1967 when it was sold to the Gulf & Western conglomerate, blossomed from a tiny, inauspicious stripling of a situation comedy that, just prior to its debut in October 1951, *TV Guide* modestly described as a show "revolving around problems arising in a household where the wife is stagestruck and the orchestra leader husband thinks she should stay home." Hardly something to rush right out and buy a new twelve-inch Motorola for.

But in a short six months, or twenty-six episodes later, *I Love*

Lucy became the first television program to be seen in ten million homes. In fact the April 7, 1952, broadcast was viewed in 10,600,000 households, according to the American Research Bureau (ARB), one of the five rating services operating in the early 1950s. That figure might not seem overwhelming by today's mass media standards, but remember that at the start of 1952 there were only fifteen million TV sets in operation in the United States.

In New York, *Lucy* was the Number One show after only four months, ranking well ahead of Arthur Godfrey, *Your Show of Shows,* Milton Berle, and *Fireside Theatre.*

Writing about *I Love Lucy* in the *New York Times,* the dean of TV critics Jack Gould observed: "The series has engendered as much public interest as anything since the days when the world stood still every evening to hear *Amos 'n' Andy* on the radio."

For, indeed, if the world stood still for *Amos 'n' Andy,* America came to a grinding halt every Monday night when *I Love Lucy* came on the air.

The *Lucy* mania was so widespread that the telephone company actually reported a "substantial reduction" in calls during that half-hour period. Families without TV sets crowded into neighbors' living rooms to watch. If the nearest set happened to be a taxi ride away, fans in New York City might have been out of luck: Cabbies disappeared into bars to catch a glimpse of Lucy and Ricky and Fred and Ethel uncoiling their latest plot, and didn't turn on their ignitions again until 9:31 P.M.

The mammoth Marshall Field department store in Chicago switched its evening shopping hours from Mondays to Thursdays when it became financially clear that the biggest clearance sale in the store's history was no match for *I Love Lucy.* So that customers and employees could watch the show, the management put up a sign in the window on State Street declaring: "We love Lucy, too, so we're closing on Monday nights."

Likewise, doctors and dentists in many cities changed their Monday-evening visiting hours to prevent cancellation of appointments by *Lucy* fans.

PTA leaders in Lynn, Massachusetts, picketed their local CBS affiliate, demanding that *I Love Lucy* be broadcast at an earlier hour so schoolchildren could get to bed at a reasonable hour.

Members of a Lion's Club in Santa Barbara, California,

chipped in and bought a TV set, then installed it in their meeting room, declaring a half-hour recess so everybody could watch *Lucy*.

George J. Van Dorp, water commissioner of Toledo, Ohio, had his own rating system in 1953. A glance at a chart from the main water pumping station, a few seconds work with his slide rule, and he could tell that *I Love Lucy* was Toledo's favorite TV show. Van Dorp contended, "There's an amazing correlation between the degree of attention that people pay to a television show and the amount of water they use. While *I Love Lucy* is being shown, pressure in the main is consistently high. As soon as the commercial comes on, the pressure drops because people are using the bathroom or whatever. That lasts only one minute: I don't need a watch; all I do is look at the water-pressure gauge. When the show is over and people once again avail themselves of water services, the pressure sometimes drops as much as thirty percent, enough to burst a twelve-inch main." Checking charts, Van Dorp was able to report, for instance, that on April 20, 1953, when Lucy and Desi went on the air, use of water in Toledo dropped thirteen percent, and at the end of the episode ("No Children Allowed"), it shot upward by twenty-one percent. Translating for us landlubbers, Mr. Van Dorp decreed: "*I Love Lucy* is always the leader under the Van Dorp system."

Whatever rating system you subscribed to, *I Love Lucy* came out ahead. The series won more than two hundred awards, including five Emmys (it was nominated twenty-three times) and the coveted George Foster Peabody Award for "recognition of distinguished achievement in television."

One of the reactions to the show was its tremendous children's following. Awards poured in from sixth-grade classes at one school, from a seventh-grade class at another. Lucille Ball and Desi Arnaz were constantly asked to judge high school contests of one kind or another.

Formal studies, such as one sponsored by the Nuffield Foundation in England in 1956, proved that *Lucy* was the favorite of seventy-three percent of all thirteen-to-fourteen-year-old girls.

Boys loved *Lucy,* too. A junior high school teacher in Fort Madison, Iowa, recalled a particular fifteen-year-old student who arrived fifteen minutes late, at 9:15, every morning. When he asked

4

the boy why he was so consistently tardy, the young man non-chalantly replied, "Because *I Love Lucy* isn't over 'til nine o'clock."

Today, in certain cities like San Diego, California, fans can enjoy *I Love Lucy* four times daily: twice on local station XETV (Channel 6) at noon and 5 P.M., and twice on Los Angeles' KTTV (Channel 11) at 9 A.M. and 7 P.M., reception permitting.

Such mass exposure once prompted TV writer Harold Mehling to speculate: "At last report there was no one left in the United States who has not seen at least one of Lucy's escapades, and arrangements may shortly be made to exhibit them to the newborn as soon as they can see."

These so-called escapades (192 of them), if screened in succession without interruption, would consume four days, seven hours, and fifteen minutes. They also are available dubbed in Japanese, Portuguese, Italian, French, and Spanish (*Yo Quiero a Lucy*) from Viacom (formerly CBS Films, Inc.), which promotes the reruns by claiming: "Today more than ever, Lucy's madcap antics with Desi Arnaz, Vivian Vance, and William Frawley are praised as priceless performances with timeless appeal. Show a new generation of viewers the queen of comedy in her finest half hours. They'll repay you with an audience worth a king's ransom."

In Washington, D.C., the series holds the record for the "most reruns of a TV show," with a grand total, as of 1974, of 2,904 telecasts of the original 179 half-hour *I Love Lucy* episodes. It is also "the most widely watched program at 6 P.M.," according to an ARB report, "when you would expect most television sets to be tuned to a news broadcast."

Hedda Hopper, who was in the Capitol the night Little Ricky Ricardo was born (January 19, 1953), said, "I remember that the 1953 inauguration party that Colonel Robert R. McCormick, publisher of the Chicago *Tribune*, gave came to a temporary halt while everybody had to watch *I Love Lucy* in silence. Bertie was wild about the show and wanted to witness the birth."

Incidentally, this particular episode is listed in a United States history book as "one of the great emotional events of the decade."

When presidential candidate Adlai Stevenson cut in on *I Love Lucy* for a five-minute campaign pitch in the fall of 1952, his office

5

was flooded with hate mail. One lady, obviously a Republican, wrote: "I love Lucy. I like Ike. Drop dead." Stevenson chose not to preempt *Lucy* when he ran again in 1956.

I Love Lucy fans are, from all available indications, a hearty lot. When WNEW-TV, New York City's Channel 5, decided to cancel the twice-daily telecasts of the vintage series in September 1975, a picket line formed in front of the station's East Sixty-seventh Street studio. Mail also poured in, ordering Lucy's immediate reinstatement.

One letter, handwritten in pencil by a young fan from New Jersey and addressed to the "Program Manger [*sic*]," said, "Dear Sir: I am eight and a half years old. I am writing to find out why you took off my favorite TV show. . . . It was a very bad idea to take off Lucy. She has the best show. Even my mother watches the show. So you better put it back on because evryone [*sic*] loves Lucy."

Reporting the problem in the second anniversary issue of the "We *Still* Love Lucy Fan Club" newsletter, president Donald M. DeLuccio informed his burgeoning membership: "I've been receiving distressing letters from both members and nonmembers in the New York area concerning a local station no longer showing *I Love Lucy* reruns. The channel informed me that they were just giving the show a six-month to one-year rest. If any of you from other areas have the same problem, simply contact the local station and find out why the show has been taken off. If they didn't do it for a similar reason—panic!"

Somewhat overwhelmed by the public reaction to his decision, Len Ringquist, vice-president and director of television programs at the New York Metromedia outlet, commented, "I used my best judgment in taking off the series. I wanted to rest her a little bit. There is something to be said about overexposure. Lucy is an institution; I want her to remain so. Her *I Love Lucy* series has been Channel 5's keystone, the anchor onto which we have scheduled all of our other programming for fifteen years."

Fifteen years ago, *I Love Lucy* actually was banned on Saudi Arabia's single TV station located at Dhahran. It seems that the sitcom depicted a local taboo: Lucille Ball "dominated" Desi Arnaz in too many episodes, and since the Saudi women traditionally were subservient to their men, *Lucy* was persona non grata

6

as far as the Arabs were concerned. Times have changed, though, and today Saudi Arabia is one of the eight foreign countries still beaming *I Love Lucy*. The others are Nigeria, Kenya, Mexico, Argentina, Costa Rica, Canada, and Ecuador. The show remains a favorite in Latin America partly because of Desi Arnaz, but in emerging African nations, Lucy has become a favored name for newborn girls.

In general, comedy is the most difficult TV form to market overseas. According to syndication specialist Charles McGregor, "Some of the American humor just doesn't translate to foreign audiences."

Lucy's basic plot, which goes Ricky *vs.* Lucy, Husband *vs.* Wife, Men *vs.* Women, can be understood even in Zulu. Lucille Ball agrees: "Because of the physical stuff which is not very difficult to understand the comedy of—if you don't mind ending in a preposition. Foreign viewers don't have to follow the words. There's a lot of action, not just spoken gags."

What made *I Love Lucy* one of TV's four all-time hits, according to media specialists and television historians (the others are Milton Berle, *The Beverly Hillbillies,* and *All in the Family*)?

TV writer Jack Sher with his wife, Madeline, put it this way: "The captivating thing about Lucy and Ricky is the fact that they hold a mirror up to every married couple in America. Not a regular mirror that reflects the truth, nor a magic mirror that portrays fantasy. But a Coney Island kind of mirror that distorts, exaggerates, and makes vastly amusing every little incident, foible, and idiosyncrasy of married life."

Jess Oppenheimer, one of the show's three creators, harbors the same opinion: "The funniest single line ever uttered on *I Love Lucy* came when Lucy summed up in epigram what happens to a lot of marriages: 'Since we said, "I do," there are so many things we don't.'"

In Jess' learned opinion, the line was not particularly funny in itself, but it gave viewers a sudden, deep insight into themselves—a shock relieved by means of laughter. An interesting sidelight is that this line was continued in the premiere episode of the series, "The Girls Want to Go to a Nightclub."

Charles Pomerantz, a former Philip Morris PR consultant and now Lucille Ball's personal press agent, insists the series had "heart": "When you went to a rehearsal and looked at the crew and other people there, half of them would put their hands over their hearts—a signal that the episode they were working on had it, heart. No matter how outrageous the outcome of a segment, everything had to be believable up to that last great hilarious moment of truth."

Pomerantz's client, Miss Ball, agrees: "Believability. I had to believe things that were childlike. I had to have a childish belief in everything I did because it was so exaggerated. If I had to bake a loaf of bread that was literally thirteen feet long, I believed it. It could be dumb—well it *was* dumb. It was baked in a bakery, and then it came out of my oven which was really the only unbelievable thing about it."

After the first season of *I Love Lucy* was over, Jack Gould made this statement: "The distinction lies in its skillful presentation of the basic element of familiarity. If there is one universal theme that knows no age limitations and is recognizable to young and old, it is the institution of marriage—and more particularly the day-to-day trials of husband and wife. It is this single story line above all others with which the audience can most readily identify itself.

"*I Love Lucy* has no monopoly on the humor inherent in marriage," Gould continued in his *New York Times* column. "The idea is as old as the theater itself. But it is the extraordinary discipline and intuitive understanding of farce that gives *Lucy* its engaging lilt and lift.

"Every installment begins with a plausible and logical premise. Casually the groundwork is laid for the essential motivation: Lucy *vs.* Ricky. Only after a firm foundation of credibility has been established is the element of absurdity introduced. It is in the smooth transition from sense to nonsense that *I Love Lucy* imparts both a warmth and a reality to the slapstick romp which comes as the climax."

Put more simply, *Lucy* was marriage projected to larger-than-life size, but never distorted so that it lost its hold on the viewer. Through the art of cleverly devised exaggeration, Lucy and Ricky (and, to a great extent, Fred and Ethel) put marriage into sharp focus.

A social psychologist who belongs to the school that main-

CREDIT: JUDY AND JERRY ERVIN

tains the American woman dominates the American man and despises him for letting her do it, offers his reasoning for the *I Love Lucy* appeal: "The extraordinary success of *Lucy* is based upon its ability to assuage two guilt factors deep in the American subconscious. A, the woman is in despair over the state to which she has reduced the man. Therefore she thanks heaven that in the Ricardo house, at least, Ricky's the boss [despite the thinking of Saudi Arabian TV bigwigs in the 1950s] and Lucy knows it and the American woman knows it and that makes all of them together glad. For a half-hour, anyway.

"B, somewhere in the background of most Americans there is a foreign-born relative whose alien accent embarrassed them, and they're sorry for it now. But Ricky speaks with a foreign accent, yet everybody respects him. By sharing their respect for Ricky, the audience appeases its conscience."

How does Ricky (Desi Arnaz) sum up this mass infatuation? Very simply. "*I Love Lucy* wasn't slick or cerebral—and it never insulted anybody," the fifty-nine-year-old Arnaz acknowledges. "It had one mission: to make people laugh honestly."

In 1966 there was one man who wasn't laughing about *I Love Lucy,* Fred W. Friendly, president of CBS News. On February 10, the United States Senate was conducting hearings on the Vietnam conflict during which former Ambassador George Kennan was being interrogated by Senator J. William Fulbright. Feeling a moral compunction, Friendly wanted to preempt a morning rerun of *I Love Lucy* in order to air the hearings live, as ABC and NBC were doing. His immediate superior, John A. Schneider, would not permit it.

"Not running *Lucy* at 10 A.M.," Friendly bitterly recalls, "would have meant a loss of about five thousand dollars." Five days later, Friendly resigned and hasn't loved *Lucy* since.

It is not surprising to note that *Lucy* enjoyed a better rating that infamous winter morning than the Senate hearings televised by the competition. But then again, it isn't surprising that thirteen years before, more people watched *I Love Lucy* on the occasion of Little Ricky's birth than the 1953 inauguration of the thirty-fourth President of the United States, Dwight D. Eisenhower, or the coronation of Queen Elizabeth six months later.

At one time you could buy official *I Love Lucy* aprons and

genuine *I Love Lucy* dolls. Thirty-two thousand white, heart-bedecked aprons and eighty-five thousand dolls were grabbed up in one thirty-day period in late 1952. One year later a Little Ricky doll made its appearance in department and toy stores, and their maker couldn't keep up with the reorders. Neither could a furniture manufacturer who sold a whopping one million *I Love Lucy* bedroom suites in just ninety days! Years later, a Connecticut real estate agent chose as a selling point "a cocktail table that is the replica of the one on *I Love Lucy*" in trying to rent a summer cottage.

Three thousand retail outlets carried Lucille Ball dresses, sweaters, and blouses; ditto for Desi Arnaz robes and smoking jackets (which had gone out of style, but because of *Lucy* had a resurgence in popularity); He and She pajamas, which the Arnazes were forced to wear on the show according to merchandising agreements, Desi Denims, Lucy Lingerie, costume jewelry, desk and chair sets, three-dimensional picture magazines with Polaroid eyeglasses, nursery furniture (after Little Ricky was born), dressing gowns, toys, games. Conceivably, an enterprising architect designed an *I Love Lucy* house; it had everything . . . but a toilet, just like on the TV show.

If you couldn't catch *Lucy* on Monday nights, you could enjoy her antics every morning in one of the 132 newspapers that carried the King Features Syndicate comic strip (December 8, 1952, to May 30, 1955), drawn by Bob Oskner and written by Lawrence Nadler.

If you possessed neither TV set nor newspaper, you could have listened to one of the *I Love Lucy* records on the radio. Columbia released in 1953 "There's a Brand New Baby at Our House" and the *I Love Lucy* theme song, both sung by Desi Arnaz with Paul Weston and his orchestra and the Norman Luboff Choir. Both records soared to the top of the Hit Parade within ten days of their release.

If you were too young to stay up for the show, there were thirty-five *I Love Lucy* comic books released from 1954 to 1962 by Dell Comics, all meant to keep you laughing at Lucy's lunatic antics (at ten cents an antic).

If you were really into *I Love Lucy* and could have persuaded your stagestruck friends to join you, the Dramatic Publishing Company of Chicago would have sold you copies of one-act plays based on various *I Love Lucy* episodes. The amateur thespians at West View High School in Pittsburgh, Pennsylvania, had to hang up a SRO sign both performance nights.

If you happened to have found yourself in Las Vegas in January 1955, you could have witnessed a musical version of *I Love Lucy* as performed by Lucille Ball, Desi Arnaz, Vivian Vance, and William Frawley at the Tropicana Hotel.

Even if you didn't write one of the ten thousand fan letters Lucy and Desi received each month, or send one of the five hundred gifts they opened the day after Desi, Jr.'s, birth, or were among the sixty thousand fans who had the privilege of seeing an *I Love Lucy* filmed in Hollywood, you'll want to remember Lucy and Ethel working at Kramer's Kandy Kitchen, and Lucy being caught up in a wine vat in Turo, Italy, and the Ricardos and Mertzes loose in Hollywood.

I promise you that these reruns will not be interrupted by commercials.

2

Lucille Ball and Desi Arnaz had been married a decade in 1950 when CBS told their manager, Donald W. Sharpe: "We want to transfer Lucy's radio show, *My Favorite Husband,* to television. Jell-O will continue its sponsorship but only if Lucy and Richard Denning continue as the leads."

Disenchanted with her film career, and particularly with a bad deal at Twentieth Century-Fox, Lucy had escaped to radio to headline a comedy series based on Isabel Scott Rorick's novel, *Mr. and Mrs. Cugat.* Since the summer of 1947, she had played the role of Liz to Dick Denning's George, her fictional, midwestern banker husband.

When CBS came through with the TV offer, Lucille Ball was not thrilled with the terms. She had nothing personal against Denning, whom she liked very much, but she wanted her real-life husband Desi to play the role in the projected video version. Therefore, loyal Lucy ordered manager Sharpe to relay her demands to the network.

"No," the television officials responded quite positively. "We don't think viewers will accept Desi, a Latin with a thick Cuban accent, as the husband of a typical, redheaded American girl like Lucille Ball. Of course, we *adore* Lucy and want *her* to be in the TV show."

Mrs. Arnaz, then thirty-eight, was adamant: no Desi, no TV show. Her rather unprecedented devotion was born more of desperation than a desire to be stubborn. Coming as no great shock to anyone in or out of show business, the Arnazes' ten-year marriage, solidified by a Catholic wedding ceremony on June 19, 1949, was crumbling as the 1940s faded.

While Lucy was busy with her radio show and a few picture commitments, Desi was traveling around the country with his rumba band, doing mostly one-nighters. During this period of absence, the Hollywood couple talked daily by long-distance telephone. "We got into arguments," Lucille remembers. "And arguments simply cannot be resolved by long distance. Desi once figured our phone bill up to that time was about twenty-nine thousand dollars.

"The long-distance operators got so used to us that they kept joining in the conversation. Once when we were in the middle of a heated quarrel the operator's voice cut in to say, 'Now, enough of this argument! You two kiss and make up.' "

Lucille and Desi met in May 1940 at the Hollywood studios of RKO Pictures. Arnaz had been summoned to the West Coast to reprise his Broadway role as Manuelito in the movie version of the Richard Rodgers and Lorenz Hart musical *Too Many Girls*. The *New York Times* said of his stage debut: "As a South American broken field runner, Desi Arnaz is a good wooer of women." Director George Abbott introduced Desi to Lucy in the studio commissary one lunchtime.

"I didn't like her at first. She looked awful. Very tough," Desi says. "She was made up like a burlesque queen for a role in *Dance, Girl, Dance*."

Lucy did look pretty unusual. She was sporting a stage black eye she had received earlier that day in a rough-and-tumble scene with costar Maureen O'Hara. So when Abbott informed the twenty-three-year-old Desi that Lucille Ball would be playing the part of Consuelo Casey, the ingenue, in the *Too Many Girls* film version, he told the veteran director: "What kind of girl is this? She's no sweet, ingenue type."

Later that day, when the cast was called together for a briefing, the pair "met" again. This time Lucille was dressed in a yellow skirt and cashmere sweater, and Desi then turned to a studio employee and, in his Cuban accent, observed: "Wot a hunk o' woman!"

"I asked her if she knew how to rumba," Desi recounts, "and when she said no, I offered to teach her."

"Some line he had!" Lucy counters. "We went out all right, but all we did was sit and yak all night. Never got to dance once."

They fell in love almost immediately. "But the studio didn't want us to get married. The gossip columnists kept telling the reasons we shouldn't get married," Arnaz offers. "We spent the better part of our courtship telling each other it would hurt our careers."

Lucy completes the story: "We talked about marriage, but it seemed impossible. Then, on a personal appearance tour in the fall of 1940, I flew to New York where Desi happened to be playing with his band at the Roxy Theatre."

Lucille was met at the airport by a columnist who was bent on getting an interview to prove the actress and Cuban would never marry. After it was over, Desi surprised both Lucy and the columnist by proposing marriage. At 5 A.M. the next day, November 30, 1940, the couple drove to Greenwich, Connecticut, and at the Byram River Beagle Club at ten o'clock in the morning they were married by a justice of the peace.

As they drove back to New York City they heard a radio broadcast describing their marriage. When Desi led his bride onto the Roxy stage to explain why he had missed the first show, thousands of voices roared good wishes—and they were pelted with a barrage of rice, supplied to the crowd by the theater management.

Says Lucille: "I threw away all my conservativeness and took the plunge because I loved him. It was the most daring thing I ever did. Hollywood gave our marriage six months; I gave it six weeks!"

The "daring" redhead was born in Jamestown, New York, on August 6, 1911, to Fred and Desiree (De-De) Ball. He was an electrician whose job of stringing telephone wires carried him around the country; she was a concert pianist. When Lucille was only four, her father died of typhoid in Wyandotte, Michigan. De-De and Lucy moved back to New York State to the village of Celeron (near Jamestown) to live with Lucy's maternal grandfather, Fred C. Hunt.

From the time she was ten, the little traveler took summer jobs: "The first one was to lead a blind man around while both

15

of us sold soap. After that I worked as a soda jerk in a drugstore, as a salesgirl in a dress shop, and I sold hot dogs and popcorn in an amusement park." She even organized the neighborhood children to act out plays, using the family chicken coop for a stage. "I can't remember not wanting to perform."

De-De Ball, now eighty-four-years-old, remembers Lucille's first show business fling: "As a child, Lucille was in the Elks. They always put on little plays, and somehow she got into them. Then I was the producer of the plays in the school where she went. That's how we raised money for the things we wanted, like the senior class trip. Even then, Lucille had a faculty for choosing the part that would stand out. I'd tell her there was nothing to the part, but she'd come back with, 'I don't care. I want that part.' And I swear to God, she was right every time!"

By then, Grandpa Hunt had introduced his "Lucyball" (the family nickname) to the world of vaudeville. She loved the world of laughter and fantasy.

By the time Lucille had quit high school at age fifteen, she had staged virtually a one-man (woman) performance of *Charley's Aunt*. "I played the lead, directed it, cast it, sold the tickets, printed the posters, and hauled furniture to the school for scenery and props."

Jamestown citizens still remember her explosive personality with wide-eyed wonder; it took quite a while for the dust to settle in the little town near Buffalo when "Lucyball" finally left for Manhattan. Neighbors were horrified. Remembers Lucy's cousin Cleo, who was raised by De-De Ball and, hence, has a sisterlike relationship with Lucy: "De-De was never bound by the social conventions of the day. She didn't mind the ridicule of the neighbors. She allowed us to express ourselves. She taught us character, values, involvement. She operated on the theory that none of us would ever do anything to disgrace Grandpa Hunt. It was a relationship based on trust. She was the one who decided to let Lucille go to New York City at fifteen."

Lucy enrolled in the John Murray Anderson dramatic school (Bette Davis was the star pupil) and at the end of the first year of study, Anderson tactfully told De-De that her daughter should try another line of work.

Determined to make her teacher eat his words, Lucy went out

the next morning and landed a job in the chorus of the third road company production of *Rio Rita*. After five weeks of rehearsal, she was canned. The director's opinion was the same as her teacher's. A Ziegfeld aide then told her, "It's no use, Montana [Lucille's preferred nickname then]. You're not meant for show business. Why don't you go home?"

Lucy stayed. Three more chorus jobs followed, and she was fired from all of them. Her first job "on Broadway" was as a soda jerk in a west-side drugstore. (For that, she had experience.) In the meantime, she studied modeling, and finally graduated to become a model for Hattie Carnegie, the famous dress designer. As a hat model, Lucy called herself Diane Belmont, choosing the moniker in honor of the Belmont Park Race Track, a nearby Long Island horse arena.

An automobile accident sidetracked her for a few years (she spent eight months in a hospital and the next three years learning how to walk again), but she was back as a model when the ordeal was over. She was once the Chesterfield (cigarettes) poster girl on billboards blanketing New York.

It was now 1933, and Lucille Ball was twenty-two. She was no closer to an acting career than she had been seven years earlier when she impulsively left high school. One afternoon, while strolling up Broadway past the Palace Theatre, she met agent Sylvia Hahlo coming down from Sam Goldwyn's office. Sylvia grabbed Lucy and cried breathlessly: "How would you like to go to California? Goldwyn just picked twelve showgirls for an Eddie Cantor picture. Six weeks work. One of the girl's mothers has refused to let her go. They're desperate . . ."

At that time, famed musicals director Busby Berkeley was instrumental in selecting the so-called Goldwyn Girls. Before his recent death, he said: "Goldwyn called me in one day and said, 'I want you to come up to the projection room. I've made some tests of girls from New York and I want to see whether you like them.' We ran them and there were two girls that I liked very much. But Goldwyn didn't like them.

"The next morning I went by his office and asked his secretary, 'Mary, did he send for the two girls that he didn't like but I did?' She smiled and said, 'Yes, he did, Mr. Berkeley.' The two girls I had picked were Barbara Pepper and Lucille Ball."

Within a matter of days Lucy was aboard a westbound express train headed for Hollywood. The movie was *Roman Scandals,* and it was six months instead of six weeks in the making. Columbia Pictures soon signed her to a contract ($50 a week) as a stock player, and Lucille, convinced that her luck finally had turned, wired her family—mother, brother Fred, cousin Cleo, and Grandpa Hunt—to come and live with her. The morning after she'd sent for the family, the studio decided to dissolve its stock company. By the time the foursome arrived by bus, Lucy was toiling as an extra at Paramount.

Determined to make a name for herself in the movies, she landed a succession of bit parts in such films as *Moulin Rouge* and *The Affairs of Cellini,* and worked for three months with the Three Stooges. A role in *Roberta* impressed RKO officials who signed her to a contract. After a series of B pictures, she began making movies with comics like Jack Oakie, Joe Penner, and the Marx Brothers (*Room Service*). Her salary rose to $1,500 a week, and her hair, already turned blond from its original brown shade, now became a brilliant but indescribable hue that has been variously called "shocking pink" and "strawberry orange."

She appeared in other RKO films, among them *Dance, Girl, Dance.* It was while she was finishing photography on this Erich Pommer-directed movie that Lucille Ball, then twenty-eight, met Desi Arnaz, twenty-three.

The only child of a Cuban senator and the *Alcalde Modelo* (model mayor) of Santiago, Cuba, Desiderio Alberto Arnaz y de Acha, III, was born March 2, 1917. His mother, Dolores de Acha, was considered among the most beautiful women in Latin America.

Three ranches totaling one hundred thousand acres, a palatial home in the city, a private island in Santiago Bay, an armada of speedboats, a fleet of automobiles, and a stable of racehorses were all at the command of youthful Desi. By the time he was sixteen, he had become, by his own admission, a fathead. His future already had been planned for him by his father: He would attend the University of Notre Dame in Indiana, study law, and then return home to a ready-made practice.

His father's grandiose plans did not include the first Batista revolution in Cuba, which came on August 12, 1933. Papa Arnaz

18

Above: Cast of *Too Many Girls* (RKO, 1940); *left to right:* Richard Carlson, Lucille Ball, Desi Arnaz, Ann Miller, Hal LeRoy, Frances Langford, Eddie Bracken, Libby Bennett. *Right:* Lucy tending her 50-by-90-foot garden of victory vittles at the Chatsworth ranchette while Desi's away in the army.

was jailed instantly, his property confiscated. Within twenty-four hours, everything was gone except $500 Mrs. Arnaz had socked away. Young Desi and his mother fled to Miami where they devoted the next six months to efforts to free the elder Arnaz from prison. During this period Desi attended St. Patrick's High School in the beach city where one of his classmates was Sonny Capone, Al's son.

During this difficult period of adjustment, Desi worked at a number of odd jobs to help pay the rent at the dingy rooming house where his family lived. His first job was cleaning out canary cages for a local bird buff bent on selling the warblers in drugstores. Desi was paid twenty-five cents per cage.

He also worked at truck driving, train-yard checking, taxi driving, and bookkeeping. Desi spoke little English at first; once when ordering a meal at a restaurant he mistakenly got five bowls of soup.

In 1937 the show business bug bit. With a borrowed suit, he auditioned at the swanky Roney-Plaza Hotel in Miami Beach. The overflowing crowd cheered—they were his St. Pat classmates. Fooled, the owner hired Arnaz at a huge salary, $50 per week.

"My first band job was with the Siboney Septet. I don't know why it was called a septet since there were only five of us. I guess septet sounded better," Desi claims.

It was during this gig that Xavier Cugat spotted him and hired the handsome twenty-one-year-old as a singer for $35 a week. After a year's apprenticeship with Cugat, Desi decided to strike out on his own. After a few months, he was back in Florida where he bluffed his way into a new club, the swank La Conga Café, at a whopping $750-a-week salary.

The local critics agreed on Desi's meager musical gifts. "He was always offbeat," one of his bosses contended. "But he's an awfully nice guy—a clean-cut Latin."

Before too long, his good looks and effervescent humor landed his band in New York. There he was singled out by George Abbott and given a leading role as a Latin football player in the new stage musical *Too Many Girls*. When RKO bought the film rights, they beckoned Desi, along with co-players Richard Kolmar, Eddie Bracken, and Hal LeRoy, to Hollywood to reprise their Broadway roles. Pretty Marcy Wescott, who had the femme lead in the legit musical, did not go west. Her part in the film went to an RKO contract player, Lucille Ball.

Following Lucy and Desi's 1940 marriage, he had parts in two or three other pictures (his best was *Bataan,* directed by Tay Garnett), but as he puts it: "I didn't take well with movies and they didn't take well with me."

At the same time, Lucy's movie career was soaring. Her first really big break was in Damon Runyon's *The Big Street,* in which she portrayed a showgirl who was paralyzed from the hips down. She played the role so convincingly that she soon had every studio bidding for her services. On August 6, 1942 (her thirty-first birthday), Lucille signed with M-G-M who immediately cast her in the title role in *DuBarry Was a Lady,* with Gene Kelly.

Her proud Cuban husband, not content to loaf at the couple's San Fernando Valley home in Chatsworth and let Lucille be the breadwinner, hit the road again to make nightclub appearances. The enforced separation their respective jobs occasioned put their marriage on an erratic course, headed for divorce.

The crackup was postponed by World War II. Desi was drafted into the infantry and later transferred, because of a broken kneecap, to Army Special Service where he made sergeant and spent much of the war guiding U.S.O. troupes from one California camp to another.

But the war gave their marriage only temporary respite. Lucille sued for divorce in the fall of 1944, but the couple subsequently patched up their differences. But then the same old arguments about Desi's out-of-town engagements versus Lucy's movie career began all over again.

Lucy succeeded in keeping Desi home for two years in the late 1940s by approaching Bob Hope and suggesting that Desi and his orchestra replace the departing Stan Kenton on Hope's popular NBC radio show.

By this time Lucy was busy with her own radio show, *My Favorite Husband,* which CBS wanted to transfer to the new medium of television. That's when the Ball ultimatum was handed down: no Desi, no TV show. CBS, of course, balked. They thought Lucille was being obstinate. Jess Oppenheimer, Lucy's radio producer, liked the idea of a television show starring Lucy and Desi, but he could not convince the advertising agency men and the

21

broadcasting bigwigs. These rejections did not please Miss Ball who was more determined than ever to cast Desi as her TV spouse.

Richard Denning, Lucy's radio hubby, comments: "She said it would help her marriage. Also the show. And, of course, she was right."

The Arnazes finally decided to take themselves—husband and wife—directly to the people. "Let's go out and 'test' it," Lucille put in.

And that's just what they did. The Cuban and the redhead put together a series of slapstick routines involving a movie star who tries to join her bandleader husband's act. They armed themselves with a wardrobe of eccentric costumes and billed themselves as "Desi Arnaz & Band with Lucille Ball."

"If no one will give us a job together, we'll give ourselves one," Lucy reportedly told Desi before dreaming up the idea. The first thing they did was form Desilu Productions (their ranchette in Chatsworth already had been christened thusly). In order to go on the road, the pair needed more than an idea—they needed an act. Desi took the scheme to an old fishing friend, Pepito, the Spanish Clown. The famed showman concocted a few bits for Lucy and Desi to perform, and even taught them how to do the skits in a hotel room near San Diego.

"Pepito built me this incredible cello," Lucille explains. "It was an entire act. Real Rube Goldberg stuff. I pulled a stool out of it, a horn, a toilet plunger, gloves, flowers, a violin bow. I wore a fright wig and we set out on a twelve-week vaudeville tour."

The act opened at the Chicago Paramount Theatre on June 2, 1950. About their twenty-minute act, *Variety* commented: "One of the best bills to play house in recent months. Most of it revolves around Desi Arnaz and his frau, Lucille Ball, who have developed a sock new act.

"Turn really gets hilarious," the review continued, "when a Red Skelton-type character in oversized tails and crushed hat comes running down the aisle seeking an audition with the band. It breaks up the audience.

"Leader [Desi] brings on a group of horns, similar to those the seals play in circuses, and Miss Ball makes like a seal burping out the notes, flipping her tails and overlong sleeves, waddling on her tummy across the stage.

"For finale, she joins her Latin friend, dressed as a denizen of lower New York, in a green split skirt with spangles and sequins, and pops the eyes out of the first-row viewers with her hip-slinging activities to hyped beat of 'Cuban Pete.' "

Next the pair hit New York's famed Roxy Theatre. Following a one-week bill starring TV's Sid Caesar, Imogene Coca, and Faye Emerson, the Arnazes opened on Friday, June 9, 1950, for two full weeks. The New York reviews echoed the earlier Chicago reactions—all excellent. Lucille and Desi celebrated their tenth wedding anniversary on June thirteen in their Roxy dressing room, the same suite where Desi had carried Lucille over the threshold on November 30, 1940, after their Greenwich, Connecticut, ceremony.

Lucy recalls an incident that took place during the New York run: "I had been taught about props by Buster Keaton. Especially attention to detail which was the most important thing. He taught me that my prop is my jewel case. Never entrust it to a stagehand or anyone else. Never let it out of your sight when you travel, and rehearse with it all week. 'Honey,' he told me, 'if you noodge it, you've lost the act.'

"Well, wouldn't you know it, it happened at the Roxy. I was supposed to run down that seven-mile aisle when some maniac sprang my cello by leaping up and yelling, 'I'm that woman's mother! She's letting me starve!' It scared me to death. I ad-libbed around it, and I am one lousy ad-libber," Miss Ball reveals.

After playing only a few days in New York, Lucy began to feel ill. "Suddenly I feel tired all the time," she confided to Desi one night after the last show. At first they believed it was merely the fatigue of performing seven shows daily, including a belly-flop entrance at each performance. But when the illness persisted she went to see a doctor.

"Are you pregnant?" he asked. The thought hadn't entered into Lucy's mind. She had had a miscarriage in her first year of marriage, and for nine years after that she had been unable to conceive. She underwent a thorough physical, including the rabbit test for pregnancy. It was a Friday, and the results would not be available until Monday morning at the earliest.

As it turned out, they learned the results sooner than the doctor. Between shows on Sunday night, she and Desi tuned to

Walter Winchell's weekly broadcast, and were dumbfounded when he announced: "Flash! After ten years, Lucille Ball and Desi Arnaz are expecting a bundle from heaven."

They were. An anxious laboratory worker had reported the news to Winchell first. The Arnazes made immediate plans. They canceled the last half of their tour (they were supposed to play the London Palladium) and slightly revised Lucy's onstage acrobatics. "In the seal bit, I no longer wiggled around on my stomach," she said. "But I still did backflips and barked."

In newspaper accounts dated June 27, 1950, Lucy reported that she would be expecting the child in January. She and Desi rested up a few days in New York before heading for their next vaudeville stand, a four-day engagement at the Paramount Hotel in Buffalo (June 30–July 3). After that they played the Riverside Theatre in Milwaukee, opening July 6. It was the theater's first vaudeville bill in weeks, and it was breaking records with a hefty $30,000 grossed in a matter of a few days.

After closing in Wisconsin, they flew back to California on an American Airlines flight, and as soon as Lucy reached their home in Chatsworth, she went to bed. She still wasn't feeling right. Within two days, she was rushed to Cedars of Lebanon Hospital in Hollywood where a team of doctors tried for a week to save the baby. On July 26, just a month after making the baby announcement in New York, Lucy suffered a miscarriage, her second.

"I need say little about that," Lucy injects. "It is one of the most tragic and shattering experiences a woman and her husband can have. I received thousands [2,867] of letters from women and girls who said, 'Try again, Lucille. You'll be lucky next time.' I thanked everyone personally, although it took me five months to do it."

The couple escaped to Del Mar, a favorite seaside resort town north of San Diego, where they tried to shake off the trauma of the tragedy. But Lucille still had her *My Favorite Husband* commitment and a number of solo TV appearances to fulfill, so she plunged back into her work while at the same time prodding manager Don Sharpe: "Please find a way for Desi and me to do a television show together. *Please*."

In late October 1950, three months after losing her unborn baby, Lucy discovered she was pregnant again. Determined not to take chances this time, she canceled all of her engagements except the radio show, which was relatively easy to do.

"And then it was decided," Lucille Ball recounts, "that, unless Desi and I could act together in the future, I would never act again."

3

By late December 1950, Don Sharpe had negotiated a deal with CBS for a pilot film starring Lucille Ball and Desi Arnaz. The West Coast director of network programs, Dartmouth-educated Harry S. Ackerman, was impressed by the excellent reviews Lucy and Desi had collected on their road tour several months before. However, Ackerman's boss, William S. Paley, who ran CBS from its corporate headquarters at 485 Madison Avenue in New York, was not enthusiastic and, therefore, refused to underwrite the cost of the test film. Instead, he ordered Ackerman to advise Sharpe and the Arnazes that CBS would be glad to sell them air time if they could get their proposed TV program off the ground.

As Lucy now puts it, "Everyone warned Desi and me that we were committing career suicide by giving up highly paid movie and band commitments to go for broke on TV, but it was either working together or good-bye marriage.

"It was then that I dreamed about Carole," the comedienne claims, referring to her late friend Carole Lombard. "She was wearing a very smart suit, and she said, 'Honey, go ahead. Take a chance. Give it a whirl!'"

Although Lucy was three months pregnant, she managed to complete *The Magic Carpet,* the last picture under her long-term Columbia contract (she was paid a hefty $85,000 for a six-day shooting hitch). Desi and his band had closed recently at the

Chi Chi, a swanky new Palm Springs nightclub, and were booked into Ciro's on Hollywood's Sunset Strip. Also, he had just debuted in his own CBS radio show, *Your Tropical Trip,* a half-music/half-game show mélange that Harry Ackerman put together for him. Despite these two birds in the hand, the Arnazes gambled on four in the bush as they kissed away an estimated $500,000 in movie and band commitments.

Under their new Desilu Productions banner, they borrowed $8,000 from General Amusement Corporation, the agency responsible for booking their vaudeville tour, matched it with eight grand of their own funds, and suddenly found themselves in the TV production business.

Jess Oppenheimer, who had served his Arnaz apprenticeship for three years as Lucy's producer and writer on the *My Favorite Husband* series, assumed the same dual position. Madelyn Pugh, Bob Carroll, Jr., and Oppenheimer then sat down to fashion a pilot script about the real-life Arnazes.

As Desi now says: "The first script wasn't about Ricky Ricardo at all. It was about a successful orchestra leader, Desi Arnaz, and his successful movie star wife, Lucille Ball."

In short, what the three comedy scribes had done was expand the essence of Lucy and Desi's vaudeville act, which they had written, by writing continuity scenes around Pepito's ingenious clown bits that had tested so successfully. These bits, which included the cello routine, the seal act, and the "Cuban Pete"/"Sally Sweet" medley, consumed twenty minutes of the half-hour test film. Hence it was more vaudeville than situation comedy.

To direct the pilot (which eventually yielded a poor-quality kinescope) Jess chose thirty-one-year-old Ralph Levy, a remarkably ingenius Yale graduate whom CBS had dispatched to Los Angeles in 1949 to set up its TV studios. When tapped for the Lucy-Desi assignment, Levy was busy producing and directing *The George Burns and Gracie Allen Show,* which was in its first TV season, and Jack Benny's radio series. In addition, he was producing Alan Young's television variety show (Young subsequently starred in *Mr. Ed*).

"I was anxious to direct Lucy's pilot because I had worked with her on Ed Wynn's TV show," Ralph remembers, referring to Lucy and Desi's television debut as a team a year earlier. "I recall

Jess and his writers having a lot of trouble with the script. They couldn't seem to get it just right. But it was clearly Lucille who walked away with the whole show. She was so professional. I recall having her parade around the living room with a lampshade on her head—trying to prove to Desi she could be a Ziegfeld girl. I didn't think she was walking quite the right way so I showed her how it should be done, not knowing that she had been a Ziegfeld girl at one time. Instead of telling me off, she simply watched good-naturedly.

"We shot the pilot at Studio A on Sunset Boulevard and Gower Street in Hollywood where all CBS radio and TV shows emanated. There were only two sets—one was a living room and the other was the nightclub where Desi worked. It was shot live, of course, as all TV shows were being done then. There was no tape yet. Later, the images were recorded on film from a TV screen, providing us with the required kinescope."

The pilot version, which incidentally went to New York without a title, did not contain two key elements that eventually helped make *I Love Lucy* such a hit—characters Fred and Ethel Mertz.

To serve as Desi's best friend and confidant, Oppenheimer cast Jerry Hausner to play Jerry, the agent. The forty-one-year-old character actor and ex-vaudevillian had played parts on Lucy's *My Favorite Husband* and had become a minor celebrity as the voice of Robespierre, Baby Snooks's little brother in the Fanny Brice radio show, which Oppenheimer also wrote. When the *Lucy* pilot sold, Hausner figured he had landed a steady job in television—any actor's dream—until Jess phoned him to say he would not be a regular character. "He told me they decided to go in a different direction, with different subsidiary characters," Hausner adds.

Of course, as any *I Love Lucy* fan already knows, Mr. Hausner popped up as Ricky's agent Jerry in scores of segments.

At the end of March 1951, Don Sharpe packed up the test film and took it to New York to find a sponsor willing to underwrite its cost as a regular TV series. Contrary to popular belief, the program did not find a firm buyer right away.

According to the late ad agency head Milton H. Biow, Sharpe's show got the cold-shoulder treatment all along Madison Avenue.

"Don got turned down by six or seven agencies before bringing his film to Biow. He had heard rumors, all true, that our client of long standing [since 1933], Philip Morris, was disenchanted with the results of its first two TV-show-sponsorship ventures—video versions of radio's *Truth or Consequences* and *Horace Heidt's Youth Opportunity.* I must be candid and say I was not overwhelmed by the pilot, but I thought it had a better than average chance for success," says the adman who created the famous "Call for Philip Morris" campaign.

When asked why other agencies had given the Ball-Arnaz outing the cold shoulder, Biow conjectured, "They may have envisioned it merely as it was originally presented, a routine vaudeville show with a comedy couple, a guest star, and a band. We envisioned it differently."

Biow continued his version of the *Lucy* lore by divulging that it was his close friend lyricist Oscar Hammerstein, II, who, upon viewing the film, "developed the idea of a warm human story built around a wholesome, lovable, dizzy couple." Oscar, who knew from much experience what "hit" meant, predicted the show would be a smash, likening it to radio's undefeatable *Fibber McGee and Molly.*

Biow told Sharpe that if Lucy and Desi were willing to talk new format, Philip Morris would be willing to talk money. Biow flew to the Coast, sat down with Lucy, Desi, Don, and Jess, and said: "If you can create characters for yourselves with whom the average person can associate—*everyday* people, not Lucille Ball, the movie star, and Desi Arnaz, the one hundred and fifty thousand dollar-a-year bandleader—I'll make a commitment here and now." In order to accomplish this new down-to-earth approach, Biow further advised "guest stars only when they are an integral part of the episode, and the same is true of the band."

Desi, whose chief concern was to keep his small band together, sweated: "We pay the boys every week, Mr. Biow, and if we only use them now and then, who's going to stand the cost?"

"Don't worry about that," Biow assured Arnaz. "Include the band in the cost of the program. If the show doesn't go, we won't stay with it anyhow. If it's a success, the cost of the band won't matter."

This new turn of events delighted Lucille, who was scheduled to give birth at the end of June 1951, just two months off. She liked the housewife image this revised format would allow her to portray. "Of all the thirty or forty films I had made up to that time," she states, "I could find only three or four scenes in those pictures that I cared anything about. When I put them all together, I discovered they were domestic scenes, where I was a housewife."

Jess immediately huddled with his two cohorts, Bob and Madelyn (the latter had to be called back from a Paris vacation), and created Lucy and Ricky Ricardo, a just-making-ends-meet married couple who lived in a modest New York City brownstone apartment (4-A) at 623 East Sixty-eighth Street. (If you're up on Manhattan geography, you'll realize they lived in the middle of the East River.) Ricky worked at the Tropicana nightclub for $150 a week. Lucy was the typical housewife with one story-pregnant twist: She longed for a show business career.

"We liked the idea of Ricky being a nightclub orchestra leader. It gave the character reality and also allowed us to use musical numbers and variety acts in the continuity of a story," Lucille reasons. "That helped us keep up the entertainment value."

To replace the Jerry Hausner-created pilot film character, the writing team concocted a pair of foils who would be the Ricardos' friends, neighbors, and, as the plot-planning continued, landlords —the Mertzes.

Ralph Levy recounts the hoopla surrounding selection of an appropriate series title: "It created quite a problem. Up to this time most TV shows, especially sitcoms, used the star's name in the title, such as *The Ed Wynn Show, The George Burns and Gracie Allen Show,* et cetera.

"Also CBS didn't want to give Desi star billing at all. They wanted the show named *The Lucille Ball Show,* and, in smaller letters, 'costarring Desi Arnaz.' Lucy hit the ceiling and told the network to forget the whole thing. When they suggested *The Lucille Ball and Desi Arnaz Show,* she again balked: Her name was first, his last. Finally, when someone from the Biow Agency offered *I Love Lucy* as a title with a good 'ring' to it, Lucy gave her approval. Why? Because the 'I' would be referring to Desi."

It was now May 1951. Desi was busy building a nursery wing on to the Arnaz ranchette in Chatsworth in anticipation of the up-coming blessed event. Having experienced two previous miscarriages, Lucy spent most of her time just relaxing. They wouldn't be starting rehearsals on *I Love Lucy* until late September, it being a "live" show like all the others.

All of a sudden one morning their collective complacence started crumbling. Milton Biow phoned Desi from New York asking him when he and Lucy would be moving to the East Coast to begin the show. This stunned the Cuban, who had no intention of uprooting his wife and family-to-be. He explained to Biow that Lucy was expecting their first child and that this was the first time in their married life they could look forward to being together, to say nothing of the fact that they loved California.

The situation boiled down to a simple matter of economics and market statistics. Biow argued that doing the show live from Los Angeles would mean that the East Coast watchers would have to settle for the inferior-quality kinescope. And since more potential Philip Morris smokers lived east of Chicago than west, it was essential that the show originate from New York.

Grasping at straws, Desi suggested that *I Love Lucy* be shot as a motion picture on 35mm film. Biow reminded the novice filmmaker that the budget for each episode was only $19,500. Desi continued his headstrong extempore: "Let us film the show in California—that way you'll have a much better quality print than that lousy kinescope which all places outside the live transmission range get; and we can stay here."

The idea of high-quality films sounded great to Biow, Philip Morris, and the network. However, Lucy's three-year run in radio's *My Favorite Husband* had proved one thing to CBS's Harry Ackerman: "I learned that Lucy was 'dead' without an audience, so I insisted that we film her TV series with one. It was for the performers' benefit at first and it also kept them on their toes—though, of course, we recorded the audience reaction and learned to 'sweeten' it when necessary."

According to Arnaz, the extra expense of doing *Lucy* on film caused additional haggling, "They wanted to know how much more it'd cost 'that' way; I had no idea so I picked a number out of the air—five thousand dollars more a week. At this point, Lucy and I were to get five-thousand-dollars-a-week salary between us, plus fifty percent of all rights in the show.

"CBS came back and said okay, they'd give us an extra two

thousand dollars and Philip Morris would cough up an additional two grand if we would take a salary cut to four thousand dollars a week. I said, 'Okay, but then we have to own one hundred percent of the shows—never thinking they'd say yes. But they agreed, and that's how we wound up owning everything!"

The burden of planning this new method fell heavily on Desi's shoulders. No one had attempted a situation comedy on film, shot before a live studio audience; he was plowing virginal fields. He had no time to waste if he was going to meet the October 15, 1951, premiere date the network had set. He hurriedly pounded the last nail into the baby's nursery wing and started right in building *I Love Lucy*.

"I'll never forget the day Desi and Don Sharpe drove up to my house on Woodrow Wilson Drive in the hills," smiles Ralph Levy, the director of the nameless pilot. "They asked me to direct the series. They even offered me ten percent of the show as an incentive. They came up sort of frightened that I'd say no.

"Well, I *did* say no. I had to—I was already up to my ears producing and directing three other shows. Who had the time? Especially when Desi and the rest were planning these innovations."

Though Desi had been successful bluffing his way through the early negotiations with CBS and Mr. Biow, he could no longer afford the luxury. He was committed to film a TV show. I repeat—*film* a TV show. Consequently he contacted cinematographer Karl Freund whom he had met in 1943 on the set of *DuBarry Was a Lady,* Lucy's first M-G-M film. Known to his friends as Papa, Karl had the distinction of photographing three Greta Garbo films, including *Camille,* and had won an Oscar in 1937 for his *The Good Earth* photography. It was common knowledge in the industry that Freund was a genius: He had developed the exposure meter and was credited with inventing the "process shot." He had become a wealthy man and, having retired from active film work, headed his own Photo Research Corporation headquartered in Burbank, California.

Desi finally tracked down the German in Washington, D.C., where he was serving as a consultant to the Film Research and Development Laboratory. A man of few words, Papa listened carefully as Desi described his ideas on the phone: do *I Love Lucy* like a stage play, and film it in sequence in front of an audience, using four 35mm cameras running simultaneously, each picking up a different angle.

"Impossible," answered Papa. "Every shot requires different lighting. You couldn't photograph three or four angles at the same time and come up with a decent piece of finished film."

Freund reeled off a long list of other reasons why the idea was unworkable, including the fact that the fire department would not permit an audience on a standard sound stage, and if you didn't do it on a sound stage, finding a theater with a stage wide enough to accommodate three or four sets side by side on it would be equally troublesome. "Forget it. It's impossible," Freund concluded.

Knowing Papa as a proud man, Desi tried a little psychology on the man whose film career already spanned forty-five years: "If you think you can't do it . . ."

In the next breath, Freund asked Arnaz when he wanted him to start work; Desi informed him that immediately was not soon enough. Karl then learned that he would be working for basic union scale, hardly justifiable compensation for an Academy Award winner who was used to earning $75,000 a year in the forties at M-G-M.

Within two weeks Karl Freund was back in Hollywood working like a demon to develop a logical system for filming *I Love Lucy* according to Desi's original brainchild.

In the midst of all the technical confusion, and two weeks overdue, Lucille gave birth to Desi's other "brainchild," Lucie Desiree, by cesarean section on Tuesday, July 17, 1951, at 8:34 A.M. at Cedars of Lebanon Hospital. Weighing in at seven pounds, six ounces and measuring twenty-one inches in length, little Lucie (as she is still called) was the most exciting event of the almost-eleven-year marriage of Lucille Ball and Desi Arnaz. So proud of his new role as father, Desi rushed out and bought a respectable 1951 blue Cadillac sedan to escort his wife and daughter home from the hospital.

Since Lucy's services as an actress would not be needed for about six weeks, she enjoyed her new role as mother, caring for the infant in the new nursery Daddy built. Daddy also wrote a song for his little Lucie the very day she was born, "There's a

Brand New Baby at Our House," which he would sing less than two years later in an *I Love Lucy* episode celebrating Little Ricky's debut.

One afternoon between feedings Lucy received a phone call from William Frawley, the character actor whom she had met in 1946 while doing *Ziegfeld Follies* for Vincente Minnelli. With droll self-assurance, Bill asked, "Do you need a good actor to play Fred Mertz?"

Frawley's agent, Walter Meyers, responsible for establishing the Beverly Hills offices of the William Morris Agency before going freelance, had alerted his client to the casting rumor. A film actor since 1931, Frawley had learned the hard way that you have to get out there and pitch for yourself.

Lucy obviously could not make any commitments without consulting Desi but she did promise Bill that she would discuss it with him as soon as possible.

Gale Gordon, who appeared in Lucille Ball's later two TV series ventures, was actually the first choice for the Fred Mertz role. "It sounds a little egotistical for a performer to say something like that, but Lucille once told me that she had hoped to have Bea Benadaret and me playing the Mertzes," says Gale, speaking from his Borrego Springs ranch north of Los Angeles.

"We had played Mr. and Mrs. Rudolph Atterbury on her radio show, and she wanted us both in her new TV venture. I had worked with her way back in 1941 in *Look Who's Laughing,* an RKO movie version of the *Fibber McGee and Molly* series. But when *I Love Lucy* came along, I was under an exclusive contract to CBS Radio to do *Our Miss Brooks* with Eve Arden, and Bea had already begun Burns and Allen's television show and couldn't do it either."

Ironically, both Gale and Bea made guest appearances on *I Love Lucy* during its first season. Gale played Ricky's Tropicana boss, Alvin Littlefield, in two episodes aired during the month of June 1952, and Bea shared the *Lucy* spotlight with Edward Everett Horton in a segment that had her portraying Miss Lewis, a shy spinster neighbor of the Ricardos'.

Gale knew Bill Frawley well and had worked with him a number of times: "He was a dear, wonderful man and a fine performer. We once costarred in a TV pilot called *Mr. Harkrider and Mr. Sweeney;* I think it was in late 1959."

Aside from the competition, there were other circumstances that almost prevented Frawley from being hired. After Lucy told Desi that Bill had phoned inquiring about the job, they agreed it would be great to have an old movie veteran, who had acted so brilliantly in *The Lemon Drop Kid, Mother Wore Tights, Miracle on 34th Street,* and a hundred other films, do the TV role. However, when Señor Arnaz mentioned Frawley's name to network officials (although Desi alone had final approval) they warned him of the actor's instability and chronic insobriety.

Bill, then sixty-four years of age, was living with his sister in a suite at the old Hollywood Knickerbocker Hotel on Ivar Street, just a few hundred feet north of Hollywood Boulevard. Desi made an appointment to meet him at a mutually convenient location, a popular restaurant/bar right next door to RKO on Melrose Avenue. Seated in a back booth, Desi leveled with Bill immediately, making him privy to CBS's opinion. Claiming moderation in drinking, Frawley called the network and its myriad vice-presidents every name imaginable, interrupting himself only once to order another Scotch. When the Frawley flack died down, Desi laid it on the line. He would hire him with one provision—if he was late to work or unable to perform except because of legitimate illness more than once, he'd be written out of the show. This was acceptable to Frawley who, despite the fact that he had a successful picture in release at the time, *Rhubarb* with Ray Milland, was experiencing hard times in the industry.

A steady job for Frawley in a soap opera *The First Hundred Years*—the first of its genre on TV—lasted only thirteen weeks beyond its May 1, 1950, premiere. Before that, things had got so desperate at one point that Bill went to CBS at Gower and Sunset, and pleaded with the producer of a popular TV variety show for a $50 loan. A soft touch, the producer instead instructed his writers to think up a couple of lines for Bill to say in the next show. They had him play a hot dog vendor at a ball game. Bill didn't need the loan any longer; he had earned the fifty bucks.

Born in Burlington, Iowa, on February 26, 1887 (some sources report 1893), Frawley started out at age nineteen to become a newspaperman. His ambition was short-lived. A month later, he was working as a clerk for the Union Pacific Railroad in Omaha. Two years after that, at twenty-one, he landed a job in the chorus of a musical, *The Flirting Princess,* in Chicago. His domineering mother forced him to leave the show and return to a "respectable" job, so he went back to bookkeeping, this time for the Rock Island Railroad. The lure of show business got the best of Bill, and without his mother's sanctions he formed a vaudeville team with his younger brother Paul. The act broke up six months later when Mrs. Frawley ordered her younger son home. Then with a piano player as a partner, Bill played the Pacific Coast vaudeville circuits for four years, introducing the song "Melancholy Baby," much to the distraction of its authors.

In 1914 he married and, hence, formed a new act, Frawley and Louise, with his young wife. Until their divorce in 1927, they played the Orpheum and Keith circuits, including the Palace Theatre in New York.

Even though he once said of the *Lucy* series toward the end of its nine-year run, "It's like eating stew every night—stale and not a bit funny," Frawley was grateful for the steady work. In 1960 he told a reporter, "That Fred Mertz character on *I Love Lucy* has made me the hero of all husbands. Just last week, a fella came up to me on the street and said, 'Mertz, I've gotta buy you a drink . . . the way you tell that Ethel off is beautiful!' "

What the man on the street probably wasn't aware of was that Bill had plenty of practice. While the Desilu press department did everything imaginable to foster the image of a happy foursome on the *I Love Lucy* set, it wasn't the case. After *Lucy* went off prime time, and Bill was engaged in his new role as Bub in *My Three Sons,* he made this remark about Vivian Vance, his TV wife, his so-called honeybunch: "She's one of the finest gals to come out of Kansas but I often wish she'd go back there. I don't know where she is now and she doesn't know where I am and that's exactly the way I like it."

36

4

Signing Vivian Vance to play Ethel Mertz was the result of a casual remark made to Desi by Pittsburgh-born Marc Daniels, the young director chosen in late July 1951 to direct the first season of *I Love Lucy*. Daniels had been introduced to her by Robert Bell, an instructor at the American Academy of Dramatic Arts in New York, his alma mater, about ten years before and had subsequently directed Miss Vance in *Counselor at Law* with Paul Muni.

Daniels had served during World War II in a Special Service unit under the command of Willard Josephy where he soon found himself assisting on a Hal Wallis film, *This Is the Army,* which Warner Brothers released commercially in 1943. When Josephy returned to civilian life he joined forces with Kurt Frings who happened to be Lucy and Desi's agent.

When Marc Daniels arrived in Hollywood from New York in July to direct the CBS pilot of *My Friend Irma* (shooting August 9), he looked up his commanding officer for old times' sake. Impressed with Marc's credentials, Josephy hinted to his partner Frings that Daniels be considered as director of *I Love Lucy*. The young man had experience using multiple cameras, having directed *The Ford Theatre,* TV's first hour-long dramatc anthology on CBS in the late forties; he had even won a few awards for his work.

Marc was staying at the Chateau Marmont, a chic hotel tucked into the hills on Sunset Boulevard in West Hollywood, when the phone rang. It was Josephy, suggesting that Marc meet with Desi

Arnaz, Don Sharpe, and Jess Oppenheimer regarding the possible *I Love Lucy* position. He did just that and promptly landed the job. During the course of the conversation, Jess routinely reminded Desi that no casting decision had been made regarding the Ethel Mertz role. It was a difficult character to cast. For one thing, the actress had to look like she could be married to a William Frawley, and she had to have stage as well as film credits. The more Marc heard, the more convinced he was that they should consider his old pal Vivian Vance.

"Vivian who?" the other three bellowed.

"Vivian Vance," Marc repeated. "I've known her for years. She just finished a film with Jane Wyman and Charles Laughton that RKO will release in a few months, *The Blue Veil,* and I understand she is appearing this very week at the La Jolla Playhouse."

On Saturday, July 28, 1951, Marc accompanied Desi and Jess to the 850-seat summer theater at 1121 Prospect Avenue in La Jolla, a quaint oceanfront town north of San Diego. Founded by Mel Ferrer, Dorothy McGuire, and Gregory Peck in 1947 as an artistic venture, the playhouse was enjoying moderate success in its fifth summer season. The theater's policy was to produce a different play every seven days during its nine-week schedule.

This particular week, the fourth, it was John van Druten's *The Voice of the Turtle* in which Vivian portrayed the acid and hateful "other woman," Olive Lashbrook. Diana Lynn and Ferrer (who also directed) co-starred. A Los Angeles *Times* critic wrote: "Miss Vance is excellent as the thick-skinned but essentially tenderhearted actress."

Apparently Desi harbored the same opinion because after the first act he leaned over to his two companions and said, "I think we found our Ethel Mertz." Oppenheimer agreed.

Daniels describes what happened next: "I went backstage during the intermission and told Viv they wanted her. Then she said to me, 'What do I want to get mixed up in that for? It's only a television show. I'm up for a picture at Universal.' I was furious with her, and said, 'You goddamn idiot, take the job! It's going to be a great series. I've seen six or seven scripts already and the pilot. It's going to be terrific!' She hedged, but finally agreed."

Vivian, who was once advised by a Hollywood agent to go home because her eyes were too close together, remembers all too well that July at La Jolla: "Fate sure is a funny thing. When Mel Ferrer called me in New Mexico to play in *Turtle,* at first I said no. I had a good reason."

It was in Chicago in 1945 while appearing in a road company production of that same play for producer Alfred de Liagre, Jr., that Vivian Vance had a nervous breakdown. "One day I was up and around, the next I was lying in bed in my hotel room, my hands shaking helplessly, in a state of violent nausea, weeping hysterically from causes I didn't know.

"A few nights before, on stage, a piece of business called for me to pick up an ashtray. I began to do it and found I couldn't move. The brain ordered, but the arm declined. It was one of the most sickening moments I have ever gone through," Miss Vance recounts. "My husband, Phil, was playing in *Dear Ruth* in San Francisco but I didn't want to burden him."

After two more seizures in Chicago, her husband of four years, actor Philip Ober, was summoned to her side, whereupon he accompanied her back to San Francisco. She barely managed to play six extra weeks in *Turtle* in the Bay City before the couple fled to New York, their headquarters. For two years she was incapable of doing anything but follow Phil around like a puppy. Then she met a woman psychiatrist at a party in Philadelphia who changed her life.

After four months in analysis, she was on her way to health. Following a brief visit to Phil's parents in Maine, Vivian retired to her small ranch in Cubero, New Mexico, just outside Albuquerque where she grew up. She had just about shaken off the tag end of the breakdown when Ferrer phoned with the La Jolla offer.

She hemmed and hawed about it for weeks until Phil put his foot down, practically dragging her out of the house. He was certain that a return to work was not only auspicious but also therapeutic. And as it turned out, it was profitable, too.

She was born Vivian Roberta Jones on July 26, 1912, in Cherryvale, Kansas. After a brief period, her family moved to Independence, Kansas, where she began to show some theatrical talent. Her father, R. A. Jones, relocated the family near Albuquerque where her talents continued to flower, now in a little theater group. Eventually, the citizens turned out for a special performance of *The Trial of Mary Dugan,* starring Vivian, the proceeds of which were to send her to New York to study with Eva LeGallienne.

Upon arriving in New York, Vivian was disappointed to learn that the enrollment at the school was already greater than it was supposed to be, so she started going to auditions on her own. Lo and behold, she was hired the very first time out for the Jerome Kern-Oscar Hammerstein musical *Music in the Air,* which ran two years at the Alvin Theatre. During her spare time, she even sang in local nightclubs, boasting quite a following. (Her two best songs were "Danny Boy" and "Japanese Sandman.")

Her big break came in *Hooray for What!* in 1937 when Kay Thompson left the cast of the Ed Wynn vehicle before opening night. Vivian stepped in at the last moment and, under Vincente Minnelli's expert direction, managed to get her name up on the marquee. Roles in *Anything Goes* and *Red, Hot and Blue* followed. Then on October 29, 1941, she opened at the Imperial Theatre in *Let's Face It,* sharing the stellar billing with Danny Kaye, Eve Arden, and Nanette Fabray for an eighty-five-week Broadway run. It was clear that Vivian had the training and experience necessary for a TV show that was to be filmed like a stage play.

If July of 1951 was hectic, what with Lucie's birth and other minor exigencies—like a new TV series—August proved to be twice as bad. With a little over four weeks before the first *Lucy* episode had to be filmed to meet the premiere date CBS had set, Desi still had not found the proper filming facility. He and Karl Freund, who was already engineering a revolutionary new lighting system for the show, were frantic. They had searched out every available theater, dance hall, and nightclub; none was suitable. And time was slipping away fast.

On the twenty-fourth of August, just two weeks before the first segment was shot, Frank Falknor, a CBS executive from New York, and A. E. Joscelyn, the West Coast director of operations for the network, prompted Desi to make an immediate decision. As *Daily Variety* reported: "Being given first consideration are the Fox-owned Belmont Theatre at First Street and Vermont Avenue, which has been shut for a month, and the Civic Auditorium on Culver Boulevard in Culver City near M-G-M Studios. If the Belmont is leased it would have to undergo considerable reconstruction due to its small stage. Also scouted for the past few days were independent picture studios."

One of these "indies" was General Service Studios, a seven-and-a-half-acre lot consisting of eight sound stages built in 1920 located at 1040 North Las Palmas Avenue, just south of Santa Monica Boulevard in Hollywood. Operated since 1947 by the four Nasser brothers—James, Henry, George, and Ted—the studio had enjoyed better times. With film production at an all-time low in 1951, the brothers were on the brink of bankruptcy, with the threat of losing the studio that played home in 1946 to the Marx Brothers' *Night in Casablanca* romp.

Suddenly a thirty-four-year-old Cuban appeared. Arnaz already had learned from various city agencies what bureau requirements he had to surmount if he intended to carry out his original plans, utilizing an ordinary motion picture sound stage. The fire department, for instance, insisted that if three hundred people were going to watch the show being filmed, there had to be sufficient exit doors, especially a double door leading onto a city street. Also a complete overhead sprinkling system would be necessary.

The most suitable General Service building seemed to be Stage 2. Although it was a little too small, it was adjacent to a city thoroughfare, Romaine Street. There were no private homes in the vicinity—across the narrow avenue was the Department of Water and Power and the headquarters of both Glen Glenn Sound and Consolidated Films—so there were no neighbors to complain about noise. It was the same stage where Shirley Temple had made her first film in 1931. It was soon to become The Desilu Playhouse.

CBS, on good old Harry Ackerman's say-so, put up $25,000 overnight to underwrite the cost of renovating the building. Desilu Productions, as the program packager, signed the lease for one full year with options for another, finally renting not only Stage 2 but also the adjoining Stage 1.

On August 30, nine days before the first show was to be filmed before a live audience, an army of carpenters, plumbers, electricians, and assorted technicians swarmed into the thirty-year-old movie studio, tore out partition walls to make two sound stages into one, broke through the wall on Romaine to make a proper exit (officially giving The Desilu Playhouse its own address—6633

Romaine Street, Hollywood 38, California, as it was printed on *I Love Lucy* tickets), and built a more or less permanent four-room set.

The existing floor was wood—full of holes, camera tracks, and nails, and badly warped—the same inferior surface found in most movie studios. If Desi's system of using three or four cameras, each mounted on a special "crab dolly" capable of turning 360 degrees in any direction, was to work at all it had to do so silently. So the existing floor was ripped out and replaced with a special composition, smooth as cement and capable of withstanding heavy weights. Karl Freund had discovered it while prowling around the loading platform of The May Company, a Los Angeles department store.

Though the physical plant was well under way, *I Love Lucy* still had no crew and no staff. From another Philip Morris-sponsored show, the just-canceled *Truth or Consequences,* Desi corralled Al Simon as his production manager. Al had already used three 35mm cameras in shooting the Ralph Edwards game show, so he was somewhat familiar with the impending problems. Al brought with him his secretary/production assistant, Felice Greene.

Lucy called her favorite makeup man, Hal King, who happened to be Max Factor's brother-in-law, and said, "I don't care what you do the rest of the week. You just be here every Friday night!" And he was, for the next twenty-three years, until 1973 when Lucy reportedly slapped him in the face on the set of the film *Mame* when King told the queen (of television) he was going to retire because of illness.

In two or three days, a complete staff was assembled. As announced that week in industry trade papers, it was as follows:

Producer: Jess Oppenheimer
Director: Marc Daniels
Writers: Jess Oppenheimer, Madelyn Pugh, and Bob Carroll, Jr.
Director of Photography: Karl Freund
Production Manager: Al Simon
Art Director: Larry Cuneo
Film Operations Manager: George Fox
Film Editor: Alan Jaggs [replaced by Dann Cahn after three weeks]
Musical Director: Wilbur Hatch (conducting the Desi Arnaz Orchestra)
Assistant Director: James Paisley

42

Original Music: Eliot Daniel
Casting: Mercedes Manzanares
Sound: Glen Glenn Sound (Cameron McCulloch in charge)
Stage Manager: Herb Browar
Choreography: Lee Scott
Wardrobe: Della Fox
Announcer: Johnny Jacobs
Makeup: Hal King (courtesy Max Factor)
Production Assistant: Emily Daniels
Office Manager: Felice Greene
Script Clerk: Maury Thompson
Janitor: Lou Jacoby

There were many others. In fact, ninety-one people were required to put together the average *I Love Lucy* episode, including grips, camera operators, sound technicians, gaffers, prop men, and so forth.

Maury Thompson, who began as script clerk and was later upped to camera coordinator status on *I Love Lucy,* looks back on the summer of 1951: "When I took the job a friend told me I'd have to fit into the family." Thompson remained in the "family" (with Miss Ball, at least) for twenty years, later assuming the prestigious position of director on *Here's Lucy.* He eventually quit —and then retired from the industry completely—when it became painfully clear that Lucy really wanted to be the director of the show.

With less than five days to put together the first *I Love Lucy* segment and get it on film, Marc Daniels scheduled his first rehearsal for Monday, September 3. At the morning reading Lucy met Vivian Vance for the first time and they seemed to get along splendidly. As the four principals read the script titled "The Diet," several dozen carpenters and electricians continued to remodel the building and install the sets.

"I can remember quite vividly," claims Marc Daniels, "that we were working under the gun. The distractions were constant. If Desi wasn't being called away to make a decision, I was. Karl Freund's new lighting system was being installed right up to the last minute, and that was a very intricate process. I recall at one point during the rehearsals for that first show suggesting to Larry Cuneo, who designed the sets, to put in those louver shutters which separated the Ricardo living room and kitchen. As he had it, it was a dead wall, and I felt I could get a lot of mobility out of being able to shoot through an opening."

By the time Thursday, September 6 rolled around, it became clear that the company would not be ready to shoot "The Diet" on schedule the next evening, as announced. Harry Ackerman flew back from Las Vegas, where he was in meetings with Frank Sinatra concerning a possible television program, and seeing the problems Desilu was experiencing, suggested they postpone the filming until the following evening, Saturday. This meant overtime for the crew as well as the construction people who were now working around the clock to complete the renovation. CBS had already spent a small fortune in a few short weeks on the Lucy-Desi show, so what was a few extra thousand?

While the bleachers to seat the audience of three hundred people were being installed under a control booth just completed, Marc and his players had their first opportunity to rehearse *I Love Lucy* with the cameras. With Karl Freund adjusting his lighting for every shot and Emily Daniels, Marc's young wife, marking the floor with masking tape for the cameras, Lucy, Desi, Vivian, and Bill tested "The Diet." To make matters worse, the Oppen-heimer-Pugh-Carroll script called for a dog to appear in a scene. It was nothing short of a nightmare.

"What made it impossible was the fact we were actually using four cameras on that first show, not three," Marc adds. "Because Desi wanted to do the show as if it were live—without ever stopping—to give it the genuine look of a stage play, it had to be shot straight through. It was so complicated because each camera wasn't capable of holding thirty minutes of film—the most we could fit into those babies was ten minutes worth. That meant we had to have footage counters in the control booth so the camera co-ordinator could inform each cameraman when to change film. That fourth, the backup camera, would fill in while another was being loaded with new stock.

"It was not only ridiculously expensive, but we also had to have an extra camera crew on hand. The floor was one mass of men, dollies, and cables. You could barely see through the crowd of people and equipment.

"The company was also using a new technique known as the Q-Track System developed by George Fox which supposedly made

44

Above: Karl Freund (*left*) confers with Marc Daniels, as Desi rehearses scene from an early *I Love Lucy* episode (1951). *Below:* Director Marc Daniels (*center*) listens to advice from the chairman of the board of Philip Morris, Alfred E. Lyons, as assistant director James Paisley looks on. Note conflicting signs in the background: one for Philip Morris, the other a "Positively No Smoking" warning (1951).

the clapstick unnecessary by replacing it with an automatic synchronization of sound and picture tracks via a "pop" sound. It was ingenius but it drove us a little crazy and we finally abandoned it after the third show."

On the day of the first filming, Saturday, September 8, 1951, the cast was still in rehearsals, attempting to iron out all the technical problems that were plaguing the production. The sets had not even been completed, let alone "dressed," and an audience was expected to file in at 7:30 P.M. It was an exhausting day, the end of an exhausting week. The Arnazes were beginning to wonder whether they had made the right decision in the first place, but it was obviously too late to turn back now.

After dinnertime, a long line of people began forming along Romaine Street. The exterior of the sound stage had been transformed into a summer theater. A gay candy-striped canopy, which marked "The Desilu Playhouse," hung over the new double doors.

Inside, CBS executives (biting their nails), Biow Agency representatives (biting their nails), Philip Morris big shots (biting their nails), and assorted members of the press (tripping over nails) inspected the refurbished facilities. Imagine how the Philip Morris people reacted upon seeing a barrage of fire department signs ordering, "Positively No Smoking"! As the last nails were being pounded and the CBS ushers were putting down multicolored cushions on the rising tier of bleachers, the cast was receiving last-minute instructions backstage from Daniels.

Suddenly an inspector from the Los Angeles Department of Health and Welfare summoned Desi. He calmly announced to the nervous Cuban, "I'm afraid you won't be able to do your show tonight."

Desi had been thrown some wild curves, but none as unexpected as this. There was a regulation that required men's and ladies' rooms for the public attending the filming. Upon inspection, the official had discovered only one, for the men. Desi instructed an aide to solve the problem and went back to huddle with Marc.

Moments later, the inspector returned. The only available toilet was in Lucy's dressing room. Upon overhearing the dilemma, Lucy obligingly offered the use of her dressing room to the ladies. "Tell them to be my guests," she offhandedly instructed the city official.

As the audience filed in, never thinking they were about to

46

witness a runaway hit, and took places on the bleachers, Desi's orchestra, under the direction of forty-nine-year-old Wilbur Hatch, was playing an appropriate Latin number. Urged by Jess to "go out and warm 'em up," Desi reluctantly took a hand mike and proceeded to ad-lib his way through yet another obstacle. Surprisingly deftly, Desi welcomed the people, explained to them the nature of the new system, told a few corny jokes, and then introduced his co-stars Bill Frawley and Vivian Vance. The pair was greeted warmly, particularly Frawley whose face was as familiar as an old friend.

Then, as the band segued into Eliot Daniel's new theme song, Desi introduced the star of *I Love Lucy*. Lucille breezed on stage, waved to the audience, kissed Viv and Bill, and threw kisses to the back row of the bleachers where her mother, Desi's mother, and the writers sat nervously.

Suddenly, Marc's booming voice from the overhead control booth interrupted the proceedings. "Please take your places," he announced to the cast.

It was now the moment of truth. A quarter of a million dollars had been shelled out so far to mount *Lucy*—a lot of money for TV, in those days. Harry Ackerman's CBS job was on the line, and the Arnazes' careers were at stake.

There was no need to worry. For the next thirty minutes, the audienced howled. Lucy Ricardo's antics while trying desperately to lose twelve pounds in four days in order to fit a particularly small costume for a Tropicana revue could not have been received more enthusiastically. The scene where she wrestled the dog for a scrap of meat was greeted with wails of laughter. And when the Arnazes reprised the numbers they did during their vaudeville tour fourteen months prior (and also in the pilot), "Cuban Pete"/"Sally Sweet," the audience of three hundred went wild with praise. It should have been obvious to everyone—the show would be a smash hit when it premiered Monday, October 15, just as Oscar Hammerstein had predicted. Not so.

For one thing, there were serious technical problems. Marc Daniels explains: "After that first film came back from the lab, we all had a look at it on Monday morning. It was painfully clear that using four cameras and doing the show without stopping was not only ludicrous, but injurious to the show's pace. I asked them, 'Why can't we stop between scenes? What's the big deal?' They felt that an audience wouldn't sit still that long. 'They sit two or three hours to see a stage play. What's an extra half hour?' I argued.

"Then Jess suggested that Desi could talk to the audience during the breaks and have the band entertain them with a few songs. Finally, everyone agreed with me. Madelyn and Bob were particularly pleased because now they could write scripts that didn't require instant costume changes and carefully timed entrances. If we stuck with the original method—running the show straight through, without stopping—we could never have done shows like 'Pioneer Women' [where a huge loaf of bread pops out of the oven], or any theme that required outlandish costuming, bizarre makeup, or a really difficult piece of business."

The second week had its difficulties too. Alan Jaggs, the film editor, was having a difficult time piecing together a rough cut (he was soon replaced by Dann Cahn) because the standard Moviola was capable of holding only one reel of film at a time. Having film of three different angles of every scene available to choose from, the editing got to be quite a headache until a special, four-headed Moviola was developed especially for Desilu.

By some miracle, a print of "The Diet" was available by Friday morning, September 14. Desi was anxious to see the reaction of an audience watching the actual film. That night, after rehearsing the second show, a makeshift audience was gathered on Stage 2 for a showing of the film. The reaction was good, but not judgmental enough to prevent Desi from taking the first two episodes the next weekend to a theater near Riverside, California, to "sneak" them. Again, the reaction was the same, but the paranoia continued.

The day after Lucie was christened on October 2, Desi, Jess, Don Sharpe, and Marc Daniels walked into Harry Ackerman's CBS office and sat down. "They were all nervous and worried about the series," Marc says, looking back twenty-five years. "None of them smiled and the only thing on their minds was, 'What are we going to do?'

"I couldn't understand what the hell they were so worried about. I felt it was a marvelous show right from the beginning. The audience killed themselves every week. Ten days later the show went on the air, and they never looked back."

48

5

On Monday, October 15, 1951, in the nine o'clock time slot va-
cated by Horace Heidt and his *Original Youth Opportunity* show,
I Love Lucy made its debut on the CBS television network, which
then consisted of a few big stations and seventy-four local affiliates.
The competition on NBC was formidable: *Lights Out,* a popular
video version of the radio classic with a Top Ten history of its
own. *Lucy* didn't stand a chance, or so the critics predicted before
they saw the first episode.

For the *I Love Lucy* company, the day was like any other. The
cast spent the better part of the day reading the script for the
seventh show to be filmed the following Friday evening. Saturday
shootings had been discontinued as the routine and new system
became more comfortable and less frantic. Soon, they would be
able to enjoy a four-day work week, beginning each Tuesday
morning, but on this particular fall week, Monday was a workday
—and a busy one at that, keeping the cast and crew toiling until
almost eight o'clock.

Finally it dawned on someone that the premiere *Lucy* episode
would be on the air shortly. The Arnazes lived about thirty miles
from the studio and would barely make it home in time to witness
the fruits of their labors. In the next breath, Emily Daniels, Marc's
wife and efficient assistant (also television's first camera coordinator), made a welcomed suggestion.

"We invited everyone to watch the show at our house at the

end of Laurel Canyon in Horseshoe Canyon where we had just moved," Emily looks back. "I remember because I made dinner for everyone and had the plates in the oven to keep them warm. While we were watching the show, I forgot all about them, so when it was all over we had to wait another ten or fifteen minutes for them to cool off before we could eat. When we were finished, it was like eleven o'clock."

The first *I Love Lucy* that went out over the CBS network facilities was not "The Diet," the first segment shot on September 8. Because of the technical problems inherent in it, Jess and Desi chose the second *Lucy* installment as the premiere show. Titled "The Girls Want to Go to a Nightclub," the half hour was described in an official CBS press release as follows:

"When the curtain rises, Ricky and Fred are plotting to attend the boxing matches despite the announced plans of the wives to go nightclubbing in celebration of Fred and Ethel's wedding anniversary. When the girls refuse to go to the fights, the boys arrange for a pair of blind dates. Later Lucy and Ethel deck themselves out as a couple of hillbillies to substitute for the blind dates."

Watching quietly in the Danielses' living room were Lucy and Desi, Vivian Vance and her husband, Phil Ober, Jess Oppenheimer, and their hosts. According to Marc, "The only one who was laughing a lot was Phil Ober because he hadn't seen it. And he had this deep baritone laugh like 'HO HO HO.' But the rest of us just sat there motionless staring at the set."

To make the half hour more frustrating for the group, there were projection room problems at local station KTLA, causing reception to be impaired, although the first Philip Morris commercial came in crystal clear. It featured an interviewer cooing confidentially into a girl's ear, "Now I want to ask you a personal question: Do you inhale?" (And they poke fun at today's commercials?)

The following day, the reviews came in. Columnist Dan Jenkins, writing in one of Hollywood's trade papers, called Lucy's eyes "the brightest, clearest, and bluest in existence" (which was quite an accomplishment for a black-and-white show). Later in the week he hailed the series as "situation comedy at its very best, serving the double purpose of giving the TV film industry a tremendous shot in the arm."

The *New York Times* decided *Lucy* "has promise of providing a refreshing half hour of video entertainment," but ended its review by stating, "Although a poor second act spoiled the first show, the basic characterizations are sound enough to go on to better things provided the situations are not permitted to get completely out of hand."

Other reports dubbed the series "high-quality slapstick," "refreshingly unpretentious," "sprightly comedy," "entertainment of a high level," "just what the doctor ordered."

Daily Variety was a little more reserved in its enthusiasm: "This initial teevee effort of Lucille Ball and Desi Arnaz should have carried the foreword: not to be taken seriously. As story-line comedies go, it is the better part of appreciation not to ask yourself too many questions and just go along with what transpires on your screen."

Its sister publication, the weekly *Variety,* reported:

"CBS and Philip Morris fell heir Monday night to one of the slickest TV entertainment shows to date. It's costing P-M $30,000 a week (exclusive of time) for the half-hour film series (without even enjoying the benefits of residual rights, which revert back to the packagers), but on the basis of this week's preem installment, it should sell a lot of cigarettes.

"*Lucy's* emergence as refreshing and big-time video is significant from various angles. It cannot help but strengthen the growing belief that video programming, to save face and sponsors, must of necessity detour into such avenues where the writing and the material, the human equations and comedy formulas inherent in well-produced situation comedies, will take TV out of its present rut. . . ."

But as sometimes happens even with a Broadway smash hit, one cardinal critic dissented. On Tuesday morning, just twelve hours after the first show's airing, O. Parker McComas, president of Philip Morris, called Terry Clyne, vice-president in charge of television at the Biow Agency, to ask, "What would it cost us to cancel the contract for *Lucy*?"

Clyne, backed up by his West Coast counterpart, Edward H. Feldman, urged the Philip Morris mogul to reconsider and give the series a little time to find its niche. He did, but it was not the only time the puffery threatened such drastic action.

51

"When the ratings came out on the first show of the second season ["Job Switching"], after *I Love Lucy* was established as the biggest hit in television history," states Feldman, "they were unusually low. This sent everyone into a tizzy, particularly Philip Morris, who had just signed for another year. No one could understand the reason for the poor showing.

"Mr. Biow nearly dropped dead. He felt the reason was 'too much Vivian Vance and William Frawley,' while the Philip Morris people shouted, 'less Lucille Ball and Desi Arnaz.' They agreed that the best thing to do would be to fire Jess Oppenheimer immediately.

"Suddenly we realized that the reason for it was that *Lucy* was sharing a 'split-rating' with *My Little Margie,* its summer replacement. In those days, the ratings were issued only every two weeks, and then it was an *average* of the two shows. *Margie* wasn't doing that well—at least not nearly as well as *Lucy*—so it dragged the rating down sufficiently to cause all the upset."

From all indications, the new filming technique developed by Desi with Karl Freund was working well. Following telecasting of the first three films in the series ("The Girls Want to Go to a Nightclub," "Be a Pal," and "The Diet"), Karl was being acclaimed by his American Society of Cinematographers colleagues for his technological excellence. Early in 1952, the A.S.C. awarded Desilu Productions the society's Scroll of Achievement at an informal ceremony held right on the *Lucy* set at General Service Studios.

It was just one of the twenty-five awards and plaques that poured in during the first season. At the Fourth Annual Emmy Awards dinner held in Los Angeles at the Cocoanut Grove of the Ambassador Hotel on February 2, 1952, after accepting the second of two Emmys for excellence in comedy, Red Skelton remarked: "Ladies and gentlemen, you've given it to the wrong redhead. I don't deserve this. It should go to Lucille Ball." The overflowing audience of industry bigwigs cheered loudly. The Arnazes could not contain their elation, and broke down and wept.

The so-called multicam system, included and described many years later in the *Encyclopedia Americana,* meant that the show was not filmed in separate shots but was picked up by three cameras (hence, multicamera) simultaneously in sequences that some-

times ran for ten minutes. Between scenes the program was interrupted to set up the cameras and prepare the next action. A film
editor put the program together by selecting the best shots from
those made by the various cameras. The method permitted the
production of a program before an audience to which the performers played and which, in turn, provided laughter for the
sound track. This made it almost unnecessary to add laughter
later by using recordings or a "laugh machine."

The same system, with very few differences, is still in use today
by such top-rated shows as *The Mary Tyler Moore Show* and
Rhoda. And why not? The ofttime director of these popular sitcoms, Jay Sandrich, started out as a second assistant director in
1956 on *I Love Lucy*.

The show was photographed on 35mm film by three Mitchell
BNC cameras mounted on dollies adapted by Freund from standard TV camera operations. Since all three cameras shot the action simultaneously, the camera in the center (number 1) made
all the long shots with a 40mm wide-angle lens. The cameras at
either side (numbers 2 and 3) recorded the action in close-ups,
using three-inch and four-inch lenses.

Cuing of camera operators, grips operating the dollies, and
the gaffer handling the light dimmers was a minor miracle. While
a segment was being photographed, the camera coordinator in the
booth overlooking the "stage" was in direct contact with key
technicians at all times via two-way intercom. Although each man
previously was briefed on the operation and in many cases had
floor marks to guide him, the camera coordinator insured against
any possibility of error by the cues. It was amazing how quickly
the crews were able to change setups and start shooting again;
delays averaged ninety seconds.

A major factor making such speed possible was the unique
lighting arrangement Freund developed for the production. Since
invariably the players were in action over almost the entire set
("intercommunicating"), the light intensity had to be uniform over
the entire area at all times. There were no light changes, other
than those made by dimming. All set illumination, therefore, had
to be from overhead. There were none of the usual floor lamps
found in most motion-picture production units, and the only illumination from a lower level came from portable fill lights

mounted just about the matt box on each camera. The set lamps were rigged carefully on catwalks suspended above the set. This overhead lighting method also kept cables off the floor, making feasible the unobstructed operation of camera dollies as well as quick movement of equipment to subsequent setups.

Freund once described the unique challenge with which he was faced: "To light a set for three cameras operating simultaneously and from different positions is a problem in itself. We have to light as uniformly as possible, yet watch for opportunities to add highlights whenever we can. This is very important, inasmuch as *Lucy* is a comedy show requiring high-key illumination.

"Contrast also has to be watched carefully," Freund continued, "since the tube in the film image pickup system of the television station is quite contrasty. Any contrast in the film therefore is compounded if not exaggerated in each step of the transmission of the picture. This makes it necessary to keep the contrast in the original negative down to what we call a 'fine medium.' "

This matter of contrast was further revealed in the decor of the *I Love Lucy* sets. They were painted in various shades of gray. Props likewise followed the demands of correct contrast, as did the wardrobe of the players. Even newspapers used in scenes had to be tinted gray to satisfy the overall uniformity of color and tones required by Freund's illumination formula.

Although each weekly show went before the cameras at eight o'clock Friday evening and was photographed entirely in an hour, the preceding four days were employed by the company in rehearsals, preproduction planning, and script revision.

At ten o'clock sharp on Tuesday morning, the director (during the first season, Marc Daniels; thereafter William Asher, James V. Kern, and Jerry Thorpe), actors, and writers gathered around a rehearsal table for a first reading. "We never saw a script until Tuesday morning," Lucy once told a visiting reporter. "We trusted the writers implicitly."

Until 6 P.M. the cast rehearsed, incorporating changes the writers had made during the day's reading. Sometimes a phrase was reworked slightly, and other times an entirely new passage was substituted. Sometimes an entire page or two or three didn't work, so Bob and Madelyn went off to their office and came up with something different. The cast members also made suggestions that were often incorporated into a script. Desi was particularly concerned that his husband role not become as moronic as so many TV hubbies were then being portrayed.

A similar schedule prevailed for Wednesday, but now the cast rehearsed on the sets, not around a table. Hopefully, over the preceding evening, the lines had been memorized—some forty-five to fifty pages of dialogue. By 4:30 P.M. the company was ready to run through the show for Karl Freund. No cameras were on the set at this time, nor were any members of the camera crews present. During this run-through Freund studied the players in their directed movements about the sets and took note of how and where they entered and exited, and planned his cameras accordingly.

A late "call" for the actors was the order of Thursday as Freund and his electrical crew began the arduous task of lighting the sets, hoping to complete the exacting job by noon. By this time the members of the camera crews came on the set and were briefed on camera movements and other pertinent details. With the various crews and cameras assembled on the stage, camera action with the cast was rehearsed until six. This enabled Freund to make any necessary changes in the lighting or operation of the camera dollies. Cues for the dimmer operator also were worked out at this time. Chalk marks and masking tape were placed on the floor indicating the positions the cameras were to take for the various shots or the range of the dolly action for a given shot.

A dress rehearsal was held at about 7 P.M. The writers, who had been kept very busy the preceding days creating an entirely new script for another episode, were present, as were network officials. Freund, his camera operators, gaffers, and grips were on hand—but the cameras were not wheeled on the floor. From eight until ten (or later—sometimes as late as 1 A.M.), a fine-toothed-comb session was conducted at which time lines of dialogue were cut, action shortened or deleted, camera movements analyzed—in short, everything that would tighten up the show, scene by scene, from beginning to end.

On Friday, the cameramen were present at nine o'clock in the morning, blocking out their lines on the floor; the lighting men used stand-ins to mark cue sheets and to crisscross the stage for the regular players. At 1 P.M. the entire cast and full company rehearsed again. If any major changes in the action, dialogue, or camera treatment were decided in the previous evening's discussions, these would be worked into the show.

A final dress rehearsal would take place at about 4:30 with the cameras on the floor. Freund gave his lighting a final check and made any necessary last-minute changes before the company broke for dinner.

A typical Friday found Lucille Ball in slacks and sweater, curlers still in her hair, acting as hostess at dinner to sometimes as many as one hundred actors, guests, and crewmen on an adjoining sound stage. Usually the dinners turned into cake-cutting parties, because she liked to commemorate birthdays, anniversaries, or just about any event she could think of.

After dinner, the company and cast returned to the stage, and there followed a general "talk-through" of the show. At this time, further suggestions were considered and immediate decisions made on any remaining problems, so that by eight o'clock the company was ready to film the show.

In the meantime, an atmosphere reminiscent of a summer theater took over. The audience filed in, after waiting for up to an hour along Romaine Street, and was seated in the bleachers. As in radio days, they were supposed to work a bit for free admission. One of the assistant directors gave them their cues for laughter, cheers, groans, or applause. Nothing, not even a bum funny bone was left to chance, although an emphasis was made as to the importance of natural, spontaneous reaction.

At this point Desi would be brought on. Grabbing a microphone for the "warm-up," he would introduce not only his costars, but also stagehands, Jess, Bob, and Madelyn, Wilbur Hatch, and sometimes even Lou Jacoby, the janitor.

Then for approximately sixty minutes the show was filmed. As soon as action was completed for one setup, the cameras, crews, and players moved rapidly to the next setup, and the action was resumed. All scenes were shot in strict chronological order to keep the flow of the story moving for the studio audience.

Due to the meticulous planning and thorough rehearsals, retakes were seldom necessary. In this respect, each camera operator had a major responsibility. He had to get each "take" right the first time—every time. Of course, he could hardly miss, considering the careful preparation that went into the filming phase of the production beforehand. Focus was carefully measured and noted for each camera position; chalk marks had been placed conspicuously on the stage floor; there were the numerous rehearsals; and, of course, there was vigilant Emily Daniels (during the first season) overlooking the proceedings from the control booth, relaying instructions over the intercom system.

The three cameras shot an average of 7,500 feet of 35mm film per show. It was taken across the street to Consolidated Film Industries, Hollywood's largest processing lab, for developing. After Dann Cahn's editing process (using the special Moviola, a "rough cut" could be produced in as little as one day), each episode was turned into a master print at a cost of about $2,500, which included the negative, plus charges for developing, and mixing the optical effects, such as fades, dissolves, and wipes. Adding a minute for the opening titles and another sixty seconds for the closing titles and credits to the twenty-four and a half minutes of actual *I Love Lucy* accounted for a reel of film totaling twenty-six and a half minutes, a print of which cost approximately $30. These prints then were sent out to the various CBS outlets across the country in just enough time to meet the specific air date.

In a *Time* magazine cover story dated May 26, 1952, the phenomenon of *I Love Lucy* was analyzed: "In about six months [Lucille Ball's] low-comedy antics, ranging from mild mugging to baggy pants clowning have dethroned such veteran TV headliners as Milton Berle and Arthur Godfrey.

". . . The television industry is not quite sure how it happened. When *Lucy* went on the air last October, it seemed to be just another series devoted to family comedy . . . But what televiewers see on their screens is the sort of cheerful rowdiness that has been rare in the U.S. since the days of the silent movies' Keystone Comedies. Lucille submits enthusiastically to being hit with pies; she falls over furniture, gets locked in home freezers, is chased by knife-wielding fanatics. Tricked out as a ballerina or a Hindu maharanee or a toothless hillbilly, she takes her assorted lumps and pratfalls with unflagging zest and good humor. Her mobile, rubbery face reflects a limitless variety of emotions, from

57

maniacal pleasure to sepulchral gloom. Even on a flickering, pallid TV screen, her wide-set, saucer eyes beam with the massed candlepower of a lighthouse on a dark night."

Attempting to explain Lucy's unprecedented TV triumph, Jess Oppenheimer said about his contribution: "You took the greatest living comedienne and worked from there . . . For every word you write in this business, you figure you're lucky to get back seventy-to-eighty percent from a performer. With Lucy, you get back one hundred and forty percent."

It was no secret that Lucy possessed an unfailing instinct for timing. This was evident in every *I Love Lucy* scene ever filmed. Marc Daniels adds his praise: "Not only was she a fantastically instinctive actress, but she was great at handling props."

Lucy, of course, credits her old M-G-M pal Buster Keator, with whom she never had the opportunity to work, with teaching her about props: "You'd be amazed at how many people cannot pick up a prop, let alone work with a conveyor belt and do the things that I had to do with a whole kitchen full of props—toast up in the air or pancakes. Viv could never do it. She just died every time she had to touch a prop.

"I haven't had a great many fights with directors but I had a real battle with my first director on television. I guess it's because I was frightened. I had to handle a pop-up toaster and during rehearsals he had me use balsa wood instead of real bread. And it was popping way up here," Miss Ball recalls, indicating an area high over her head. "So I said, 'I'm going to have to eat this bread. Don't you think we ought to start working with the real thing?'

"By the second day of rehearsal with the balsa wood, I said, 'Sir, don't you think we should be working with the bread?' 'For what?' he asked. 'Because of the weight,' I explained. 'The balsa's taking off like a ping-pong ball.' So he got a little miffed. And I said, 'May I use the bread?' 'No.' So I insisted: 'It's *my* bread, bring it in!' And what a helluva difference."

One character actor who made many appearances on *I Love Lucy* is Ross Elliott. An old army buddy of Marc Daniels's, he was cast as a TV director in a segment ("Lucy Does a TV Commercial") that called for Lucy Ricardo (posing as Lucille Mac-Gillicuddy) to act as spokeswoman for a liquid vitamin product, Vitameatavegamin. "Lucy was fantastic," says Ross who was thirty-five at the time he did his first *I Love Lucy*. "An inspired clown in the classic sense. She was always the hardest worker on the set. Everything had to be perfect."

Elliott, who is remembered to this day by fans of the Vitameatavegamin episode, made a habit of bringing his dog Chloe, whom he smuggled all through Europe during World War II, with him to the Desilu sound stage each day. "Lucy loved Chloe, and if I didn't bring her in she would ask me why and insist I bring her the next day," Ross recalls. Years later as a tribute to Miss Ball, the actor named his second dog Lucy.

His allegiance to *I Love Lucy* was so fervent that Elliott actually postponed his wedding in 1954 because of the show. "Jess wanted me for an episode titled 'Don Juan and the Starlets.' It was to shoot the week Sue and I were to be married. We decided to postpone the ceremony until after the December ninth filming. We got married on December 11. We didn't want to disappointment Lucy and the staff."

Ross wasn't the only actor to admire Lucille Ball's stamina and perfectionism. "I can remember a scene in one of the episodes during her pregnancy in 1952 which required her to jump up and down on the bed," explains Jerry Hausner. "Lucy became ill, went off the set, threw up, and was back within minutes doing the scene over again. She was a fantastic trouper."

During one rehearsal the first season, Lucy set fire to her dress with a cigarette but continued the scene. "It was right in the middle of a good rehearsal and I was afraid to stop," she explained. Luckily, Vivian noticed the smoldering fabric and screamed. Another time, the script called for a running leap toward Desi. Lucy jumped, missed him, and ricocheted fifteen feet. Bruised, she got up and redid the scene.

Her physical stamina notwithstanding, by the close of the first season, Lucy's doctor, Mark Rabwin, insisted that she spend her weekends in the hospital to rest because she was precariously close to exhaustion. To make matters worse, she and Desi had committed themselves to play New York's Roxy Theatre (where they appeared two years before on the vaudeville tour) for two weeks and the London Palladium for another two weeks in July. The deal, negotiated by General Amusement Corporation, called for $57,000, plus a hefty percentage of the gross over $100,000.

Business was good. So good, in fact, that Desi commissioned Eddie Sedgwick, the Arnazes' dear friend and director of countless Buster Keaton M-G-M comedies, to convert three *Lucy*s into a feature film for experimental release in the United States and Latin America.

Newsweek reported in the February 18, 1952, edition: "Desilu's success has sent a stream of Hollywoodites to tour the Arnazes' sound stages. Among them are Rosalind Russell, Eve Arden, Arlene Dahl and Lex Barker, Laraine Day and Leo Durocher, and Bing Crosby, who told Lucille he would probably use the Desilu technique when he makes his long-awaited television debut. The Durochers were so impressed that they had Desilu film a baseball series for them. Red Skelton uses the facilities for his commercials. And last week Eve Arden was making a pilot film of *Our Miss Brooks*."

By May, an estimated 11,055,000 American families were inviting the Ricardos and Mertzes into their living rooms every Monday night. The April 7 broadcast, "The Marriage License," broke a TV record. On this evening, ARB reported 10,600,000 households tuned to *Lucy,* "the first TV show to be seen in ten million U.S. homes," the report stated.

"*I Love Lucy* was the top program in the nation in April with a rating of 63.2," ARB director James W. Seiler continued. "And it was the first-ranking show in practically every major city."

With an estimated 2.9 viewers watching each TV set, the April 7, 1952, *I Love Lucy* show was seen by approximately 30,740,000 individuals. Of these, thirty-two percent, or 9,836,800, were men, forty-four percent, or 13,525,000, were women, and twenty-four percent, or 7,377,600, were children.

TV Guide's endorsement defined *I Love Lucy* as "the season's most popular program—smooth, deft, solidly produced, and funny."

Concerning the classic Vitameatavegamin TV commercial, Ross Elliott confirms: "I chewed the inside of my mouth out to keep from laughing out loud. Lucy would do new stuff that wasn't rehearsed, like an extrafunny face. Then, at one point, she became 'drunk' and started making eyes at me, flirting, and I almost broke up again."

The ability to evoke laughs came easily to the four principals.

A backstage bulletin board listed the names of cast and crew with a series of gold stars next to each name. The stars represented off-camera ad-libs. Frawley's stars ran the length of the board, and then some, so quickly that the project was soon abandoned. "Lack of competition," Lucille explained.

A year or so later, Bob Carroll and Madelyn Pugh, the two *Lucy* scribes, developed their own method of recognizing comedic excellence among the cast and crew. If something caused the studio audience to burst into spontaneous applause, the writers awarded the person responsible with a shiny silver dollar. Lucy surely earned an accolade or two the night of the filming of "The Ballet" early in 1952. During a scene with actress Mary Wickes who played a strict dance teacher, Lucy inadvertently got her leg stuck in the practice bar. It was all Miss Wickes could do to keep a straight face as she watched Lucille ad-lib around the mishap. As always, Lucy managed brilliantly, making the writers wonder why they hadn't thought of writing it in the script.

Very rarely did Lucille Ball make a mistake. Rehearsals were too thorough. However, one wag remembers an occasion when she hopelessly stumbled over a speech eight or nine times in succession, until she broke the tension by yelling out into the audience to her mother, De-De (who missed nary a one *I Love Lucy* filming), "Don't worry, Mom, I'll get it!"

"Pioneer Women," the twenty-fifth episode filmed, and originally telecast March 31, 1952, created a number of production problems that were almost unsolvable. The basic premise of the script was the men (Ricky and Fred) versus the women (Lucy and Ethel) in a contest (bet: $50) to determine which sex could withstand better the rigors of the pioneer days (actually the 1890s) when there were no modern conveniences. In one scene, the girls bake their own bread, and, having put in too much yeast, an eight-foot loaf explodes from the oven, pinning Lucy against the sink.

"When we went to a prop shop to find out what it would cost to have a loaf of bread made that long," says Marc Daniels, the director, "we found out it would be enormously expensive. So someone had the bright idea to go to a regular bakery. They were happy to do it for one tenth the cost. After the filming was over, we invited the entire studio audience down to the Tropicana night-club set where we served huge slices of bread to them and provided

61

butter, jam, and the like.

"In another scene in the same episode, we had Desi riding a horse, since he wasn't permitted to use modern public transportation. We rehearsed the hell out of that horse all week. He even had to walk up a short flight of stairs in the apartment building. But the night of the filming the horse took one look at the three hundred people sitting in the bleachers laughing at him and refused to cooperate any longer. Desi couldn't get him through the apartment door, so we improvised a scene on the back porch set. It was a helluva mess."

Although three of the total thirty-eight *I Love Lucy* episodes that Marc Daniels directed were aired during the early weeks of the series' second season, he quit after the first season, in late May 1952. As he explains, "I left because the show was getting more and more difficult to do. I now admit it was a mistake."

Perhaps the confrontations with Lucille were part of the reason for his departure from TV's Number One program, although he immediately accepted the position as director of *I Married Joan,* a sitcom often likened to *I Love Lucy,* which comedienne Joan Davis masterminded.

The real challenge, especially during the first *Lucy* season, was met by writers Bob Carroll, Jr., and Madelyn Pugh ("Pug" to her friends) who were required to turn out one script every week. Luckily, they were able to capitalize on their knowledge of both Lucy and Desi's real-life characteristics, having known the couple since 1947 when Lucy began doing the radio series Bob and Madelyn wrote with Jess Oppenheimer. Consequently, they were able to parlay the real-life Lucy and Desi into the family situation-comedy Lucy and Ricky. When the writing pair sat down together to do their work (Bob always clad in Bermuda shorts), their reaction to suggestions was based always upon whether Lucy or Desi—in reality—would or would not do certain things or act in certain ways.

The writers carefully tailored their material. Knowing, for instance, that Lucille Ball superstitiously knocks on wood, they wrote an episode, "The Seance," in which Lucy Ricardo spoiled a business deal for Ricky by consulting a horoscope. Similarly because Lucille likes to imitate Tallulah Bankhead, Bob and Madelyn fashioned a sequence in "Lucy's Fake Illness" where Mrs. Ricardo imagined herself to be a famous actress known as "Taloo." Lucy loves bop musicians so the writers dreamed up "The Saxophone," an episode that required Lucille to learn how to play "Glow Worm" in several days, in order to do it well enough in the segment.

"I never can get cool; Desi is never warm," Lucy once remarked, explaining the inspiration for a scene in "Break the Lease" in which each sought to outsmart the other by surreptitiously opening and closing windows after going to bed for the night.

There were more important similarities to the real-life couple. For instance, Lucy and Desi were married in 1940; so were the fictional Ricardos. Lucy Ricardo says she went to high school in Celeron, New York; that's where Lucille Ball attended school. The make-believe pair were married at the Byram River Beagle Club in Greenwich, Connecticut, according to "The Marriage License" segment, in which they repeated their marital vows. The Arnazes, too, were married at the Byram River Beagle Club in Greenwich and once repeated their marriage vows in 1949. Marion Strong was one of Lucy Ricardo's best friends; Marion Strong was also the real name of a person from Jamestown, New York. Lucille Ball grew up with her.

So personal a project was *I Love Lucy* that both Lucille and Desi made sure their friends had acting assignments (and their relatives jobs). Barbara Pepper, who got her start in the movies along with Lucy as a Goldwyn Girl in *Roman Scandals,* appeared in countless *Lucy* episodes, usually portraying a matronly woman bystander. This was years before she played the role of Doris Ziffel, Arnold's (the Pig) "mother," in the bucolic sitcom *Green Acres.* Desi was just as loyal. Besides keeping his entire band on the payroll, he made certain his buddy from the Xavier Cugat days, Louis A. Nicoletti, got acting jobs on the show. He usually played waiters. Years later "Nick" became an assistant director and before his death in 1969 was performing that function on *Here's Lucy,* Lucille Ball's third and last TV series. Even Vivian Vance's husband, actor Phil Ober, showed up in a few *Lucy*s.

Desi's fractured English, which evoked a great deal of laughter throughout the years, was *not* written into the scripts, as one might assume. However, his Cuban accent often made retakes necessary: Once his reading of "recognized talent" came out distinctly as "recognize Stalin." He said "ever thin" for "everything," "mushing peectures" for "motion pictures," "widdout furderadoo" for "without further ado." "Won't" was "wunt," "stage" was "staitch," "apartment" was "apparrmin," "partner" was "parner," and, best of all, "Fred Mertz" was "Frat Mers." Someone once put a sign on Desi's dressing-room door: "English broken here." Remember Ricky Ricardo's classic Spanish outburst, usually delivered nonstop at Lucy? *"¡Miraquetienecosalamujeresta!"* was merely an extension of the real Desi Arnaz who generously punctuated his English with peppery *español*.

However, no real-life similarity could possibly have matched the circumstances surrounding Lucille Ball's pregnancy in 1952 when it was decided that Lucy Ricardo would also have a baby on *I Love Lucy*.

6

"One day Desi walked me off the set so we could be alone," recalls Jess Oppenheimer about an afternoon in May 1952 just prior to filming one of the last *I Love Lucy* episodes of the first season. "I could see that, whatever the news, it could only be bad. Swallowing hard Desi said, 'We just came from the doctor. Lucy's going to have a baby.'

"He looked to me for answers: What could we do? How long would we have to be off the air? How much would it hurt the show? Without thinking twice, I said, 'Congratulations! This is wonderful. It's just what we needed to give us excitement in our second season. Lucy Ricardo will have a baby too.' As Desi rushed off to tell Lucy, I started wondering whether I shouldn't have thought twice before making that decision." Never before had a pregnant actress portrayed a pregnant woman on television.

"We could have filmed enough shows in advance to tide us through until the baby came," Arnaz states, "but I wanted to talk about my son. I didn't want to put Lucille in a closet for nine months. Having a baby is a perfectly natural happening."

While Desi went about trying to get permission from CBS, the Biow Agency, and Philip Morris to carry out these new plans, other problems arose. Marc Daniels wanted out as director, so a replacement had to be found before the season was over and schooled in the system. Luckily, Jess found the right guy in William Asher, a young director who would remain for several seasons before going out on his own, eventually marrying Elizabeth Montgomery and producing her *Bewitched* series.

At this time, the company also converted Stage 1 into a second Desilu Playhouse, moving into it in July to make way for *Our Miss Brooks,* the Eve Arden comedy that CBS bought and scheduled for a fall 1952 premiere.

Already having proved to the Hollywood community that he was more than just a bongo-beater, thirty-five-year-old Desi continued to show his mettle as a businessman. "Desi had a mathematical mind, but he had never used it much up to that point," Lucille Ball points out. "Then CBS sent over a new budget for the second season and he began to study it. He said to me, 'They've made a million-dollar mistake.' I said, 'That's impossible.' 'No,' he said, 'I know there's a million dollars more in here for us to spend on production. They've got their figures wrong.' The next day he took the papers to Harry Ackerman at CBS and said, 'You've made a million-dollar error.'

"Ackerman said, 'That's impossible. Look, Desi, stick to your acting. We'll handle the business details.' So he spread the papers out all over the office. He proved to them that they were wrong: There *was* an extra million in there to be used for production. From then on, when he talked, CBS listened. That gave him a boost of self-confidence."

With the baby on the way, Lucy and Desi decided to cancel the four-week personal appearance tour they were set to do in New York and London in July. The May 23, 1952, issue of *TV Guide* carried this explanation: "Lucille Ball and Desi Arnaz have canceled two weeks of personal appearances at the Roxy and another at the London Palladium. They don't want to leave their nine-month-old daughter, Lucie Desiree, and their San Fernando Valley home. They are turning down an estimated $200,000." No mention was made of Lucy's pregnant condition since plans regarding the second season of *I Love Lucy* were as yet unresolved.

CBS, having been approached by Desi about writing Lucy's pregnancy into the series, didn't like the idea. Years later, Harry Ackerman commented, "We had every intention of keeping *I Love Lucy* right where it was—Lucy always trying to get into show business. When Lucille Ball announced that she was going to have a baby, all we could think of at first was complete disaster. As it

66

turned out, it was the best thing that ever happened to *I Love Lucy*. It gave the show a change of pace, a change of perspective.

"After the first season of any show, it becomes necessary to find new things for the characters to do and talk about, new places for them to go, and even new characters for them to bounce off."

Hindsight is fascinating, but Arnaz kept running into brick walls with his "baby" plans. Philip Morris and its ad agency, run by strong-willed Milton Biow, issued statements urging Desi to consider one or two shows about Lucy's pregnancy, but no more. They advised him to hide Lucy behind chairs, or not feature her at all during her pregnant period. Desi's temper flared quickly, and he fired off a letter to the Philip Morris chairman of the board, Alfred Lyons, who was away in England on business. After all, it was Lyons who essentially controlled the company and it would be his decision that would be final.

Carefully worded, the letter said, in effect, that if Philip Morris was satisfied with Desilu's track record—having produced the nation's Number One television program—then the cigarette company would have to relinquish any and all creative control it had or might have had during this period, if their association was to continue. Lyons's immediate reply came in the form of a memorandum addressed to his New York office and the Biow Agency. It warned all concerned not to mess with Arnaz.

Once the flack subsided, Desi knew he could proceed with his "baby" plans. But this was easier said than done. In order to film enough episodes and still leave Lucy with sufficient time to rest before the baby was due in January, production had to begin almost immediately.

Bob and Madelyn were called back from their vacations to produce new scripts. The first episode of the new season would have to be filmed on July 18 in order to meet the prescribed deadlines. Vivian and Phil Ober were vacationing at their little ranch in Cubero, New Mexico. They were contacted and advised of the new start date.

The Arnazes managed a quick vacation at Sun Valley, Idaho, with little Lucie. Lucy was exhausted after a grueling thirty-eight-episode first season. She desperately needed a rest. While they were away, and despite fervent efforts to keep her pregnancy a secret until the propitious moment, Louella Parsons broke the news in her "Louella O. Parsons in Hollywood" column on June 18, 1952. She apologized in the piece to Lucy and Desi for revealing the news without their permission, but said it would be a disservice to her many readers to withhold such important information.

This immediately led to widespread speculation that *I Love Lucy* would be canceled. No one knew of the "baby" plans outside the company. Hastily, Desilu, through its PR man Ken Morgan, issued this statement, which appeared in the July 18, 1952, edition of *TV Guide:* "Lucille Ball's pregnancy won't keep her off TV. The approach of the stork will be written into *I Love Lucy.*"

With no time to waste, Jess sat down with Bob and Madelyn. "We finally decided that although it had never been done before, we could tackle the job of a pregnancy on TV," Oppenheimer recalls of his two partners, who were both single at the time. "We felt certain we could extract all the inherent humor from the situation while staying within the bounds of good taste. To further insure that we offended no one, we arranged for a Catholic priest, a Protestant minister, and a Jewish rabbi to approve the scripts and see the shows being filmed."

In the meantime, a new situation comedy, *My Little Margie* starring Charles Farrell and Gale Storm (in the role originally meant for Mona Freeman), took over the *I Love Lucy* time period for thirteen weeks beginning June 16, 1952. Although it later became a popular hit, it was a critical disaster, dubbed "unfunny," "pointless," "pathetic," "tired," "trite," "dreary," "hackneyed," "dismal," and so forth. Where Walter Winchell decided he "loved Lucy," he was "just mild about Marg." Lucy had set a precedent difficult to challenge or even come close to. In fact, when the 1952–1953 season blossomed, there were fourteen new sitcoms—from *Leave It to Lester* to *Doc Corkle*—all trying to copy the basic *I Love Lucy* formula.

On Tuesday, July 15, 1952, the *Lucy* cast and crew assembled on Stage 1 to begin rehearsing the thirty-ninth episode in the series, titled "Job Switching." It was Bill Asher's first crack at directing Lucy (now just entering her fourth month of pregnancy), Desi, Viv, Bill, and guest star character actress Elvia Allman. As was the usual procedure, they rehearsed for four days before filming the now-classic segment on July 18.

Despite its poor showing in the ratings (due to the *My Little Margie* split-rating mixup) when it was televised as the premiere episode of the new season on September 15, Jack Gould wrote this review in his *New York Times* column: "*I Love Lucy* is back in fine fettle. The top program of last season . . . once again proved a delightful slapstick romp for Lucille Ball. The success of *Lucy* is proof of the old adage of show business that what you do often is far less important than how you do it. Incorporated in Miss Ball's weekly endeavor is probably every pat comic situation ever devised, yet withal her program consistently achieves a hilarious level. It is a triumph of familiar nonsense beautifully turned."

As the summer of 1952 progressed, the company managed to rehearse and film episodes forty to forty-four, which were "The Saxophone," "Vacation from Marriage," "The Courtroom," "Redecorating," and "Ricky Loses His Voice." None of these even hinted at Lucy Ricardo's pregnancy. Following these productions, five additional episodes, forty-five to forty-nine, were put on film to serve as the postbirth shows. This was possible because Lucy didn't "show," the result of some valiant dieting on her part (she eventually gained twenty-seven pounds during the pregnancy).

During this same period, Bob and Madelyn were busy preparing the seven episodes that constituted Lucy Ricardo's entire pregnancy. "We didn't want to do anything that would upset the public," Desi admits. "There was nothing we had to throw out except the word 'pregnant.' CBS didn't like that, so we used 'expectant.' CBS thought it was a nicer word."

Philip Morris put its two cents in. They requested that during Lucille's pregnant state, she should not be viewed smoking cigarettes.

The first "pregnancy" episode was scheduled for filming on Friday, October 3. Titled "Lucy is Enceinte" (a Latin word meaning pregnant), it was the crucial script that had to set the tone for the series and the tone had to be just right. The night before the filming, a special performance was given, without cameras, for the three local religious leaders—Monsignor Joseph Devlin, head of the Catholic Legion of Decency, Rabbi Alfred Wolfe of the Wilshire Temple, and Reverend Clifton Moore of the Hollywood Presbyterian Church. Scripts had been sent to them in advance, but they watched the performance. When they were asked for their opinions—"Was there anything objectionable?"—the three said in unison, "What's questionable about having a baby?"

From then on every script in the baby series was submitted to the three men for their opinion. They never changed a word of Bob, Madelyn, and Jess' scripts:

ETHEL: Good morning, Lucy.

LUCY: Oh, hi, Ethel.

ETHEL: Where are you going so early?

LUCY: Oh, I thought I'd go down to see the doctor.

ETHEL: What's the matter, honey? Are you sick?

LUCY: No, I just want to get a checkup. I need a tonic or something. I've been feeling real dauncey.

ETHEL: Dauncey?

LUCY: Yeah, that's a word my grandmother made up for when you're not really sick but you feel lousy.

ETHEL: Oh.

LUCY: I don't know what's the matter with me. I've been getting a lot of rest and then I wake up feeling all dragged out in the morning. I don't have much energy and yet I've been putting on a lot of weight. I just feel blah.

ETHEL: Well, maybe you need some vitamin pills or a liver shot or something.

Next Lucy swears Ethel to secrecy because she doesn't want Ricky to worry needlessly over what might prove to be nothing. Then Lucy reveals something that causes Ethel to speculate in amazement.

LUCY: Gee, I'm gonna have to go on a diet. You know I could hardly get into my dress this morning?

ETHEL: Hey, Lucy, wait a minute. You don't suppose . . .

LUCY: I don't suppose what?

ETHEL: You don't suppose you're gonna have a baby?

LUCY: Of course not. [*Long pause*] A *baby*??

ETHEL: Yeah, baby. That's a word *my* grandmother made up for tiny little people.

Lucy goes off to the doctor and returns in a dreamy trance. She tells Ethel the good news, then again makes her promise not to tell anyone else until she has had the opportunity to break the news to Ricky. Ricky comes home for lunch and Lucy is determined to tell him, despite his bad mood. After a number of telephone and doorbell interruptions . . .

RICKY: Oh, what a business. Sometimes I think I go back to

	Cuba and work in a sugar Plantation. Just the two of us.
LUCY:	Just the two of us?
RICKY:	Yeah. I don't mean to get you all involved in my affairs, but you should be happy you're a woman.
LUCY:	Oh, I am, I am!
RICKY:	You think you know how tough my job is, but believe me, if you traded places with me . . . you'd be surprised.
LUCY:	Believe me, if I traded places with you, *you'd* be surprised.

Ricky has to return to the Tropicana before Lucy has the chance to tell him about the baby, so she decides to go to the club herself and tell him there. With musicians and stagehands everywhere, Lucy can't bring herself to reveal such personal news. After a long silence, Ricky asks her what she wants. Looking back at the two-dozen staring faces, Lucy asks: "Do you have the correct time?" Foiled again, she decides to return to the nightclub that evening, even if she has to tell Ricky during the mdidle of the show.

In the last scene, Lucy manages to relay the news to Ricky. The script called for Desi to become excited and bellow with joy. Instead, as the three cameras rolled, he unexpectedly broke down and cried. Many members of the audience cried right along with him. Believing that the film and sound track had been ruined by all the tears, Bill Asher halted the cameras and ordered a retake.

After viewing the rushes a few days later, Jess and the others agreed that the crying scene had more of a dramatic impact than the funnier, more upbeat version. Desi and Lucy agreed, and when "Lucy Is Enceinte" aired for the first time on December 8, 1952, the nation shed a tear, too.

By the time this first "baby" episode was shot, Desilu had already begun a major publicity campaign. At first they had decided to have the Ricardo baby the same sex as the Arnaz offspring, who was expected to be delivered via cesarean section on January 19, 1953. (The original due date had been January 12, but upon closer examination by Lucy's physician, Dr. Joseph Harris, the later date was pinpointed.) It happened to be a Monday, the same day *I Love Lucy* aired, only because Harris performed all his cesarean operations at Cedars of Lebanon Hospital on that day. On October 13, a magazine reported that the

71

Lucy producers were "leaving the sound track open and later will insert whether it's a boy or girl." That was a short-lived idea, as a little child psychology prevailed.

It was for little Lucie's sake that they decided to make the baby in the script a boy. The Arnazes were concerned that when their little daughter saw the films she would wonder why she had been left out. If it had been a girl on the show, she would have reasoned that this was her sister, not herself. Not to be overlooked was the fact that Desi wanted a boy.

At a solemn conference with a battery of press agents was born a five-part, five-page memo titled "Various Aspects of the Ricardo Baby in the *I Love Lucy* Publicity and Promotional Campaign." All present swore "that there must be absolutely no word about the baby released out of any office before December 8." Only then were 40 million televiewers to be let in on the secret of Lucy's pregnancy, although it had been hinted at as far back as July (*TV Guide*).

Plans were developed to tie in the show with a new Columbia record of "There's a Brand New Baby at Our House" (which, you'll remember, Desi had written the night Lucie was born) and the series' theme song. All the PR men promised to bombard newspapers, magazines, and wire services with feature stories. Regarding the Ricardo baby's sex, the memo contained this clause, titled "The Secret Gimmick About the Baby's Sex." It required an inviolate pledge of secrecy until January 19. "The Ricardo baby will be a boy regardless of the sex of the actual Arnaz baby. Of course, if the Arnaz baby does happen to be a boy, then all writers and editors can assume that the producers of *I Love Lucy* are clairvoyant and possessed of sheer genius. If it happens to be a girl, the story (and the truth) is that Desi was so set on having a boy . . . that he went ahead and filmed the Ricardo baby as if it were, regardless."

What to do about notifying Hollywood's competitive gossip columnists: "Walter Winchell should be alerted to be given the first news of the Arnaz baby. We will phone the news to him since he will be expecting the phone call. When he is alerted, he is to be told nothing of the gimmick, but when he receives the phone call, and not before, he will be given the story of Desi's thinking concerning the Ricardo baby. Of course, the news of the Arnaz baby

Lucille poses with Richard Lee Simmons who alternated with his twin brother Ronald Lee in the Ricky, Jr., role during final rehearsals for "No Children Allowed" (1953).

will be given out simultaneously to Louella, Hedda, Johnson, Graham, all the wire services and all the local dailies. But the story of the gimmick as released to the other outlets will be a follow-up . . . to give Walter the edge."

On October 17, the cast filmed "Lucy's Show Biz Swan Song," the third episode in the "baby" series. It was like old home week on the set: Pepito, the Spanish Clown, made a guest appearance. It was he, you will remember, who devised the stunts Lucy and Desi performed on their 1950 vaudeville tour, the forerunner of *I Love Lucy*. They felt a great affinity for the man who was considered a genius in show business circles until his death a few years ago.

After the dress rehearsal, Bill Frawley sought out Lucille in a darkened corner of the deserted sound stage. "It's terrible," he growled, referring to a barbership rendition of "Sweet Adeline" called for in the script.

Frawley, a walking expert on the subject of barbershop-quartet singing, continued his gruff assault: "You amateurs are lousing up this whole thing! If we let that song go on the air the way it is now, we'll be laughed off every TV set in the country."

Lucy turned on one of her coldest stares. "What are you complaining to me for?" she asked. "I've only got one lousy note in the whole arrangement. What do you want from me?"

"And that goddamn Vivian Vance," Frawley foamed. "That Galli-Curci!"

"Look, Bill, I've only got one note to sing. Go ahead and complain to Desi."

"Desi?" Frawley groaned. "That Cuban square! What the hell does *he* know about good old American music? All right, all right. I'll go see Desi."

He stalked across the long sound stage, muttering to himself. When he got to the other end, he suddenly turned around and bellowed back at la Ball: "And as for that one note of yours, it sounds like a barrel of gravel on a baked Alaska!"

It was the evening of November 14 that Lucy appeared in her last segment before going on a four-month hiatus. "Lucy Goes to the Hospital" was telecast nine weeks later on January 19, 1953, climaxing with the birth of Little Ricky Ricardo, played in this initial half hour by eighteen-day-old James John Gouzer who had blue eyes and reddish-black hair (coincidentally the same as Desi Arnaz, Jr's, features at birth). Because of her condition, Lucy's role in the segment was minimal (she barely appeared in the second act), causing a reviewer in *Broadcasting* to speculate: "Until Lucy left for the hospital, the . . . production was up to the quality of any other in the series. It descended to routine levels, however, the moment she was out of sight. . . . Mr. Arnaz and his writers exerted every effort, perhaps too much effort, to keep the comedy going while he was awaiting the delivery of his child, but at best *I Love Lucy* was mediocre in those sequences."

Miss Ball went into temporary retirement after the November 14 production, spending all her time at the couple's Chatsworth ranch. Caring for little Lucie and preparing for an addition to the family, she rarely ventured off the San Fernando Valley property, except one night in late December to accept the *TV Guide* award as "Best Comedienne of the Year." She deserved it.

The breakneck schedule that existed during this early second season of *I Love Lucy* was often cause for strained emotions. The company worked nonstop from mid-July to mid-November, filming a total of eighteen segments that would tide them over until Lucille's expected return to work in mid-March 1953. Desi, who had observed every facet of the production diligently during the entire first season, now had begun to assert himself when it came to technical matters. Maurice Marsac, a charming Frenchman who came to the United States from Paris in late 1951, and played the Tropicana maître d' in a few *Lucy* shows, noticed the difference: "I saw a great change after the first season. Desi was into everything, every aspect of the production. He had become a dynamo. The atmosphere on the set was always demanding. There was never any fooling around. You definitely had to be on your toes on *I Love Lucy*."

Jerry Hausner maintains that Desi virtually had become the show's director after Marc Daniels left and Bill Asher stepped in. "I remember an incident when Bill was at the helm," Hausner says, "and I was playing my usual role of Ricky's agent. We had a scene in the apartment; it was to be a three-shot of Lucy, Desi, and myself. Suddenly, Desi started to take over, telling Billy Asher, 'Now we're gonna have a three-shot for the three of us. And then we say a few more lines, then a two-shot of us after Jerry leaves. And then there will be a close-up of my face, see?'

"Lucy then turned to Desi," Hausner recounts, "and asked very sharply, 'And then what after *your* close-up, dear?' Desi turned to her, smiled, and said, 'Then there will be a close-up of you, of course.' Lucy looked straight through Desi and announced coldly, 'If you value my friendship.' "

Despite claims to the contrary, Vivian Vance was beginning to feel a little spurned during this period. She already had become disgruntled with having to wear frowsy housedresses, an arrangement Desi had worked out with a clothing manufacturer during the first season. This resentment, coupled with a contractual stipulation that Vivian remain twenty pounds overweight for her Ethel Mertz role in order to appear frumpier than Lucille (who is actually one year older than Vance), fostered a few heated arguments with the star. None of these was disclosed to the press, which had been led to believe that the four principals were buddy-buddy. Even *TV Guide* once indicated, "Vivian and Bill, and the Arnazes have a four-way admiration society."

One observer recalls this incident, which took place in late October of 1952 at the height of Lucy's pregnancy: "Because of her condition, Lucy's dressing room was right next to the set and she had two or three dressers to help her with costume changes. One particular transitory scene called for a very quick change. Vivian had to run clear to another sound stage, which housed her dressing room, in order to change her outfit, while Lucy obviously had no problem with her change.

"Vivian made her costume change," recalls the onlooker, "raced back to the stage, over cables and props, and took her place beside Lucy so they could both make an entrance together. Waiting calmly, Lucy snapped, 'You almost missed your cue. You're late.' Plussed, Vivian took a deep breath, turned to Lucy, and said, 'I'd tell you to go fuck yourself if Desi hadn't already taken care of that!' "

While tempers simmered during the four-month vacation period, newspapers were responding en masse to the PR workings of the Desilu organization. Writing in *Reader's Digest,* Eleanor Harris reported: "On January 14, 1953, when reporters discovered

76

that the Ricardo baby . . . would be 'born' the following Monday, the excitement began. An electric current seemed to race through newspaper offices all over the country: Perhaps [although the Arnazes already knew] Lucille Ball's real baby would make its appearance on the same day. Reporters everywhere picked up the telephone; hundreds of calls began flooding the Arnaz home, office, studio. Voice after voice said, 'It's the greatest human-interest story of our time—when is she going to the hospital?' Newspapers published hourly bulletins and ran pools betting on the baby's sex."

Jack Gould's January 16 *New York Times* TV column carried this reaction: "Both CBS and Philip Morris have received letters from a number of viewers who for several reasons have taken exception to the subject of pregnancy as the main point of interest for a comedy series. As the matter has been handled on the screen, there seems [to be] no grounds for valid objections. Rather, there should be applause. Miss Ball and Mr. Arnaz not only handled the topic of their approaching baby with a great deal of taste and skill but also have been thoroughly amusing in the process. Far from ridiculing motherhood, *I Love Lucy* has made it appear one of the most natural things in the world."

Without meaning to be crusaders, the Arnazes did manage to lift from the shoulders of all expectant mothers a load of embarrassment and gaucherie. Where a few newspaper readers wrote in protesting the frankness (by 1952 standards) of the dramatization, the papers were subsequently flooded with irate answers in reply: "I feel sorry for the lady who protests Lucy's expectancy. Has she heard of the story of Mary, Joseph, and the Christ Child?"; "I believe that TV with this program is bringing to the children of America true facts that many parents neglect to teach in their homes"; "Did it ever occur to you that if a whole family was watching one of the recent shows, it might make it easier for parents to explain to children and would eliminate embarrassment on both sides?"

Mail that reached Desilu was more pro than con. Only 207 letters arrived disapproving of pregnancy on television. "Hundreds of thousands of women all over the country who were pregnant along with me," Lucille Ball explains, "wrote me encouraging notes, and after our baby was born, I received thirty thousand congratulatory telegrams and letters."

77

One woman whose life was devoted to charitable work for American GIs in Korea had planned to forego her position because she was pregnant and embarrassed to meet the public. Inspired by the show's treatment of Lucy's pregnancy, she wrote that she would continue until her baby arrived.

Quietly on Sunday night, January 18, Desi drove Lucy to Cedars of Lebanon Hospital where little Lucie had been born eighteen months before. That same night Vivian Vance had a dream: "Lucy came into my room clad in a beautiful white dress and said, 'Vivian, I had a boy.'"

Early the following morning, January 19, Lucy was wheeled into surgery, and given a spinal anesthetic so she could remain conscious during the operation. "We really don't care what it is, but as long as we already have a girl, it would be nice to have a boy," she said just moments before the surgery began. "I'll have a son on television tonight anyway."

Talking to James Bacon of the Associated Press, the only reporter allowed in the fathers' waiting room with Desi, the proud papa-to-be speculated, "If it's a boy—swell, but if it's a girl, the producers of *I Love Lucy* will just have to write it off to artistic license."

In the operating room, Lucy badgered her doctor, Joe Harris: "What is it? What is it? Can't you give me at least a hint?"

"Relax, honey," Dr. Harris replied, trying to calm his impatient patient. "A few more minutes and we'll know."

At 8:15 A.M., PST, Dr. Harris announced, "It's a boy!" The attending staff of nurses reacted with glee. Murmuring, "Desi will be so happy," Lucy fell instantly asleep, quite unaware of the worldwide hysteria that started one minute after Desiderio Alberto Arnaz y de Acha IV entered the world. (Had it been a girl, she would have been named Victoria Dolores.)

Grinning from ear to ear upon hearing the news of his new eight-pound, nine-ounce son, Desi burst into the hallway outside the waiting area, arms waving wildly. "It's a boy! It's a boy!" he shouted. "That's Lucy for you. Always does her best to cooperate. Now we have everything!"

Next he grabbed a nearby telephone receiver and blurted out to Jess Oppenheimer, who had been holding on the phone for nearly thirty minutes, "Lucy followed your script! Ain't she something?"

"Terrific!" exploded Oppenheimer. "That makes me the greatest writer in the world. Tell Lucy she can take the rest of the day off!"

Next Desi phoned his father in Miami. "I'm entering him in Notre Dame, class of seventy-four," Desi shouted in Spanish. The news of a grandson particularly pleased the senior Arnaz. Desi III was his only son; his two brothers each had girls. If Lucy and Desi had had no son, it would have spelled the end of the Arnaz clan.

Newspapers went wild. Headlines all over the world carried the news. Seven minutes after the baby's birth, it was broadcast in Japan. Los Angeles school officials went around to classrooms to announce the blessed event to the students. A spokesman for the Associated Press claimed, "We covered the birth on a wartime basis, with hourly bulletins."

Lucy and Desi received one million indications of public interest, including letters, telegrams, gifts, and telephone calls. Gifts of baby booties, bonnets, sweaters, and blankets arrived in such quantities that they were sent by truckload to state institutions. The day following the baby's arrival, General Dwight D. Eisenhower was inaugurated as the thirty-fourth President of the United States, and on his ABC Sunday (January 25) broadcast, Walter Winchell reported, "This was a banner week—the nation got a man and Lucy got a boy."

While 29 million people witnessed Ike's swearing-in ceremony on American television, 44 million tuned in to watch Little Ricky's birth. This audience figure represented a television first. The fifty-sixth episode of *I Love Lucy,* "Lucy Goes to the Hospital," boasted an unbelievable 71.7 Nielsen rating.

"How about that?" beamed Desi, as he perused a newspaper. "She's as important as Ike. I wonder if we could run her for President in fifty-six?"

Exactly eight days after Lucy came home from the hospital, she stepped on to a makeshift stage at the Statler Hotel on February 5, 1953, to accept from Art Linkletter her first two Emmy awards—one for "Best Situation Comedy" and the other for "Best

Comedienne" of the year. She was nominated for a third, "Outstanding Personality," but didn't really mind losing to Bishop Fulton Sheen.

The *I Love Lucy* furor did not stop there. By the start of February, Lucille and Desi had signed to star in M-G-M's *The Long, Long Trailer,* a comedy about a couple making a cross-country tour in an auto trailer, based on a Clinton Twiss novel published by Thomas Y. Crowell Company. The Arnazes' price: $250,000 for six weeks work; filming to begin when production on *I Love Lucy* shut down for the season in June. They almost agreed to appear in a different film—their first since *Too Many Girls,* the RKO musical where Lucy and Desi first met—a Universal-International flick called *Policewoman* in which Lucille would have played a lady law guardian and Desi her long-suffering police captain.

Since Lucy wasn't expected back to start filming new *Lucy* episodes until March, the time between the January 19 episode and the date of her video return, speculated at about mid-April, was filled in by the five postbirth episodes produced during late summer 1952 and by several reruns.

On February 18, despite persistent rumors that Philip Morris might drop *I Love Lucy,* CBS announced a new $8,000,000 contract with the Arnazes.

As reported in *Advertising Age:* "Rumors that Philip Morris might drop the show were based largely on the report that the company's sales had dropped from $234,346,380 to $232,559,372 in 1952, with the net profits down $2,371,990. In addition, Philip Morris dropped from fourth to fifth place in cigarette sales."

The contract, one of the biggest ever written for television, guaranteed the series' run for the next two and a half years—through the 1954–55 season. About sixty percent of the amount was paid to Desilu to produce *Lucy,* the remainder covering CBS air-time charges. At that point, the weekly program budget was between $40,000 and $50,000, a far cry from the original $19,500 figure proposed in the spring of 1951.

At the Hollywood signing, Lucy said happily: "It couldn't happen to a nicer pair of kids—I mean our two children, of course."

Several weeks later Philip Morris president, O. Parker Mc-

Comas, addressed the membership of Financial Analysts of Philadelphia, during which he gave a rave endorsement for *I Love Lucy:*

"This show is the all-time phenomenon of the entertainment business. On a strictly dollars-and-cents basis, it is twice as efficient as the average nighttime television show in conveying our advertising message to the public. It is nearly three times more efficient dollarwise in reaching adults than *Life* [magazine] or your own Philadelphia newspapers. Three times more people see every Monday night's *I Love Lucy* show than watched all the major-league baseball games last year. . . . Although the entire sum [$8 million] sounds huge, it is probably one of, if not the most effective advertising buys in the entire country. In addition, we derive many supplementary merchandising and publicity benefits from the show. As you can see, we love *Lucy.*"

The arrival of little Desi sent the popularity of the series to an all-time high and opened the door to lucrative merchandising deals. Experts referred to the new Arnaz offspring as "Lucy's $50,000,000 Baby," because revenue from certain tie-in commitments was expected to top that mark, an amazing figure for a field in which Hopalong Cassidy promotions were considered a smashing success when they passed the $3 million-a-year mark.

To shield baby Desi from the effects of too much publicity, all promotions were centered around the fictional baby, Little Ricky Ricardo. In fact, within two months of his arrival, a "Ricky, Jr." doll was introduced on the market. This was the work of A. E. (Ed) Hamilton, Desilu vice-president who was in charge of their New York office located in the Fred F. French building at 551 Fifth Avenue. He alone handled the royalty arrangements on promotions that reached into every corner of the country.

As Jack Gould wrote in the *Times* in February 1953: "*I Love Lucy* is probably the most misleading title imaginable. For once, all available statistics are in agreement: Millions love Lucy." And they kept on loving her when she returned to the screen April 20 in "No Children Allowed," the first episode filmed since November 14, 1952.

Since California law limited the posing time under lights of an actor less than six months of age to just thirty-second intervals, Desilu sought out the services of a pair of undersized, six-month-old twins who, by state child labor laws, could pose two hours each per day and spell each other in the Little Ricky role. Jess Oppenheimer sent James Paisley, the *Lucy* assistant director, to Los Angeles City Hall to examine the birth records of twins. Paisley found nine sets and, on the basis of coloring, finally narrowed the choice to Richard Lee and Ronald Lee Simmons, the identical twin sons of Mr. and Mrs. Arthur L. Simmons, a Los Angeles department store shoe buyer. Born on September 7, 1952, the infants were paid $25 each per show and were attended on the set by a nurse and Department of Welfare social worker. Stand-in dolls were used during rehearsals so that the boys had to show up only for the Friday filmings.

The Simmons twins were not the only new actors to begin recurring roles with the "No Children Allowed" *Lucy* installment. Having guest-starred in "The Marriage License" episode the preceding season, seventy-eight-year-old actress Elizabeth ("Patty") Patterson was tapped to portray Mrs. Mathilda Trumbull, an elderly neighbor of the Ricardos'. She brought with her a long list of movie credits, over one hundred, the first of which was *The Boy Friend* in 1926. Born in Savannah, Tennessee, a small town on the Tennessee River, Miss Patterson never married and lived alone during her thirty-year motion-picture career at the Hollywood Roosevelt Hotel. She died of complications from pneumonia on January 31, 1966.

Martin Lewis, a *TV Guide* staffer, was there for the March 20 filming. He recalls: "Before the filming, Desi explained to the three hundred people in the audience that Ricky, Jr., would be featured in the show, and that a doll wrapped in a blanket would be used in the long shots and a real baby in the close-ups.

"In the doll scenes, the crying was done on cue from backstage by Jerry Hausner, who had years of experience as a crybaby on radio. This was particularly important since the episode was centered around the baby's incessant crying. However, the real baby proved to be a ham. He cried during the scenes as per the script, and when the scene was finished and Lucy picked him up out of the crib, he stopped crying as though on cue and stared at the applauding audience.

"Lucy fluffed her lines only once. Jokingly, she blamed Desi because the scene had to be done over. He said it was all her fault, at which point Lucy playfully threw a roundhouse right that landed on Desi's back.

"Eight setups were required, with five-minute intermissions between scenes for costume changes. A five-piece Latin American musical group entertained during the breaks. When Lucy and Desi returned from a costume change before the camera crew was ready for the next scene, they did a rumba for the studio audience that would have made professional dancers jealous."

Earlier in the week, during rehearsals, Jerry Hausner was standing in the wings, awaiting his cues to provide the necessary baby cries, when an elderly man wandered on to the sound stage. "He insisted on knowing where I learned to cry like that," Hausner said. "I told him that many years ago, during the twenties in Cleveland, I went backstage at a vaudeville house after a clown named Pepito had done it on stage.

"I was just a teen-ager at the time, and I told him I was interested in learning how to do it. At first, the clown refused, telling me, 'You might take my job away.' But finally he relented and showed me how to constrict my throat in order to effect the baby cry.

"We were right in the midst of the *Lucy* dress rehearsal, so I hardly noticed, but the old man was crying. He looked up at me and said, 'I'm Pepito.' I couldn't believe it. Here it was almost thirty years later, and I had been making a very good living in radio, mostly from that baby cry he taught me."

The remainder of the 1952–1953 season was hectic. The staff and crew had become accustomed to a certain production pace before the baby boom began. There was usually a six-to-eight-week postproduction schedule for an average *I Love Lucy* segment. For instance, an episode filmed January 1 was not likely to air until late February or early March. Miss Ball's period of convalescence following little Desi's birth prohibited the luxury of such a time span. Instead, the eleven episodes filmed upon her return to work were broadcast about a month after they were put on 35mm celluloid, requiring the staff to maintain a vigorous pace.

These episodes included such gems as "Lucy Hires a Maid," in which delightful Verna Felton, a character actress seen earlier in the season as Lucy's nemesis in "Sales Resistance," played a no-nonsense household helper; "Lucy's Last Birthday," where Lucy joins Friends of the Friendless, a Salvation Army-type group, to teach Ricky a lesson ("about the meaning of friendship") for forgetting her twenty-ninth birthday (in this classic episode, Desi sang the *I Love Lucy* theme song for the first time); "The Ricardos Change Apartments" (from 4-A to 3-B), a clever half hour through which the *Lucy* living room set gained a window upstage; and the last televised episode of the season, "Never Do Business with Friends," which depicted the hilarious misadventures when the Ricardos sold their used washing machine to the Mertzes.

After the last filming of the season on May 29, 1953, the cast and crew embarked on a well-deserved three-month hiatus, during which time *Racket Squad* filled in for the vacationing *I Love Lucy*. Reed Hadley as Captain Braddock hardly could compare with the antics of Lucy and Ricky and Fred and Ethel, but he did manage to corral crooks for thirteen weeks while Philip Morris picked up the tab.

84

7

While most of the Desilu people enjoyed a summer of rest and relaxation, Lucille and Desi plunged into production on *The Long, Long Trailer* feature after only nine days vacation. (Vivian interrupted her summer break by appearing with Mel Ferrer in a stock version of *Pal Joey* at the La Jolla Playhouse, the site of her discovery by Desi for the Ethel Mertz role two summers before.)

Trailer, not so incidentally, became M-G-M's most successful film comedy despite a large sampling of lukewarm reviews, one of which accused the ninety-six-minute movie of being "a long, long *I Love Lucy* decked out in CinemaScope."

Metro wanted no part of it at first. They subscribed to the theory that the audience wouldn't pay to see actors they could get at home for free. But Pandro S. Berman, the film's producer, insisted that these were different parts, and Lucille Ball and Desi Arnaz could make the picture hilarious. If the picture were funny enough, he had no worries about whether people would pay to see it.

Vincente Minnelli, who had directed Lucille in the M-G-M musical *Ziegfeld Follies* in 1945, was director of *The Long, Long Trailer.* "She and Desi were at the height of their television popularity. I thought the story was perfect for them," contends Minnelli in his autobiography. "There were times when the action was broad and those were the opportunities Lucy grabbed hold of and ran away with.

"It was an inexpensive picture to make, and a painless one. All the film editor had to do was clip off the end slates of the film to make this a smoothly flowing picture. Lucy is one of the few comedic talents who can be broad and uniquely human at the same time. She can get away with things that less talented people wouldn't even presume to handle. On television, week after week, she's handled manufactured situations and passed them off as real."

At times the film came precariously close to resembling *I Love Lucy,* especially in the slapstick sequences. The roles Lucy and Desi played were Tacy and Nicky Collini, which even sounded like Lucy and Ricky if you said it fast enough.

After six weeks of *Trailer* photography, Lucy and Desi bundled up their two children and escaped to a rented house in Del Mar. They had intended to do personal appearances for *I Love Lucy* that had been postponed from the previous summer, but they were too exhausted to travel. Instead, they planned to enjoy the four or five weeks at the beach.

As executive producer of *Lucy,* Desi initiated some important changes during the summer. Because General Service Studios did not have enough sound stages that could be converted into Desilu "playhouses," he sought suitable space elsewhere. He found it several blocks east at Motion Picture Center, a seven-acre lot that boasted nine stages, six of which could be converted into "summer theaters" to accommodate the growing number of situation comedies that Desilu was producing, coproducing, or about to produce. Located at 846 North Cahuenga Boulevard in Hollywood, the new Desilu headquarters began to take shape late in the summer so that rehearsals for the first new *Lucy* of the third season could begin after Labor Day. The sets and equipment had to be trucked over from the Las Palmas Avenue address and installed. Lucy was delighted with the move: She gained her own kitchen so she could rustle up short-order snacks between *Lucy* sessions. Her hatred for studio-commissary food was well known.

In addition to physical changes, Desi implemented a number of personnel changes. He promoted assistant director James Paisley to the status of Desilu production manager and hired Jerry Thorpe to replace him as first A.D. on *Lucy.* Son of veteran M-G-M director Richard Thorpe (*Night Must Fall, Three Little*

Words, Ivanhoe, etc.), Jerry was Vincente Minnelli's assistant on *The Long, Long Trailer.* Desi was so impressed by young Thorpe's dedication to detail (the Number One requirement of an assistant director), he hired him for *I Love Lucy* halfway through *Trailer* photography. Thorpe's only stipulation was that Desi also hire his assistant Jack Aldworth as second A.D. Since they worked so well together on the M-G-M comedy, Arnaz agreed.

However, Thorpe's first assignment in August of 1953 was to find a new set of twins to portray Ricky Ricardo, Jr., during the third *Lucy* season. Child labor restrictions prevented the company from fully utilizing the "talents" of the Simmons twins who were not yet one year old. Arnaz had a good lead—he had seen what he thought was an ideal pair pictured in a newspaper layout, so he instructed Thorpe to contact the boys' parents and offer the fourteen-month-old twins the role.

Mrs. Max Mayer, mother of Michael and Joseph Mayer, and member of the nationwide Mothers of Twins Club, was skeptical when Jerry called. There had been many news accounts of fraudulent talent agencies bilking parents of so-called talented kiddies.

"I thought this was phony, too," she said, "because we'd never given a thought to placing our children in TV. I told Jerry I'd bring them in for an audition, but emphasized that the minute it cost me a penny, he could count us out."

Thorpe was amused. "I've got a whole corridor full of doting mothers with their kids, looking for this job," he told Mrs. Mayer. "I give you first whack at it and you call me a crook!"

Mrs. Mayer dressed the twins simply in seersucker playsuits, quite a contrast to the sartorial splendor of some of the other applicants. One look at the boys and Desi signed them to a contract. They remained in the role for three full seasons, amassing an educational trust fund and, as a gift from Lucy, all the clothes they wore on the show.

"It's an unnatural life for children, especially after they reach school age," Mrs. Mayer now confides. She promptly retired them from show business at age four.

With the move to Motion Picture Center and accompanying increase in production, Desi needed a key executive to carry the bulk of the load. Instinctively, he went to the one man at CBS who, in the long negotiations for the original *I Love Lucy* deal, had given him the most trouble. "It figured," Arnaz said simply. "There was this one guy who kept costing me money and saving it for CBS. I figured I had better get him on my side where he could start saving me money for a change." This is how Martin Leeds, formerly in charge of business affairs for CBS in Hollywood, joined Desilu Productions as executive vice-president.

Another key figure who joined the *I Love Lucy* staff that summer was Academy Award-winner (in 1950 for "Color Costume Design," *Samson and Delilah*) Elois Jenssen. "Lucille first came to me in 1951, asking if I'd design her clothes for a new TV series she was starting," relates Elois, a lovely and articulate lady who's pretty enough to be a movie star herself. "At the time, I was under exclusive contract to Twentieth Century-Fox and couldn't do it. When my three-year hitch was up, I decided to freelance.

"Jack Chertok, who had produced Lucy's film *Lured* for which I designed the costumes, was starting a new TV series starring Ann Sothern, *Private Secretary,* and he asked me to design Ann's clothes.

"After a season of *Secretary,* I decided to get together again with Lucille to see if she still wanted me to design clothes for her. I knew I could handle both assignments at the same time. Up to that point," Elois reveals, "all of her dresses for *I Love Lucy* were either cut out of two or three of the same dress patterns and put together by Madame Sara [Mancilas], or purchased at Ohrbach's.

"I drove out to M-G-M where Lucy and Desi were filming *The Long, Long Trailer* and told her some of my ideas. She thought they were great, until she questioned me about salary. I told her that Jack was giving me a flat rate of two hundred dollars per episode on *Private Secretary.* Lucy said, 'Oh, we couldn't afford *that.*' She claimed the most she could pay was half of that."

It wasn't the first account of Desilu's thriftiness. Academy Award-winning cinematographer Karl Freund started out at scale. So did Marc Daniels and most of the creative staff. One veteran character actor offers: "It was supposed to be a privilege to appear on *I Love Lucy.* It *was* nice, but they were awful cheapskates. We got paid the absolute minimums. If your part was small, they just hired you for one day—the day of the actual filming—which gave you just one or two rehearsals. They didn't want to pop for a full week's pay which was pretty much the standard practice." (Because *I Love Lucy* was the first *filmed* TV series, it came under the Screen Actors Guild jurisdiction. SAG minimums, until the summer of 1955, were as follows: a "day player" received $70; for three days work, $175; and for a five-day, or weekly, assignment, $250.)

Typically, then, Elois Jenssen—Paris-educated at Parson's School of Fine and Applied Art, Oscar-winner, designer of costumes for over twenty-five films, and still under the age of thirty— waited over a month for a decision to be made on the *Lucy* assignment.

"Even Kurt Frings, who was Lucy and Desi's agent, had to okay this 'major' expenditure," jests Miss Jenssen, recalling the incredible hoopla over a measly hundred-dollar-a-week outlay. "Not only did I have to design Lucy's costumes [Vivian, by insistence, now was receiving a weekly allowance with which to purchase her own wardrobe], but I also had to set up an entire wardrobe department from scratch. They didn't have much of anything, and it was like pulling teeth to buy even a spool of thread, let alone a sewing machine. Everything had to be approved."

Elois herself was "approved" the Friday before Labor Day 1953, exactly seven days before the filming of the first new *Lucy* episode of the season. "I immediately sat down and started sketching designs for her. I wanted to build up the kind of wardrobe that would be becoming to Lucy. I worked all night and then on Saturday drove out to Chatsworth to show Lucy my sketches. She had just come back from her summer vacation in Del Mar. Desi wasn't due back until Tuesday morning, when rehearsals were set to begin.

"When I got there, we walked toward the pool where we could sit down and go over my drawings. I'll never forget what happened next," Elois shudders. "As we turned a corner, we saw little Lucie, two years of age, face down in the pool. She had apparently fallen in. Lucy became panic-stricken and couldn't move, she was so upset. I dove into the pool with all my clothes on and pulled her out. Thank God she was all right. Needless to say, Lucille hardly could concentrate on costume sketches."

Something else that happened that Labor Day weekend caused

Lucille some unnecessary anguish. Several weeks before in Del Mar, she had received a phone call from a member of the House Un-American Activities Committee, asking if she would volunteer to appear at a closed meeting on Friday, September 4 in Hollywood. "We simply want to go over the statements made at your previous appearance before our committee last year," explained an aide of Representative Donald L. Jackson, chairman of the committee, referring to an April 3, 1952, closed meeting at which time Lucy had been questioned concerning her intention to vote on the Communist ticket in 1936. She had explained her Grandpa Hunt's role in her political activities that year, and when the hearing ended she shook hands with the various committee members and left, completely cleared. No word of the interview went beyond the committee room.

Having returned early from Del Mar especially to make a second appearance before the committee, Lucy again testified that she had registered her intention to vote the Communist ticket only to please her grandfather. After two hours of intense questioning, the hearing ended. Investigator William Wheeler concluded by telling Miss Ball, "I have no further questions. Thank you for your cooperation." When the handshaking ended, Lucy was assured by committee members that she was completely cleared, again. She was also assured that her testimony would remain secret.

Two days later, with Desi still in Del Mar playing poker at movie producer Irving Briskin's ocean-view home, Lucy put the children to bed and settled down in a comfortable rocking chair in the den of their Chatsworth home to catch Walter Winchell's weekly, Sunday night broadcast. Toward the end of Winchell's infamous "Mr.-and-Mrs.-America-and-all-the-ships-at-sea" program, he punched across a "blind" item: "The top television comedienne has been confronted with her membership in the Communist party."

Winchell's emphasis on the word *top* left little doubt that he was referring to Lucille Ball. Instantly in Del Mar, Desi's poker game was interrupted by an urgent phone call from Desilu PR representative Ken Morgan. "Desi," Morgan began, "did you hear Winchell's broadcast?" Desi had not, but after being told the details, he immediately phoned Lucy. "I'll be right home," he exclaimed, slamming down the receiver.

Within an hour Howard Strickling, M-G-M's publicity director and an old friend, arrived at Chatsworth with Kenny Morgan. Lucy was puzzled. She had not yet realized the impact of Winchell's cryptic statement. Strickling, whose studio had just shelled out $2 million to film *The Long, Long Trailer,* knew what the consequences could be. The era of Joe McCarthy and of the infamous Senate hearings was in full swing, and an accusation such as Winchell's could spell the end not only of the *Trailer* film but also the entire Desilu empire—including *I Love Lucy,* the nation's Number One television show. Following on the heels of Strickling and Morgan, the Arnazes' neighbor, columnist Bill Henry of the Los Angeles *Times,* knocked on their front door, offering his help. Suddenly Lucy began to realize the full impact; she was in a panic, wishing desperately that Desi were home.

Sometime around 1 A.M. Desi arrived, having sped the 125 miles from San Diego. He found Lucy in a chain-smoking state. "You're making too big a fuss over this," he said, trying to calm her. "Don't get excited."

"But why are you so cool?" she asked.

"Because I've known about it for two weeks."

"You have?"

"Yes. J. Edgar Hoover told me about it at the racetrack. He said there was nothing he could do about it."

Strickling agreed. He advised the Arnazes to ignore Walter's broadcast, play dumb, and the whole affair would be forgotten in a day or two. Dismissing his urge to fight back, Desi decided to follow Strickling's recommendation, mainly to spare Lucy and her family further embarrassment.

However, the next day, Monday, September 7, Winchell's widely syndicated newspaper column carried the same accusation. Still, Lucy and Desi intended to start rehearsing the first new *I Love Lucy* segment, "The Girls Go into Business," the following morning as if nothing was wrong. On Wednesday, amid a run-through at Stage 9 of Motion Picture Center, their new *Lucy* headquarters, someone alerted Desi to columnist Jack O'Brien's barb in the New York *Journal-American:* "Lucille Ball has announced that she intends to retire in five years. It may be a lot sooner than she thinks." He tore up the newspaper, hoping Lucy wouldn't see the item.

On Friday, the day of the first *Lucy* filming, he and Lucy drove

Opposite (from left to right, top to bottom): Emily Daniels, Milton H. Biow, Jerry Hausner, Pepito. *Above:* Wilbur Hatch, Jess Oppenheimer, Karl Freund and William Asher.

in the back gates at Motion Picture Center for a 1 P.M. "call." The front offices were jammed with reporters; the Desilu telephone (HOllywood 9-5981) had clocked several hundred calls. At noon the Los Angeles *Herald-Express* (which was also Winchell's local outlet) broke the story; in huge four-inch-high red letters the front-page banner headline proclaimed, "LUCILLE BALL NAMED RED." The evidence, printed: a Photostatted copy of the 1936 registration card on which Lucy had indicated her intention to vote for the Communist party candidates in the 1936 elections.

While the subject of all the furor, Lucy, went about her business preparing for the evening's filming, under Bill Asher's able direction, Desi picked up the telephone and called CBS in New York. He told network president Dr. Frank Stanton about the headlines and confessed that he had had no word yet from Philip Morris, the sponsor. Desi was scared—the cigarette company, fearing bad publicity, had every right to cancel their contract with Desilu. If they did, or threatened to do so, Desi was prepared to cough up about $30,000 to buy the half-hour time slot *Lucy* usually occupied, although *Racket Squad* was currently running as its summer replacement. Stanton agreed to sell Desi and Lucy the time so they could explain their side of the story to the American public.

Meanwhile, Lucy followed Desi's orders not to speak with any reporters. Instead, she continued rehearsing. Around her the other actors and crewmen tried to pretend it was an average day, although everyone knew the empire was in danger of collapsing. Nobody discussed the crisis with her.

In New York, an executive of Philip Morris put in an urgent call to the firm's independent public relations consultant, Benjamin Sonnenberg. "What should we do?" asked the cigarette man.

Sonnenberg, who had been in on the *I Love Lucy* negotiations from the start in 1951, knew strong-willed Desi. His advice to the client: "Let *them* handle it."

At 3 P.M. the call came from New York. Desi grabbed the telephone, listening to the sponsor's verdict: "If all the facts are as they now are, we're behind you one hundred percent."

Relieved and choking back tears, Desi hung up and raced fifty feet across the studio courtyard, which separated his office from Stage 9, to inform Lucy. He smiled at her knowingly and tears quickly filled her eyes. Then in a carefully controlled voice she said, "Well, that's fine. I'll get back to work."

Sponsor's faith or not, Lucy was still upset. The headlines of the day caused her to conjure up visions of the entire American public hating her. Desi decided to get Donald Jackson on the phone and insist he hold an immediate press conference exonerating Lucille of any Communist suspicion. Lucy's only concern was the night's filming—she was scared to death that she would be booed off the stage by the studio audience. Desi tried to waylay her fears even though he was thinking the same thoughts. He even considered canceling the live audience that night, but later reasoned it would be almost an admission of guilt.

Jackson agreed to hold a press conference at the Statler Hotel at 6 P.M., if he could get together a quorum of committee members. Desi then arranged to have favored newsman Jim Bacon of the Associated Press personally cover the conference for him. It most likely would be concluded just moments before the *Lucy* filming that evening. Arnaz *had* to know that Lucille had been publicly cleared before he went out to face the studio audience.

The call finally came, and Bacon relayed the news that Jackson had cleared Lucy and there would be beautiful headlines in all the morning papers. Lucy, chalk-faced and near collapse, smiled weakly. A doctor was in attendance all day just in case. Quietly the group made its way across the narrow courtyard and through the red-striped canopied entrance that led to the rear of the sound stage.

At a few minutes past eight, Desi stepped through the living room door on the set and faced three hundred people seated in bleachers extending the entire width of the building. He had a little trouble with the door and laughed nervously about it. However, instead of the usual warm-up, which included a few planned jokes, he gave an impromptu speech to the unnaturally silent throng.

"Welcome to the first *I Love Lucy* show of the season," he began. "We are glad to have you back and we are glad to be back ourselves. But before we go on, I want to talk to you about something serious. Something very serious. You all know what it is. The papers have been full of it all day."

He paused briefly to switch the mike to his other hand. Suddenly his lower lip began to quiver and his voice broke. "Lucille is no Communist!" he blurted out fiercely. "Lucy has never been a Communist, not now and never will be. I was kicked out of Cuba because of communism. We both despise the Communists and everything they stand for."

An emotional Latin, Desi was angry. His eyes had now filled with tears and his voice was shaking. "Lucille is one hundred percent an American. She is as American as Barney Baruch and Ike Eisenhower. Last November we both voted for Ike. Tomorrow morning the complete transcript of Lucille's testimony will be released to the papers and you can read it for yourself. Then you will know this is all a pack of lies. Please, ladies and gentlemen, don't believe every piece of bunk you've read in today's papers!"

He had to stop. The audience had risen to its feet in roaring approval. One man shouted, "We're with you, boy!" and Desi turned, looked over his shoulder in the man's direction, and said, "Thank you."

Glancing into the wings, Arnaz sighted Lucy. She was sobbing.

Then, as was the usual preshow custom, Desi introduced Bill Frawley and Vivian Vance. They received warm, hearty welcomes from the crowd. Desi was pleased, but now he was approaching the really difficult moment—introducing Lucy, who was quickly trying to regain her composure.

"And now," Desi began, his voice calm, "I want you to meet my favorite wife—my favorite redhead—in fact, that's the only thing red about her, and even *that's* not legitimate—Lucille Ball!"

Getting hold of herself, Lucille took a deep breath and quietly stepped out from behind a door at the rear of the set. The heavy makeup for the show concealed the lines of worry and strain. Following the last dress rehearsal, she had been in seclusion in her dressing room and had spoken to no one but Desi, her mother, and a few close friends. Suddenly, Bill Hatch's band was playing the *I Love Lucy* theme song, and the audience gave Lucy a standing ovation. She tried to smile, but was unable to speak. Instead, she punched the air lightly with both hands as if to say, "We'll fight this thing out." Grimacing with emotion, she bowed briefly and walked backstage through the set door.

Then came Bill Asher's voice from the control booth: "Please take your places for the first scene. . . . Cameras ready? . . .

Roll the sound . . . roll the film. . . . Action!" And "The Girls Go into Business" was on its way.

When it was over a little more than an hour later, Lucy and Desi came out arm in arm and asked each of the supporting players (including Lucy's dear friend Barbara Pepper) to take a bow. Then Lucy stood alone with Desi for a moment, looked at the audience, and said, "Good night, God bless you for being so kind—and thank you." It was a long walk offstage, clear across the width of the studio. She received an ovation every step of the way. When she reached her dressing room, she broke down and cried her heart out. It had been a very long Friday.

On Saturday, the Arnazes held an informal press conference at their ranch home at 19700 Devonshire Street in Chatsworth. An army of reporters fired questions at Lucy, who was now capable of answering them calmly. The *Los Angeles Times* already had printed this banner headline for all to read: "LUCILLE BALL NOT RED, REP. JACKSON DECLARES." At the end of the two-hour session, held in a garden setting, a reporter faced his colleagues. "I think," he said, "we owe both of them a vote of thanks. And I think a lot of people owe them an apology."

The apology that counted most came the following night on Winchell's telecast: "During the past week, Donald Jackson, chairman of the House Un-American Activities Committee, and all its members cleared Lucy a hundred percent, and so did J. Edgar Hoover and the FBI, plus every newspaper in America and tonight, Mr. Lincoln is drying his eyes for making her go through this." After seven long days, the ordeal was over.

Thousands of fans wired their support to Lucy. Harry Ackerman issued a simple statement that appeared in *Variety:* "People seem to feel this thing is silly, not serious, and they all love Lucy." Ed Sullivan expressed his support in his nationwide column: "It's a singularly fortunate thing for Lucille Ball that she's been a weekly visitor to millions of American living rooms. In those Monday night visits, people have come to know her well. TV cameras being as revealing as they are, so the jury of Public Opinion is an informed jury as it renders its verdict on a silly thing she did seventeen years ago."

As further confirmation of her innocence, on November 25,

1953, the B'nai B'rith named Lucille Ball "Woman of the Year," the first time the award had been bestowed on an actress. On November 26, Lucy, Desi, Vivian, and Bill were invited to the White House to dine with President and Mrs. Eisenhower who were staunch *I Love Lucy* fans; guests included Eddie Fisher and Jackie Robinson. After performing for his hosts, Desi approached Ike: "They said a foreigner with an accent wouldn't be believable playing an average American husband." The President replied: "Out in Kansas they said I'd never be President. You know what we are? A couple of walking miracles!"

The premiere episode of the third season, telecast October 5, 1953—"Ricky's *Life* Story" (actually filmed the previous May and saved)—managed to maintain the high ratings the series had become noted for. The "red" scare apparently had little effect on the popularity of *I Love Lucy*. The public still adored the antics of the Ricardos and Mertzes.

The critics, however, thought otherwise. One wrote: "The opening show was pretty funny. Just pretty funny. Last year's opener ["Job Switching"], as I recall, was a riot. This one wasn't. . . . The *Lucy* shows, let's face it, are beginning to sound an awful lot alike. Miss Ball is always trying to bust out of the house; Arnaz is trying to keep her in apron strings. The variations on this theme are infinite, but it's the same and I'm a mite tired of it. I don't think I'll ever get tired of Miss Ball though; she's a joy to watch."

In November, *Dragnet,* Jack Webb's series about the Los Angeles Police Department costarring Ben Alexander, achieved the impossible—it momentarily passed *I Love Lucy* in the Nielsen race and the two series began a neck-and-neck race for leadership. With a 61.3 rating, *Dragnet* nosed out *Lucy* with an even 60.

Karl Freund was hospitalized in early November with pneumonia, and his *Lucy* chores were taken over by one of his cameramen, Nick Musuraca. Freund returned to work on December 3. Unfortunately, he missed the surprise thirteenth wedding anniversary party that Desi threw for Lucille at the Mocambo nightclub on November 30. Lucy had expected only a quiet dinner with Desi and their longtime friend Vincente Minnelli. When they arrived at the posh Sunset Strip club, Desi escorted Lucille to a private back room.

"We can't go in there," she insisted. "Someone's having a party."

Someone was—Lucy. Forty guests helped the Arnazes celebrate their anniversary. At nine o'clock, nightclub owner Charley Morrison wheeled in a television set. It was a Monday night, and no one wanted to miss *I Love Lucy*. The crowd watched the "Too Many Crooks" (a/k/a "Madame X") episode, as did an estimated 46 million devotees of Lucy's televised high jinks.

"As the show became more and more popular, so did the theme song," says Eliot Daniel, composer of the catchy melody. "In writing a theme for the show I tried to get an opening musical phrase that would say, 'I love Lucy.' Having settled on the first four notes, the rest of the song practically wrote itself. I played it for Jess, Desi, and a few others, and we had a theme song. Not a note was changed and no other tune was submitted.

"When Ricky had to sing a song to Lucy on her birthday ["Lucy's Last Birthday," telecast May 11, 1953] we decided to use the theme song, but we needed lyrics," recalls Mr. Daniel. "I was most pleased when Harold Adamson came up with lyrics that I feel are just right for the song and the show."

Adamson's lyrics to *I Love Lucy* are as follows:

Verse: There's a certain couple that I know.
         They're strictly love birds.
         A pair of turtle dove birds.
         He's a guy who wants the world to know,
         So ev'ry day you'll hear him say:
Chrous: I love Lucy and she loves me.
         We're as happy as two can be.
         Sometimes we quarrel but then
         How we love making up again.
         Lucy kisses like no one can.
         She's my missus and I'm her man.
         And life is heaven, you see,
         'Cause I love Lucy,
         Yes, I love Lucy
         And Lucy loves me.

"Throughout the series," Eliot Daniel continues, "there were several shows that included musical numbers. In a few cases they were popular songs, but for the most part they were special material, with lyrics by Madelyn Pugh and Bob Carroll, and music by me. One show was a complete operetta ["The Operetta"], and on this one we had the help of an outside lyricist. One original song that seemed to do very well was in a baseball skit with Bob Hope ["Lucy Meets Bob Hope"]—'Nobody Loves the Ump' [Music by Eliot Daniel, Lyrics by Larry Orenstein].

"In these musical numbers the principals would rehearse with piano during the week, either with me or with Desi's pianist, Marco Rizo, and do it with the full orchestra during the filming. We were fortunate in that our four principals all handled musical numbers very well and seemed to get a genuine kick out of doing them."

Daniel describes the procedure he followed to furnish his original music for each *Lucy* installment: "After the show was edited, they would run it in the projection room for the music editor and me, and I would tell him the footages I wanted— sometimes just a ten-second bridge, sometimes three minutes of underscoring, catching various accents and moods. The editor would then send me a cue sheet with all the timings and descriptions of action, and I would go ahead with composition and orchestration.

"We recorded the music for the early shows done at General Service Studios at Glen Glenn studios which were right across Romaine Street; but when we moved to Motion Picture Center, they ran cable to the Glenn complex and we were able to record in a room right next to where the show was being filmed. Bill Hatch would conduct the orchestra from my score, and I would be in the control room with the engineer. Everything was done to stopwatch so we didn't waste time for rollback starts with the projector. I would check the balance, and Bill and I would check each other on the timings, so we soon had a pretty efficient setup.

"When all the various tracks were ready—dialogue, sound effects, music, et cetera—we had a rerecording session where all the tracks were run with the picture, balanced, and then reduced to one master track. This session was usually attended by all concerned: producer, director, film editor, music editor, ad agency representative, and myself."

Members of the versatile Desi Arnaz Orchestra, conducted by Wilbur J. Hatch, included Marco Rizo, pianist; Alberto Calderón, drums; José Betancourt, Latin percussion; Nick Escalante,

100

bass; Tony Terran, trumpet; Vince di Bari, trumpet; Felipe Hernández, trumpet; José Gutiérrez, trombone; Jack Pickering, trombone; Joe Miller, flute and sax; Jack Baker, sax; Jack Echols, sax; and Nancy Youngman, harp.

Most familiar of all musicians was pianist Marco Rizo. He was featured in dozens of episodes and referred to in many others. "My association with Desi started long before *I Love Lucy*. I was Desi's pianist-arranger when he appeared at the Copacabana in New York in the forties, then continued in the same capacity when his orchestra headlined the Bob Hope NBC radio show in Hollywood for two years. Then we did *Your Tropical Trip* for CBS Radio in 1951 which featured music from South America and the Caribbean. Then came the *I Love Lucy* pilot and there I remained until the very end in 1959," Rizo points out, adding that on his worldwide concert tour he plays his own special arrangement of the *I Love Lucy* theme song. "It meets with instant approval all over the world."

Lovely Doris Singleton, who played Caroline Appleby, Lucy Ricardo's friendly nemesis, once was approached in a shoe store in Italy by an *I Love Lucy* fan. "The woman greeted me like we were old-time friends," says Doris who is prettier today than she was during her Caroline Appleby days. "Once a man came to my table at Prunier in Paris and asked me if I was from San Francisco. He said his wife was sure she knew me. I told him that while I had visited Frisco a few times, I didn't have any friends there. A few minutes later he came back, insisting his wife knew me. Finally it dawned on me, so I told him to ask her if she ever watched *I Love Lucy*. He went off and, a few seconds later, came back grinning. 'Of course,' he said, 'you're Caroline Appleby!' "

Like many *I Love Lucy* alumni, Miss Singleton had worked with Lucille before the television series came along: She did a few parts on *My Favorite Husband*. When the TV show was under way, Jess Oppenheimer hired her to play one of the girls in the women's club.

Doris explains how her character became Caroline Appleby: "Lucy liked to use real person's names. As you know, Marion Strong, which Shirley Mitchell played on the show, was actually one of Lucy's girl friends from Jamestown, New York. When we were trying to come up with a name for me, Lucy suggested that

I use my own name, but I didn't want to. So she said, 'Okay then, Doris, you'll be Caroline Appleby.' I told her that would be fine. Later I discovered that Caroline Appleby was one of Lucille's schoolteachers." Caroline's husband was Charley Appleby. He ran a TV station. Doris Singleton's husband is Charley Isaacs. He's a TV writer. *Lucy* was just one big, happy family.

The 1953–1954 season saw one member of the happy "family" depart. It was Jerry Hausner, the actor who had appeared in the original *Lucy* pilot, and for two and a half years had played Ricky's agent Jerry. It was not a happy parting. "Desi and I had a scene in which I was to call him from a pay phone," recounts the actor about an incident that took place during the "Fan Magazine Interview" episode. "The set with the pay phone was on the opposite end of the sound stage and during rehearsals, the phones were not connected. In other words, it was impossible for us to hear each other without cues. I told Desi I didn't think it was going to work out, but he assured me the phones would be connected by Thursday night when the show would be filmed before the live audience.

"The night of the show we did the scene, but the phones still were not connected. It did not go very well, as I had expected. The audience was laughing in all the wrong places. When the scene was over, Desi stormed across the sound stage and cursed me out in front of the entire cast and crew and audience—about four hundred people. I couldn't believe it—in all my professional career I had never been treated so badly. I was so upset that I walked over to Jess Oppenheimer and told him I would never again do the show. He understood. It was terrible when Desi and I had to do another scene together in the last act. I found it very difficult looking him in the face."

Midway through the season, Lucy and Desi flew to New York for the February 18, 1954, premiere of *The Long, Long Trailer* at Radio City Music Hall. The highlight of their Gotham visit came when Lucy was honored on the Radio City stage. She recalled for the SRO audience the days she sat in the theater dreaming that one day she would be on that stage. Another thrill came when she and Desi discovered a woman in the lobby of their hotel, who wanted them to baptize her baby. The pair went from one party to another . . . Billy Reed's Little Club, the Waldorf,

102

the Astor . . . and mobs of *I Love Lucy* fans thronged each affair to pay homage to TV's Number One team.

When Lucille was asked what she thought was the main reason for the excellence of the program, she unflappingly replied, "Desi does it all."

"I found that bringing *I Love Lucy* to home screens," Desi once admitted, "was ninety percent desk work, ten percent acting. From the overwork, I soon developed an eye twitch and headaches. I was worrying myself sick trying to be everywhere at once. Then one day Bill Frawley remarked, 'Remember when you led a band? You just waved a stick and the boys took it from there. Why don't you develop faith in others?' That took some of the air out of me. Once I tried delegating authority, making each of the five hundred workers feel pride through accomplishing a task unassisted, everything went twice as smoothly."

There was not a person interviewed for this book who did not agree, however, that most of the credit for the show's superiority goes to Lucy herself. Her dedication, hard work, and incredible drive for perfection were what made *I Love Lucy* a hit.

"It was a demanding week when I worked on *I Love Lucy*," offers Doris Singleton. "It was one constant rehearsal. Everything had to be absolutely perfected. It was definitely not fun-and-games time on that set.

"I was lucky to have been in the Harpo Marx episode. He was absolutely fantastic to work with and was about the sweetest man I've ever met. He wasn't a bit funny offstage, but a very warm, lovely gentle man. When the fright wig was off, he was just Harpo. After the show was filmed, he gathered us all around and did a concert on the harp; Vivian sang.

"Every time there was a lull during rehearsals, Lucy would drag Harpo off to the other side of the stage to rehearse that incredible mirror bit. She refused to do it unless it was absolutely perfect."

Lucille Ball has always expected professionalism and perfection from those around her. After a recent Lucille Ball television special, costar Jackie Gleason remarked: "Lucy would have made a terrific top sergeant. I hate rehearsals. That's the hard part of working with this dame. She wants to rehearse over and over again."

Lucy expected even child actors to be troupers. In the episode "Baby Pictures," originally telecast November 2, 1953, Lucy pops in unexpectedly on Caroline Appleby to catch her off-guard, hoping to find her apartment in a state of disarray and the Appleby baby, Stevie, similarly unprepared for visitors.

"All through rehearsals we worked with dolls," explains Miss Singleton. "We never saw the children until the dress rehearsal, sometimes not even until the actual show. Of course, Lucy was used to the Mayer twins who alternated in the Little Ricky role, but I had never worked with the little boy who was going to play my son. So I decided to 'introduce' myself to the baby before we went on. His mother informed me that he was very cranky and had just gotten over the measles. She advised me that if he didn't behave during the show, I should pick up a toy and play with him.

"I went over to Lucy and said, 'We're in big trouble. My baby's mother says he's cranky and she expects me to play with him if he gets antsy.'

" 'The hell you will,' Lucy said to me. 'If the kid gives you any trouble during the scene, just drop him down and hold him by the hands out of view of the cameras. And get a firm grip on him so he can't crawl away and ruin the scene.' "

Evidently the perfection paid off. On February 11, 1954, at the Sixth Annual Emmy Awards ceremony of the National Academy of Television Arts and Sciences, held at the Hollywood Palladium, *I Love Lucy* walked off with "Best Situation Comedy" honors, the second year in a row, and Vivian Vance won as "Best Supporting Actress." Lucy was nominated but lost to Eve Arden for her role as Connie Brooks in *Our Miss Brooks*. Bill Frawley also received a nomination—the first of five for his Fred Mertz characterization—but he lost to Art Carney.

Years later, when asked about his numerous Emmy losses, Frawley cracked, "It didn't surprise me. I knew they didn't know what they were doing when Vivian Vance got one!" A loner, Frawley rarely socialized with anyone connected with *I Love Lucy*. "Mostly, my friends are in baseball or they're golfers. I just don't go to dinner at people's houses. I don't even know the names of the people next door at the Knickerbocker Hotel where I live. I don't mix easily, and mostly I mind my own business."

Frawley, who was associated with *Lucy* for nine years, was

well liked by his friends, among them baseball great Joe DiMaggio. One buddy comments: "He was an able performer and probably came pretty close to being Fred Mertz in real life. He was well-meaning, but obstreperous, at times vaguely ridiculous. He was moral and responsible, likable and uncompetitive. He fussed and fumed, but his bark was much worse than his bite."

Another Frawley aficionado observes, "If he didn't like you, he was just awful. He was a completely prejudiced man. Couldn't stand *any* ethnic group. But, in general, he was a warm, wonderful, hearty old guy with a great sense of humor."

Doris Singleton remembers Frawley: "He would come on the set with the *Racing Form* under his arm. He never had an entire script with him—just his scenes. As I recall, he usually spent most of his time in his dressing room."

Lucille adds a footnote: "Bill was something else. You couldn't rely on him to know where he was going or what he was doing because he just tore out what he was supposed to do, and when he came in he never knew what the story was about. But he was a funny, irascible, wonderful man for whom our writers wrote perfectly."

By the close of the season, Desi had reached the thinking-out-loud stage on plans to expand *I Love Lucy* to a full hour for the 1955–1956 season after the $8 million Philip Morris contract had run its course. This, despite some poor midseason reviews.

Jack Gould, in his March 31, 1954, *New York Times* television column wrote: "What's happened to *I Love Lucy?* At the rate the . . . program has been going in the last few weeks it's surely jeopardizing its exalted place in the popularity charts. Where once the show was a recognizable and hilarious farce on married life, it currently seems bent on succumbing to the most pedestrian and sophomoric slapstick. . . ."

In spite of poor reviews, lower ratings, the Communist scare, and a handful of mediocre episodes, *I Love Lucy* did manage to take top honors as the "most-viewed show in the 1953–1954 season," according to ARB. In May, an estimated 50,840,000 persons watched a single *I Love Lucy*.

8

"The first 100 shows are the hardest," read the inscription on the icing of the mammoth twelve-layer cake that was wheeled onto Stage 9 by two Desilu stagehands on the evening of June 10, 1954, after an overflow audience of more than three hundred people witnessed the filming of "The Business Manager," the one-hundredth episode in the *Lucy* series.

As scores of *I Love Lucy* staff and crew members looked on, Lucille Ball paid homage to the three people most responsible for keeping the show on top of the heap. "I love them dearly," she said sincerely, "I appreciate them daily, I praise them hourly, and I thank God for them every night." Every person in the studio, from janitor to network vice-president, knew to whom Lucy was referring: producer and head writer Jess Oppenheimer, and writers Bob Carroll, Jr., and Madelyn Pugh.

Earlier that year, while accepting a Los Angeles Press Club award, Lucy had said, "Without my writers, I'm dead," repeating it several times for emphasis.

From the start, the *Lucy* writers were held in an esteem at Desilu not common in television. Lucille bombarded Jess Oppenheimer with photographs inscribed to "The Bossman," and Desi once presented the producer with a statuette of a baseball player, with the punning tribute, "To the man behind the ball."

The comedy-writing team of Bob Schiller and Bob Weiskopf, who joined the *I Love Lucy* staff at the start of the 1955–1956 season, comment: "When we did our first show, we worked like the devil on it. We wrote it so well that when it was taped, it sounded as if it were unrehearsed, and there were laughs everywhere. We thought everybody would hail the writers."

But, alas, praise for the writers, as usual, just was not to be, and it didn't help any that this time the jokes appeared to be spontaneous. After the show, "Homecoming," was aired, the first review Schiller and Weiskopf saw went as follows: ". . . As always, Miss Ball carried the show. In this one she did a particularly outstanding job, because the writing was so poor. But she saved everything by making up wonderfully funny ad-libs—right on the spot."

As you have learned already, *I Love Lucy* was rarely, if ever, ad-libbed. It probably was the most carefully rehearsed show on television at the time. Perhaps this—along with the above-par writing—was the key factor in its continual success. Lucille said, "We had the same writers for three and a half years on radio, before going to TV. We concentrated on our characters and what we wanted them to do, and never vacillated from the start. Desi has two or three story ideas a year, and the writers take them and develop them. I'm not an idea girl; I'm a doer."

When the name of the series first became *I Love Lucy,* writers tended to abbreviate it in accordance with time-honored studio custom. When Lucille saw I.L.L. in the top left-hand margin of every script page, she rebelled. "I don't want a show that's 'ill,' " she said emphatically. Agreeing, Desi gravely issued a memorandum directing "the only authorized abbreviation henceforth will be 'Lucy.' "

What did an *I Love Lucy* script look like? Well, it was mimeographed, for one thing. On plain white paper. It was usually at least forty-five pages, sometimes as many as fifty or sixty. The dialogue was double-spaced, and the stage directions, or "business," were typed single-spaced in capital letters.

"My type of comedy had a lot of props, and what we call 'block pages,' " Lucy maintains. "Literally, my directions were a whole page, sometimes two, of what to do and how to do it. Bob and Madelyn—we called them 'the kids'—were sensational. They would actually do it themselves before asking me to do it. If I read a script and said, 'I don't know if I can do this,' Madelyn would

107

jump up and reply, 'Yes, you can. We did it. We acted it out. You can do it.' I learned an awful lot from doing what they wrote. They were great. Still are."

The pair often toiled more than seventy hours a week talking, testing, and dreaming, then putting their ideas and jokes on paper. Every Monday, they would start plotting an *I Love Lucy* episode with Oppenheimer, often spending the entire day—frequently many hours of the next—outlining the story scene by scene, laugh by laugh. During the next four days, Bob and Pug would go off to their boxlike office in a far corner of the studio complex and write the script. On Friday afternoon, they would turn it over to Jess for editing, and he, in turn, would run it through the mimeo mill. The two usually worked eight weeks ahead of filming and fourteen weeks before the air date.

"Sometimes I didn't touch a word of their script," says Oppenheimer about his role as chief *Lucy* scribe. "Other times, I changed a great deal. I may have been wrong when I changed it, but I had to do what I thought was right. Afterwards, I dictated the entire script so I could give it the consistency and constancy that each episode needed. Rightly or wrongly, the show sounded the same each time because it funneled through me. I knew best the mood and feel of our previous shows; I could bring it all into line so that nothing sounded too different or out of character."

Madelyn, short, cute, and utterly feminine, and Bob, whose bushy eyebrows remind one of a friendly Svengali and John L. Lewis all rolled into one, sat before facing typewriters behind a closed door marked "Writers' Room." There they would not only create the situations, but also write the lines and, most importantly, test each gag to see if it would work.

"That was Madelyn's job," says Carroll. "It was up to her to see if it was physically possible for a woman to do all the things we dreamed up for Lucy."

"You see," adds Madelyn, "if I could do it, Lucy could. The situations not only had to be funny, but believable." During her writing days for *I Love Lucy,* Madelyn had been rolled up in a rug, stuck in a loving cup, and carried off in a garbage can. She has also glued icicles to her face, filled her blouse with eggs, and tried wrapping chocolate bonbons at breakneck speed. "We got our ideas from real life, or at least things that *could* happen in real life. We also had our prejudices. Bob loved to throw pies. After all, our idols are Laurel and Hardy."

Oppenheimer, a onetime "gifted child" whose career had been closely watched by psychologists ever since he was in the second grade, held one of the toughest jobs in television. As producer of *I Love Lucy* (he was thirty-eight when the series began), he was required to keep track of thirteen separate episodes at all times. In a given week, he would discuss with Bob and Madelyn the show to be shot nine weeks in the future, and edit the finished script for the show eight weeks away. The same day, he had to check on costumes (his initials, like Lucille's and Papa Freund's, were required on all costume sketches before they were given the green light for "construction") and casting for episodes three and four weeks in the future, while taking care of production details for the show in production that week. After that, he supervised the cutting, editing, and dubbing of episodes filmed two, three, and four weeks earlier. So valuable was Oppenheimer that when he resigned at the close of the 1955–1956 season to accept a lucrative and prestigious network post with NBC, industry insiders predicted the immediate demise of *I Love Lucy*.

He was an idea man—one of the best in the business. It was he who, during the first week of June 1954, after filming "The Matchmaker" episode, called Pugh and Carroll to an important story conference meant to decide the fate of the approaching 1954–1955 season. He said, "We've got to do something new. When we started out, Desi is in show business and Lucy tries to get into the act. Later, we did more about the husband-and-wife angle, and when that got heavy, we were lucky and Lucy had her baby. Now we've got to think of something else."

It was evident that Jess, too, had read some of the less-than-rave reviews Lucy had garnered during the previous season, the series' third. The competition, particularly NBC's *Dragnet*, was encroaching on Desilu's hit, and *Lucy* was suffering. The show needed a shot of creative adrenaline if it was going to stay on top much longer.

"Let's take the Ricardos from New York to Hollywood," Oppenheimer put in suddenly. "Desi could get a studio offer."

"Let Desi take a screen test," Bob Carroll added excitedly. "That would give us a couple of funny scenes with Lucy."

109

Madelyn added the womanly touch: "Suppose Hollywood was shooting *Don Juan* and they thought Desi would be perfect for the part. This opens up all kinds of scenes. Lucy trying to play femme fatale, Lucy getting jealous of the women Desi must make love to in the show . . ."

The concept was perfect. It would give the show a logical reason to use real stars playing themselves—a surefire ratings' booster. Oppenheimer instructed "the kids" to go ahead alone and start brainstorming episodes, the first of which would be filmed in mid-September, almost three months away.

During the period following a six-week break that ended May 24 (Lucille and Desi escaped to their Palm Springs home, which overlooked the ninth and eighteenth fairways of the Thunderbird Country Club), the company managed to film five new *Lucy*s for the fall season. This backlog—"Lucy Cries Wolf," "The Matchmaker," "The Business Manager," "Mr. and Mrs. Television Network," and "Mertz and Kurtz"—would permit the entire cast and crew to enjoy an eleven-week summer vacation, during which time eighteen reruns of previous *I Love Lucy* shows would be aired. This was a departure from the past two summers when *My Little Margie* and *Racket Squad* substituted for the Lucille Ball-Desi Arnaz comedy.

While the stars themselves found summer solace at Del Mar, Bill Frawley began work on a new radio show, *Great Scott*. He didn't need the extra money but the role, that of a major-league baseball scout, was right up his alley. Such a baseball fanatic was Frawley that his agent, Walter Meyers, demanded and got from Desilu a contract that stipulated that if the New York Yankees (Frawley's favorite ball club) copped the American League pennant, his client would be free to attend the World Series. And sure enough, seven out of *I Love Lucy*'s nine seasons, that seemingly minor clause caused Desilu Productions a good deal of grief over schedule-juggling.

Desi's passion had turned from boats (the Arnazes owned a thirty-four-foot cabin cruiser, *Desilu*) to golf and skeet-shooting. In fact in September he was privileged to play golf with President Eisenhower at Palm Springs. And while vacationing in Del Mar, Desi spent a good deal of time (and money) at the racetrack. *TV Guide* reported: "For $18,000—the cost of approximately 15 minutes of one *I Love Lucy* film—Lucille Ball and Desi Arnaz have bought a brown colt by Count Speed out of Nursery School and have thus started Desilu Stables."

Desi's summer vacation was not all fun and games. There appeared in a syndicated newspaper story on July 8 an item quoting Lucille Ball as saying she would retire after the 1955–1956 season. "This whole thing is ridiculous," confirmed Arnaz, speaking from their Del Mar retreat. "Now it's possible that Lucy might have made such remarks in a very offhand way. Everybody would like to quit work and loaf for a while. It's the kind of thing everybody tosses off a dozen times a week in casual conversation. Only with Lucy, the casual remark got picked up off the floor and blown right up to the ceiling.

"In the first place, Lucy can't quit . . . even if she wanted to, which she doesn't. Our contract with Philip Morris runs until the end of the coming [1954–1955] season. After that, CBS has the right to ask us to do two more years of the show, which would carry us through the end of the nineteen fifty-six to fifty-seven season . . .

"And I want to make one more thing crystal clear. Some people have been speculating in print about the possibility of *I Love Lucy* continuing with someone else taking Lucille's place. That is the one thing we are absolutely dead sure about: "There will never be an *I Love Lucy* without Lucille Ball. Period. Exclamation point."

The use of big-name guest stars on the show helped to drive up the somewhat faltering *Lucy* ratings. The two Tennessee Ernie episodes, aired May 3 and 10, 1954, did exceedingly well on the Nielsen charts, and it was about that time, after the ratings were issued, that Oppenheimer decided on the Hollywood move. The guest stars certainly would be easy to come by—most of them were Lucille and Desi's personal friends and acquaintances. But in order to bear the extra costs and pay for other amenities, Desi called the CBS brass that summer and informed them that he and Lucy were dissatisfied. CBS would have to "come across" with something to make them "happier," he told them quite firmly.

Spencer Harrison, a powerful CBS attorney who was in charge of business affairs on the West Coast, and J. J. Van Volkenburg, the network president, agreed to sit down with Desi and talk.

Arnaz drove up from Del Mar in early August and ensconced himself in Bungalow 5 of the secluded Beverly Hills Hotel. Ken Morgan, the Desilu PR head and Desi's "brother-in-law" (actually he was married to Lucy's first cousin Cleo) joined him. Shrewd and demanding, Desi refused to budge on forty separate issues. Harrison and Van Volkenburg were getting nowhere fast. Their only hope was to call William S. Paley in New York and see if he could help. Paley, the head of CBS, flew to the Coast.

"Paley called me and asked me to meet him for breakfast at the hotel," Harrison recalls. "After breakfast we drove to the bungalow where the negotiations were taking place. It was hot and the air conditioning was barely working. We started at nine A.M. and worked until seven thirty in the evening when we finally closed the deal." Paley came to terms with all forty points on which Desi had been unyielding. "He very seldom got involved like that."

It was back to work on Monday, September 13, 1954. Lucille, Desi, Vivian, Bill, and guest player Frank Nelson exchanged niceties before sitting down to read through the one hundred and third *I Love Lucy* episode, which would be broadcast eight weeks away on November 8. Entitled "Ricky's Movie Offer," it was the first of many shows incorporating Jess, Bob, and Madelyn's original ideas on the Hollywood trip concocted the previous June.

Nelson played Ben Benjamin, a talent scout whose studio, M-G-M, was looking for a new face to portray classic lover Don Juan. When the news of Ricky's impending stardom leaked out (Ethel: "I didn't tell a soul, and they all promised to keep it a secret!"), what seemed to be all of New York wanted to audition for parts: Mrs. Sawyer and her French poodle; Pete, the grocery boy-cum-trumpet player; songbird Mrs. Trumbull; Ethel, wearing the garb of a Spanish *señorita,* complete with a rose between her teeth; Fred, the matador; and, of course, Lucy who, upon reading the *Don Juan* script, discovered a part for "a Marilyn Monroe-type." It took her little time to deck herself out in the appropriate, tight-fitting dress to impress Benjamin.

Before the first dress rehearsal on Wednesday, Lucille poured herself into the Monroe gown and strolled casually around the Motion Picture Center lot. She went from one office to another— hip-swaggling all the way—staring insolently but saying nothing.

One electrician quipped, "Marilyn Monroe can look like that, too. But can Marilyn manage to look like Lucille Ball?"

The next filmed episode in the Hollywood vein was "Ricky's Screen Test," shot the following Thursday evening. It turned out to be twice as funny as the "Ricky's Movie Offer" segment, especially the hilarious scenes featuring Lucy feeding Ricky his lines during the *Don Juan* screen test.

Two non-Hollywood shows followed, the first of which, "Lucy's Mother-in-Law," introduced us to Ricky's Cuban mother, beautifully played by Mary Emery. (She would play the same role two years later in "The Ricardos Visit Cuba.") From that point on, *I Love Lucy* concentrated solely on the Hollywood trip. In all, twenty-seven episodes, six of which aired during the 1955–1956 season, were shot using the Ricardos-go-to-Hollywood theme. Except for a few clinkers, they were pure gold.

Who could forget the time Fred Mertz bought an antique Cadillac roadster for $300 for the cross-country trip? Or the time Lucy learned to drive the new 1955 Pontiac convertible Ricky purchased to replace Fred's old clunker (Lucy to Ethel: "Oh, he makes me so mad! . . . How was I supposed to know we didn't have enough room to make a U-turn in the Holland Tunnel?")? How about the episode ("California, Here We Come!") in which Lucy's mother, Mrs. MacGillicuddy, arrived in New York, insisting on going along too (Kathryn Card's debut as Ricky's mother-in-law)? Or the brilliant half hour titled "First Stop," which found the Ricardos and Mertzes holed up in a rickety motel outside Cincinnati?

Because of Tennessee Ernie Ford's good showing in the two back-to-back *Lucy*s of the past season, the writers created another episode employing his talents. Titled "Tennessee Bound," it was set in the small (population: 54) fictional town of Bent Fork, Ernie's hometown (his real birthplace is Ford Town, Tennessee). Again, he played Lucy's Cousin Ernie; and the actor loved every minute of it. About his first *Lucy* stint, Ford once commented: "What really amazed me is the way those writers came up with a script full of genuine mountain expressions I hadn't heard in a passel of years. When I read that 'hitch in his gitalong' bit, I just lay down thar on the floor and liked to die laughin', it was so natural-like."

113

"Ethel's Home Town," the last episode before the foursome arrived in Hollywood, also made use of an *I Love Lucy* alumnus: Irving Bacon, who portrayed Ethel's father, Will Potter, had appeared in the first-season installment, "The Marriage License." Having arrived in Albuquerque, New Mexico, the group expected simply to enjoy a visit to Ethel's birthplace. Instead, they quickly learned that the town was under the impression that it was Ethel, not Ricky who was going to Hollywood to be in the movies. A theater marquee even read, "Ethel Mae Potter. We Never Forgot Her."

The new fall season had got off to a grand start. On the night before the premiere episode, Sunday, October 3, 1954, Ed Sullivan devoted his entire *Toast of the Town* hour to Lucille and Desi. During the salute, which also featured Vivian and Bill, Sullivan presented the Arnazes with the "Champions of Show Business" plaque to pay tribute to their phenomenal TV success. In addition to appearing in person, Lucy and Desi provided film clips of both old and new *I Love Lucy* episodes.

It was a hectic few months that followed. Lucy and Desi wanted a few weeks off around Christmas to spend with the kids in Palm Springs. The pair also wanted to rest up for their upcoming Las Vegas engagement to which they had committed themselves the previous summer.

Lucille and Desi opened January 1, 1955, in Las Vegas with a musical version of *I Love Lucy* in which Vance and Frawley costarred. Part of their crowd-pleasing act was featured on a January 20 TV special, "A Night in Las Vegas," with Sophie Tucker, Tony Martin, and Johnnie Ray.

Upon their return to Hollywood, Desi learned some news that scared him. Motion Picture Center, the studio complex that had been Desilu's home for a year and a half, was about to be sold. Joe Justman, the owner, had accepted an offer from none other than Harry Cohn, Columbia Pictures' head and Lucille's nemesis. And though rumor had it that Columbia would still agree to rent space to Desilu, Desi did not want to take a chance. Neither did Lucy.

Without wasting a moment, Desi summoned his tax attorney and told him the problem. The two devised a scheme: Justman would be invited the next day to Chatsworth for lunch along with

Above: Ed Sullivan presents the Arnazes with "Champions of Show Business" plaque on *The Toast of the Town*, October 3, 1954 (*CBS*). *Below left:* February 11, 1954, at Hollywood Palladium, Emmy Award ceremony (*The National Academy of Television Arts and Sciences*). *Below right:* Lucille Ball and Desi Arnaz arriving at Pantages Theatre for the 1954 Hollywood premiere of *A Star Is Born*.

the tax man. "I want you to stay," Desi told the accountant, "until Desilu owns controlling interest in Motion Picture Center." After more than eight hours of negotiation, it was all arranged. *I Love Lucy* did not have to fear eviction from its Cahuenga Boulevard home.

Another interesting financial negotiation took place that fourth season. It was no idle choice that resulted in the use of a spanking new 1955 Pontiac convertible in several *I Love Lucy* episodes. For the inherent promotional consideration, General Motors agreed to pay Desilu $50,000 cash to cover the added production costs of some exterior shooting involving the automobile. GM also tossed in five Pontiacs, three of which went to the series' writers.

In order to stifle the persistent rumors about Lucille and Desi's retirement, CBS signed the pair to a new contract before the end of 1954, despite the fact that the current agreement still had almost a year to run. The multimillion-dollar deal ensured the continuation of *I Love Lucy,* as a half-hour comedy, through the 1956–1957 season.

The first *Lucy* actually set *in* Hollywood featured William Holden, who, incidentally, would not take a dime for his guest appearance. (Neither would Eve Arden who made a cameo appearance in the same show.) This classic episode also happens to include Lucille Ball's favorite comedy routine. Titled "L.A. at Last," the show depicts Lucy Ricardo's first adventure in Tinseltown.

The episode, nominated the following year for an Emmy as "Best Written Comedy Material," aired February 7, 1955. The following morning, Jack Benny (who would soon become the Arnazes' next-door neighbor after their move to Beverly Hills in late spring) called to congratulate the couple who, in turn, offered him a guest stint on the show. The second phone call came from movie mogul Samuel Goldwyn saying he had missed it and could he please have a print to run that night for his house guests. Colleen Moore sent Lucy a telegram: "Your program last night was the funniest I have ever seen anyplace, anywhere, and your scene with the putty nose was so great that it should go down in history. My children, my husband, and I send congratulations to our favorite comedienne and her husband."

116

Lucy's long-time friend Hedda Hopper also made a guest appearance that season in "The Hedda Hopper Story." Such bosom buddies were they that upon her death in 1966, Miss Hopper bequeathed her black-and-blue Rolls-Royce to Lucille Ball.

Other big names who guested on the series were Cornel Wilde in "The Star Upstairs"; Rock Hudson in "In Palm Springs"; Van Johnson in "The Dancing Star" (segment originally intended for Ray Bolger); Harpo Marx; Richard Widmark in "The Tour"; and fashion designer Don Loper and the wives of Bill Holden, Dean Martin, Van Heflin, Forrest Tucker, Gordon McRae, and Richard Carlson in "The Fashion Show."

Dore Schary, then M-G-M production chief, was set to play himself in "*Don Juan* Is Shelved," but at the last minute, he got cold feet and backed out. Vivian's husband, Phil Ober, stepped into the role. Plans were under way to star George Burns and Gracie Allen in one segment, and Bing Crosby in other. But they, like Jack Benny, could not come to terms.

By April, Nielsen again hailed *Lucy* as the Number One television show in the nation, a rank they had enjoyed almost without interruption for three consecutive years. The series also had the longest waiting list for tickets. And if it is true that "imitation is the sincerest form of flattery," then *I Love Lucy* had registered yet another plus: In Puerto Rico, a TV comedy series blossomed that resembled *Lucy* right down to the next-door neighbors. Entitled *Mapi and Papi,* it starred another husband-and-wife acting team, Maria de Pilar Cortes and Fernando Cortes. (Coincidentally, the latter appeared with Lucille Ball in the film *Seven Days' Leave.*)

Unfortunately, on March 7, 1955, at the Seventh Annual Emmy Awards ceremony (telecast for the first time by NBC from the Moulin Rouge in Hollywood) *I Love Lucy* won no awards. This was particularly disappointing since the show had garnered a record five nominations. *I Love Lucy* lost to *Make Room for Daddy;* Lucille Ball lost to Loretta Young (*The Loretta Young Show*); Vivian Vance lost to Audrey Meadows (*The Honeymooners*); Bill Frawley lost to Art Carney (*The Honeymooners*); and Jess Oppenheimer, Robert G. Carroll, Jr., and Madelyn Pugh lost to George Gobel's comedy-writing staff.

Whether or not these multiple losses were the reason, Philip

117

Morris announced the following day that it was dropping *I Love Lucy* after its current contract expired on June 27, 1955. For some time the puffery had been sharing the *Lucy* load with Proctor and Gamble, which was hawking its Lilt home permanent; both were Biow Agency clients. Now that the cigarette manufacturer, which had sponsored the series since its inception in the fall of 1951, wanted out, the giant General Foods wanted in. With Jell-O as the product (sponsor of Lucille's CBS radio show, *My Favorite Husband*), General Foods began its three-year alternating sponsorship of *Lucy* that summer, even though the show was replaced for seventeen weeks by *Those Whiting Girls,* a sitcom created by Pugh and Carroll, and starring Barbara and Margaret Whiting, Mabel Albertson, and Jerry Paris.

Roger Greene, then Philip Morris advertising director, said his company was "happy to have had the privilege of bringing to the American public the fine entertainment of the *I Love Lucy* program these past four years. This program reached the highest audiences ever achieved by any single entertainment vehicle over a sustained period. We wish to thank the stars of the show—Lucille Ball, Desi Arnaz, Vivian Vance, and Bill Frawley. . . ."

Why the Philip Morris pullout when *I Love Lucy* was still the nation's favorite TV show? Some people are quick to count demographics as the major cause—*Lucy* viewers were not cigarette smokers, they contend.

"For some strange reason, no one seems to want to admit the real reasons," says Edward H. Feldman who was head of Biow's radio and television department on the West Coast during that period. "*Lucy* was selling Philip Morris cigarettes all right, until the Federal Trade Commission forced us to stop using the slogan, 'Philip Morris is recognized as being less irritating to the nose and throat by eminent nose and throat doctors.' On top of that, *Reader's Digest* published a 'scare' story in its July 1954 issue warning the public of possible cancer from smoking. This, more than anything, hurt our sales.

"The people that heeded the *Digest* warning switched to Winston which was one of the first filter-tipped cigarettes on the market," continues Feldman, who joined Desilu in 1955 as a vice-president in charge of film commercials. "Then Pall Mall came out with the first king-size cigarette which also didn't help matters too much. Competition was very strong and it hurt Philip Morris sales to a large extent."

Maurine Christopher, the astute radio and television editor of *Advertising Age,* has her own theories: "My guess is that [Philip Morris] fell down at the merchandising level—that they did not effectively achieve a natural association of the product with the show. Remember how everybody thought of Texaco when they thought of Milton Berle? Or Jack Benny and Jell-O? Or, then again, perhaps the program had its greatest appeal to non- or light-smokers. Hindsight is a great thing but I doubt if I would have signed for two and a half years more of such a 'high ticket' show in 1953. I would have preferred a variety show with an on-screen smoking host—Jackie Gleason, Dean Martin, for example."

When asked how he explained the fact that Philip Morris sales were lagging at a time when it was sponsoring the country's most popular television program, Thomas Christensen, assistant to the advertising director for the cigarette company, said: "I don't believe the show didn't sell. Nobody knows where we would have been if we hadn't had *I Love Lucy.* And if we had changed our copy story, we might have done better."

Accordingly, in December 1955, Philip Morris, a client of the Biow Agency since 1933, moved its $8,000,000-a-year advertising account to N. W. Ayer and Sons. A few months later, Milton H. Biow, the man who was instrumental in the formulation of *I Love Lucy,* announced the closing of his agency.

As for *I Love Lucy,* the cancellation did not hurt in the least. CBS had already ensured the continuation of the series through the 1956–1957 season. The Hollywood segments were among the highest-rated in the show's history. In fact by March 1955, Oppenheimer had decided to expand the Ricardos' horizon again next season—this time they would travel to Europe. New scenery, more guest stars, and, hopefully, a million laughs.

On Sunday, April 17, 1955, the series had the distinction of being on twice a week. Desi had leased the first fifty-two *I Love Lucy* episodes to the Lehn and Fink Corporation, makers of Dorothy Gray Beauty Preparations and Hinds, Etiquet, Lysol, for $30,000 each ($6,000 more than each episode originally cost to produce). Retitled *The Lucy Show* (not to be confused with Lucille Ball's 1962 sitcom), the show was slotted in the 6:00–6:30

P.M. (EST) time period. The deal had particular significance: Since the episodes, starting off with "The Ballet," were first shown during the 1951–1952 season, more than twenty-seven new territories had opened to television service and an estimated twenty-three million new TV sets were in operation. The scheduling on Sunday afternoons also made it possible for every member of the family, particularly youngsters, to see the original programs.

This unique move especially pleased Marion Oring who was president of the original Lucy-Desi Fan Club. The official organization, sanctioned by Desilu Productions, had only 150 members, but they were a loyal crowd. Fan mail continued at a staggering rate—ten thousand letters monthly. Sometimes the mail proved a giant headache. In one batch, for instance, Lucille and Desi received letters from a woman who wanted to sell them her home to finance a major operation; a man who wanted them to adopt his dog's puppies; a mother whose son invented a clothespin for them to manufacture; a maid with stage experience who wanted to be an actress; and several strangers seeking financial assistance. "To get to the point," one such person wrote, "could you lend me $10,000 and write it off your taxes?"

How did Lucy memorize one script per week? It wasn't easy. "Doing *Lucy,* we read the script once and we were on our feet," recalls Miss Ball who never saw a script until the first day of rehearsal, Monday. "We had to learn from fifty-two to fifty-four pages of dialogue in two days, and because we were on our feet with the props, it came easily. The next two days would be camera rehearsals, doing refinements, and getting angles set—then on Thursday night we'd be off like opening night.

"Over the weekend, the whole thing had to be erased mentally because on Monday we'd start with a new one in the same surroundings. I'll admit I've been known to walk on the set and start right in with last week's dialogue. Same set, same people—and the director would yell 'Cut! That's last week's show.'

"*I Love Lucy* completely changed my methods of memorizing; as a movie actress, I used to have great trouble remembering lines. Now I have a quicker way, worked out with cooperation from the writers. Everything is cut down to the nub before I get a script," Lucille maintains. (Lucy used to be kidded for using

120

what she calls an "alphabetical system" to remember her lines, concentrating on the order of the key verbs.)

One actress who appeared occasionally on the show had a more difficult time with the memorization process. "There were no cue cards used, so a lot of us would write parts of our dialogue on the palms of our hands," she remembers. "One time I recall Lucy and Vivian having a terrible time with a scene in the living room. It ended up that they wrote the difficult parts all over the coffee table. But before the filming began, and while Lucy was in her dressing room getting ready, a stagehand came on the set and sprayed the coffee table with something to cut down the glare from the overhead lights. Naturally, the dialogue was wiped out in the process. But, like all of us, they managed to pull it off all right."

Did Lucy collaborate with her writers on the scripts? "We never really saw them. We never discussed anything with them. We trusted them first and always," Miss Ball says. "All I ever contributed to the lines was what I call 'naturalizing'—twisting a phrase here and there to the way I'd say it—but very seldom. The writers used very graphic descriptions of what they wanted me to do. Some of their names for these expressions were in code. I'd know what they meant when they asked me for the 'Umlaut' look," she says referring to the German punctuation mark found over certain vowels.

There were code words for each of Lucy's familiar mugs. There was the "Credentials" look where Lucy's mouth would open wide as if to say, "How dare you?" Then there was the often-used "Puddling Up" when Lucy's eyes would fill with tears before breaking into one of her classic wails. "Foiled Again" was a popular countenance used when one of her cockamamie schemes went awry; "Light Bulb" referred to an expression that enveloped her face when she had a brainstorm; and then there was the "Spider" look.

Hardly a week went by without "Spider" creeping into a *Lucy* script. That was the writers' way of asking her to recreate a gawkish frown she invented years ago while playing the role of a spider in a commercial based on "Little Miss Muffet." To effect it, Lucy's upper lip would raise up and she would make a strange guttural sound. Sometimes it was called "Spider-Combined-with-the-Gobloots-Voice." (That was lemon with a jigger of Mickey Finn added.) This was developed in "Lucy's Fake Illness," a first-season show starring Hal March as a phony doctor who tells Lucy she is suffering from "a severe case of the Gobloots . . . brought into the country on the hind legs of the Boo-Shoo Bird." After being told of her condition, Lucy stares back at March and says, "I got the Gobloots from a Boo-Shoo Bird?" What followed was Lucy's infamous "Spider-Combined-with-the-Gobloots-Voice" look.

"All our key words did," says Jess Oppenheimer, "was remind Lucille to duplicate something she had invented in the past."

Too bad the writers did not remind themselves of what *they* had invented in the past. *I Love Lucy* was filled with factual errors and oversights, points that easily could have been corrected. Ethel Mertz's middle name, for example, was Louise in the 1953 episode "Lucy and Ethel Buy the Same Dress," but three months later, on "The Million Dollar Idea," it had become Roberta (Vivian's real middle name). A year after that, she was Ethel Mae in "Ethel's Home Town." (Fred's middle name was always Hobart.)

Similarly, Fred's ex-vaudeville partner was named Ted Kurtz in "The Ballet" and two and a half years later he had become Barney Kurtz. In episodes originally broadcast only a month apart in 1952, Ricky mentioned that he and Lucy had lived in the Mertzes' apartment building for five years, then nine years; and then a few segments later, he gave the exact move-in date, August 6, 1948. By 1954, it had suddenly leaped to twelve years. The longevity of Fred and Ethel's marriage bounced from eighteen to twenty-five years in twelve short months. Then, three years later, while on the *Constitution* sailing to Europe, the pair was celebrating its twenty-fifth wedding anniversary, again.

The Ricardos' telephone number vacillated back and forth during their five and a half years living at 623 East Sixty-eighth Street. At one point it was MUrray Hill 5-9975; six months later, CIrcle 7-2099; and two years after that—MUrray Hill 5-9099.

9

Production on *I Love Lucy*'s unprecedented fifth video season commenced Labor Day 1955. "I had just returned from a well-deserved vacation in Hawaii," says costume designer Elois Jenssen. "Earlier that summer before I went away, I put in for a fifty-dollar-a-week raise. You'll remember that when I started on *Lucy,* I was getting only one hundred dollars per episode; that was the 1953–1954 season. The next year—1954–1955—I got one hundred fifty dollars an episode for my costume-designing chores. But this was still short of what Jack Chertok was paying me for creating Ann Sothern's wardrobe for *Private Secretary.*

"When I got back from the islands on the Friday before the Labor Day weekend, I phoned Andy Hickox who was Lucy and Desi's business manager and one of the vice-presidents at Desilu Productions. I asked him if my fifty-dollar increase had been approved. He said no. Frankly, I couldn't believe it: *I Love Lucy* was the Number One show on television, and its costume designer was being paid peanuts. I asked Andy, in whom I had a great deal of faith (if it wasn't for him, I would never have had a spool of thread to put the clothes together with), what I should do.

"He advised me to hold out for the two hundred dollars. He said, 'Don't come to work on Monday. Lucy will call you at the last minute.' Well, Monday rolled around and Lucy didn't call. Instead, Madame Sara, who constructed all of Lucille's clothes from my designs, phoned and in an excited voice said, 'Guess who's here? Eddie Stevenson.' (Stevenson was another costume designer.)

"I raced over to the studio and sure enough—Eddie had already taken over my office. I immediately confronted Lucy who was busy rehearsing the new show. She said, 'What happened?' I told her that Marty Leeds [executive vice-president of Desilu Productions] wouldn't okay a raise for me. Lucy started to cry, and to this day I don't know whether she knew about the whole thing beforehand or not. All I knew was that Eddie Stevenson had *my* job . . . and at a salary of two hundred dollars a week, the same amount I had asked for," Elois confirms.

"That's what really hurt me. Being left out in the cold for a measly fifty-dollar raise—which they paid Eddie Stevenson anyway. And after I had done so much for them. Besides designing and supervising the construction of most of the costumes worn on the series, I designed Lucille's clothes for publicity pictures shot in connection with the many endorsements she and Desi made. For instance, when they built their Palm Springs' house, they got free carpets, free drapes, free everything, just for endorsing the products. I'm the one who designed Lucy's clothes for the advertising layouts. I even designed Desi's racing silks when he bought his first racehorse. In short, they expected a lot of you . . . for very little.

"But what *really* made the whole affair hard to take was being left out after *saving* Desilu almost ten thousand dollars on the costume budget of *Forever, Darling,* Lucy and Desi's second picture together for M-G-M," concludes Miss Jenssen, who now interrupts her busy designing career to teach a course on costume design and history at UCLA.

During that summer, the Arnazes did appear in *Forever, Darling,* a comedy script originally written in the 1940s for Lucille and William Powell. Whereas Lucy and Desi's previous tandem film, *The Long, Long Trailer,* was produced *and* distributed by Metro-Goldwyn-Mayer, this feature was produced by Zanra (Arnaz spelled backward) Productions at the Motion Picture Center lot—home since 1953 of Desilu and *I Love Lucy.*

Production on the feature began June 14, 1955, with a staff made up principally of *Lucy* workers. Desi himself produced the film with an able assist from Jerry Thorpe (on summer vacation from his *December Bride* chores); Jack Aldworth was one of the assistant directors; Dann Cahn handled the film editing assignment; and Cameron McCulloch took care of sound. And, of course, Elois Jenssen designed the many costumes used in the motion picture.

Following their seven-week film chores on *Darling,* Lucy and Desi managed a six-week holiday at Del Mar, their favorite beachside hideaway. When they returned to work on *I Love Lucy* after Labor Day, a number of personnel changes, besides the Elois Jenssen replacement, had taken effect. James V. Kern replaced Bill Asher as the show's director, commencing with "The Homecoming" episode. Kern had paid his three-camera Desilu dues on *Those Whiting Girls, Lucy*'s 1955 summer replacement.

Comedy writers Bob Schiller and Bob Weiskopf were added to the writing staff, making a total of five *Lucy* scribes. Consequently, these staff changes and additions required a new closing-credits film, which Desilu promptly ordered from a local title design firm. The result: an unexpected error. Desi's name was misspelled in "Wilbur Hatch conducting the Dezi Arnaz Orchestra." The mistake was not corrected until the start of the next season.

Just before the current year got under way, Jess Oppenheimer announced his resignation, to take effect the following spring. NBC had made him a job offer: a plum position in network programming. Jess was earning about $2,500 a week as *Lucy* producer and head writer when his five-season tenure ended. He also "owned" the name "Desi and Lucy," and, hence, received a royalty for whatever the Arnazes did under that title (for instance, *The Lucille Ball-Desi Arnaz Show,* which ran three seasons from 1957–1960). That was Desi's gift to Jess for creating *I Love Lucy.*

As soon as Oppenheimer's resignation was made public, rumors abounded about the demise of *I Love Lucy.* These were firmly spiked by Señor Arnaz: "I hate to see Jess go, but his leaving won't interfere in the slightest with whatever plans we make for the show. Personally, I would like to expand *Lucy* to a full hour every week, maybe even in color, using big-name guest stars—say, three weeks out of four—to help Lucy and me carry the load. But we'd still appear in every show. Of course, this is just my own plan and will have to be concurred in by both CBS and the sponsors. We are working on that right now. CBS, you see, has an option on *Lucy* for 1956–1957. Sure, we'll miss Jess," Desi concluded. "But who knows? By next spring Desilu might buy NBC, and we'd be back together again!"

In the meantime, NBC was the competition. And the competition was trying desperately to displace *I Love Lucy* from its lofty perch in the Nielsens. Bucking the October 3, 1955, fifth-season premiere episode of *Lucy* ("Lucy Visits Grauman's," filmed the preceding spring) was NBC's *Medic,* a powerful, dramatic hour-long series starring Richard Boone as Dr. Konrad Styner. NBC pitted the second part of "And There Was Darkness and There Was Light," the *Medic* show about childbirth, against the perennial winner, *I Love Lucy,* hoping that viewers who caught the first part on September 26 would not want to miss the climax the following Monday night at nine o'clock. It was a good and valiant try on NBC's part, but it didn't work. *I Love Lucy* was still Number One.

Overseas, the British in 1955 loved *Lucy* second only to their favorite BBC broadcast. *Lucy* had a phenomenal rating of 94 in England by the end of the year. The show had become a way of life all over the world.

In 1957, Lucille Ball was asked to comment on her series' incredible track record. Could she foresee another weekly comedy show compiling such an enviable history? "I doubt it," she answered. "The competition in TV gets tougher all the time. Even our show has never been able to match Milton Berle's highest ratings, and no other program may approach *Lucy*'s highest ratings over the years. The business has changed, that's all."

The Jack Barry-hosted evening game show, *Twenty-One,* had the rare distinction of outrating *I Love Lucy* for two weeks in 1957 when contestant Charles Van Doren appeared, finally winning $129,000 before being defeated. This was the first time in five years that *I Love Lucy* lost its foothold on the Number One spot for more than one week at a time. Lucille added wryly, "Well, I do enjoy the quiz shows on TV but the fact is that Desi and I watched Van Doren only once. And that was on a night that we had a rerun going on our own series [February 25, 1957], so we didn't feel as if we were playing hooky or anything."

The 1955–1956 fall season kicked off with the remaining "Hollywood" *Lucy*s. These were filmed before the summer break, and included "Lucy Visits Grauman's," "Lucy and John Wayne," "Lucy and the Dummy," "Ricky Sells the Car," and "The Great Train Robbery." Thereafter, four non-Hollywood shows were shot and aired: "Homecoming," "The Ricardos Are Interviewed," "Lucy Goes to a Rodeo," and "Nursery School."

With the success of "going-to-Hollywood" firmly established by the ratings, the writers now proceeded with plans formulated the previous spring to send the Ricardos and Mertzes to Europe at midseason. Ricky was to be booked with his Latin band in various European cities like London, Paris, and Rome.

In the one hundred thirty-seventh *I Love Lucy* episode, "Ricky's European Booking," Ricky informs Lucy that he is going on a three-week tour with the band; he cannot afford to take her along. Lucy: "You never take me anywhere!" Ricky: "What do you mean? We just came back from Hollywood a month ago." Lucy: "Yeah, but where have you taken me lately?" Lucy then proposes that if she can raise the money ($3,000) herself, she be allowed to go. Ricky consents, though he realizes it's a long shot.

Lucy and Ethel concoct a scheme to raise the needed cash (a thorough search of cookie jars, pocketbooks, and G. T. H. P.—"going-through-husband's-pants"—yields only $200.16): Under the phony name 'Women's Overseas Aid" (Lucy: "We're women. We want to go overseas. And, boy, do we need aid!"), the two decide to conduct a raffle (TV set donated by Mr. Feldman, owner of a local appliance store). Little do they know that what they are doing is illegal, bordering on fraud, according to Mr. Jamison of the district attorney's office. Mr. Jamison: "Fraud is punishable by one to ten years in prison." Lucy: "I can't go to prison! I'm going to Europe." Lucy manages to clear herself just hours before Ricky informs her that a major steamship company has offered his band free passage in exchange for playing on the trip to Europe. Now he can afford to take Lucy and Ethel (Fred Mertz had already been invited along to act as band manager). The steamship company in question was American Export Lines, owner and operator of the 23,750-ton *Constitution*.

"I had a heck of a time selling the idea to my company," maintains Allison S. Graham, one-time publicity director of American Export Lines. "The people in the shipping business are traditionally conservative in their approach to public relations, thinking in terms of pennies where many large-scale enterprises plan with dollars. What really surprised us most of all was the idea of rich Hollywood seeking financial aid from a steamship line." Desilu was asking $30,000; American Export finally agreed to pay $12,000.

After telecast of the two *Lucy* episodes set aboard the *Constitution*—January 16 and 23, 1956—the series was the subject of wide comment at downtown New York maritime clubs, the India House and the Whitehall Club. "The heads of American Export were very surprised at the unbelievable response to the show," recalls Al Graham, a company employee since 1940, now retired. "I attended a luncheon meeting of the American Merchant Marine Institute public relations committee on February seventh of that year. My industry colleagues were high in praise of the shows, although several reported certain executives of their respective companies were not enthused."

The *New York Times* reported, "American Export Lines voted itself the brightest steamship company of the year for doing a promotional job that was worth several times what it cost. . . .

"Other ship line officials either munched tart grapes or said the whole thing was silly. They pointed out that by law no one can land on a ship by helicopter [a scene from "Bon Voyage"]. And, in any case, no one ever gets halfway through a porthole, finding the shoulders too large to go back and the hips unable to continue through [sequence from "Second Honeymoon"]."

So authentic were these two *Lucy* episodes that a British company, after viewing 'Bon Voyage," cabled Desilu asking when the *Constitution* was arriving in Southampton. (The *Constitution* sailed nowhere near England, Lucy's fictional destination.) In Washington, Federal Maritime Board officials liked the shows so well they asked for and got copies of the films to help promote the merchant marine.

In March of 1956, with only a few segments left to film for the series' fifth season, the Arnazes engaged in a serious discussion about their future, and the future of *I Love Lucy*. "Desi and I were driving up from Palm Surings one Monday morning, headed for another hectic week at the studio, after a weekend that had brought Desi no rest. His problems had come along, crowding me out. Worried about his overwork and inability to relax, I could sense a cloud over his head. His eyes were intent on the road and his hands were gripping the wheel until they showed white. Suddenly he reminded me that five years of doing *I Love Lucy* were winding up, we had only a few shows to go, and it was time to renew our contract with CBS. We were still on top. How did I feel about it, he wanted to know.

"I spoke as if I had memorized my lines from a script, I knew them so well. Five years before, when *I Love Lucy* was just starting, we had agreed that if the show were a success, we would begin to taper off after the first five years. Not to retire, but to live graciously and work when and where we pleased, provided it didn't interfere with the pleasures we wanted to enjoy together. Desi always wanted to own a ranch, not just the five acres we had had, but one large enough so the horses he loved so much wouldn't have to crowd together like commuters on a train. We had talked of trips we would take and the adventures we would have with the children.

" 'What do you think, Desi?' I asked.

"All he said was, 'We have over two thousand people working for us now. It doesn't seem right to let that many people down because we've done what we set out to do.' "

Lucy knew by then that her fifteen-year marriage to Desi was crumbling. One cynic observes, " 'America's favorite couple' barely communicated with each other except as Lucy and Ricky Ricardo on *I Love Lucy*."

Miss Ball attempts to explain the interesting interrelationship: "Something about the make-believe world in which we played Lucy and Ricky enabled us to laugh at our genuine problems, the way Lucy and Ricky laughed at the ones our writers dreamed up for them.

"Once we got on the set, we worked nearly sixteen hours a day, from Monday morning until almost Thursday midnight. There wasn't time to think of anything else, for we were plunged into a fishbowl of creativity that was displayed every Thursday night before a live audience. To us, every Thursday evening had the tension of an opening on Broadway, and there was so much enthusiasm among our company that I could forget the silent, strained weekends, Desi's departures from home, the threats to his health. Only when I had a chance to come up for air did I have time to worry. I never worried about my work. I worried as a woman, not as a performer," Miss Ball concludes.

The Arnazes attempted a few vacations together hoping that, *sans* studio pressures, they might reconcile their differences. After the April 5, 1956, filming of the one hundred and fifty-third *I Love Lucy* segment, "Return Home from Europe," the pair disappeared for a month. Again in July, they took off for Cuba for another short holiday. Unfortunately, these mini-vacations were not the answer to their marital travails.

Except for close friends, no one knew about their difficulties. Had the news leaked out and become public, it probably would have spelled the end of *I Love Lucy,* still the nation's top-rated situation comedy.

At the Eighth Annual Emmy Awards ceremony on March 17, 1956, held at the Pan Pacific Auditorium on Beverly Boulevard near CBS Television City (telecast over NBC), Lucille Ball copped the statuette for "Best Actress—Continuing Performance," beating out the likes of Gracie Allen, Eve Arden, Jean Hagen, and Ann Sothern. However, it was the first year since the series debuted that *I Love Lucy* was not nominated as "Best Comedy Series." However, William Frawley received his third nomination for the Fred Mertz supporting role, while his TV-wife, Vivian Vance, was not nominated at all. In another category, Lucille Ball lost as "Best Comedienne" to Nanette Fabray (*Caesar's Hour*); and the *Lucy* writers, hailed for their "L.A. at Last" teleplay (a/k/a "Bill Holden") lost to the *You'll Never Get Rich* (a/k/a *Bilko*) writing group.

Business at Desilu, despite the squabblings of its president and vice-president, was burgeoning. In 1955, its various corporations paid out $5 million in salaries alone to 3,300 people. The product: 295 half-hour TV shows (of which twenty-six were *I Love Lucys*), one ninety-minute television spectacular, and one theatrical feature, *Forever, Darling.* Desi already had clearly become a television tycoon.

A CBS lawyer describes the tycoon's big plan when trying to make his first capital-gains deal: "Lucy and Desi would sell five years of *I Love Lucy* episodes to CBS and buy back a twenty-five-percent interest in Desilu Productions, which they already had sold to CBS in 1952 for one million dollars.

"Desi was asking four million dollars-plus for the *Lucy* shows in the can—and other less important properties [like *December Bride*]—but he was unwilling to pay more than one million dollars to buy back the twenty-five-percent CBS interest in Desilu. He kept raising the price on the reruns and each time he did we escalated the price he would have to pay to buy back the twenty-five-percent. He was determined to keep CBS from profiting on its Desilu investment. Paley wouldn't let him get away with it. But Desi was always in there plugging away and he generally got most of what he wanted."

In the meantime, Desi and his business associates had to deal with the increasing salary demands of Vivian Vance and William Frawley. Their respective agents made it clear to Arnaz and Desilu VP Marty Leeds that their clients were responsible to a large degree for the continuing success of the series. Vivian's mouthpiece always threatened that his client would have another nervous breakdown if she didn't receive more money.

Truth is, Vivian Vance spent a considerable part of her nine *I Love Lucy* years in psychoanalysis. She says, "I'd go from the couch to the studio every morning." According to those who worked with her, she was never visibly upset, nor did her personal problems affect her performance. In fact, Vivian credits the years in *Lucy* with a therapeutic effect second only to the analysis itself.

If Bill Frawley had personal problems, he managed to conceal them successfully from his *Lucy* cohorts, except perhaps his penchant for betting on the horses. He was highly regarded by the *Lucy* crew, especially for his easygoing manner. He bothered no one, did his job (brilliantly), and, in his own words, "took the money and ran."

A senior member of the sound crew remembers Frawley's outspokenness: "When he was around young ladies, he was like Lord Chesterfield, courtly to his fingertips. In the presence of men, he was a no-holds-barred critic of whatever he didn't happen to like which was just about everything. He would say anything to anybody, in language as colorful as it was profane, and the general rule on the *Lucy* set was that he never be allowed near a news-

131

paperman without a chaperone. If Bill's off-the-record stories had ever gotten on the record, half of Hollywood would've quietly committed suicide."

The fifth season of *I Love Lucy* came to a successful close on May 14, 1956, with the telecast of the one hundred fifty-third episode in the series, "Return Home from Europe." This was the climax of seventeen European-related shows, the first of which aired December 12. This 1955–1956 TV semester proved to be a rousing winner, both in the ratings and as a creative triumph for the five *Lucy* writers, including the departing Jess Oppenheimer.

Lucy's antics while attempting to find a copy of her birth certificate, in order to apply for her passport (she locked herself in a steamer trunk and threatened to stow away on the ship), were second only to the afternoon she spent on the Staten Island Ferry, helping Fred Mertz overcome his seasickness. Then followed the two *Constitution* episodes—"Bon Voyage" and "Second Honeymoon"—in which Lucy missed the ship, tried unsuccessfully to catch a "pilot boat" to overtake the swift liner, donned a descent harness, then finally was lowered from a helicopter onto the deck of the huge ship; later she got herself stuck in the porthole of her cabin and had to be extricated by a team of engineers wielding acetylene torches. "This could only happen to Lucy Ricardo," wrote one midwestern newspaper columnist.

If there was ever a *Lucy* episode that topped "Job Switching" or "L.A. at Last," it was the 1956 segment titled "Lucy's Italian Movie." Set in Rome, the tale dealt with Lucy's foreign-movie fling when she was offered a part in *Bitter Grapes,* the new Vittorio Fellipi film. In order to get in the right mood for her role, Lucy visits Turo, a fictional town renown for its wine vineyards and old-fashioned winemaking methods on the outskirts of Rome. There, while "soaking up local color," she becomes embroiled in the ancient art of winemaking in a huge, grape-filled vat. The scene in which Lucy climbs into the giant bin with a seasoned wine crusher (played by Teresa Tirelli, a real grape-stomper from Northern California) was nothing short of side-splitting. In fact, the show remains one of Lucille Ball's favorite *Lucy* episodes.

The overseas' comedy high jinks then continued through "Lucy's Bicycle Trip" and "Lucy Goes to Monte Carlo," two so-so half hours, aired April 23 and May 7, 1956, respectively. The

132

culmination of the European trip was the season's closing episode, "Return Home from Europe," filmed Thursday, April 5, 1956, and aired May 14, 1956, set aboard a Pan American Airlines flight #155. In an effort to smuggle a twenty-five-pound hunk of cheese on the plane for free, Lucy disguises the bundle as a baby, thinking tykes travel gratis. The ensuing scenes, with actress Mary Jane Croft playing the mother of a four-month-old infant girl, were brilliant—a true tribute to writers Bob Carroll, Bob Schiller, Bob Weiskopf, Madelyn Pugh (*Look* magazine once tagged the quartet "Three Bobs and a Babe"), and Jess Oppenheimer. Jess, as you have already learned, left to take an NBC executive post, but those close to *I Love Lucy* claimed "irreconcilable differences" with Desi Arnaz as the primary reason for the exit.

That spring Desi agreed to do another season of half-hour *Lucy*s for CBS, although he would find himself assuming the additional function of active producer, taking over Jess Oppenheimer's key position.

With Desi now producing the show, *I Love Lucy* commenced brainstorming sessions for the upcoming 1956–1957 season. One decision was to place a great story emphasis on Little Ricky, the character neglected throughout the "European" shows. In order to take advantage of this creative idea, Ricky, Jr.'s, age was jumped to five, the age of a kindergartner. The Mayer twins—Joe and Mike—were not old enough (three and a half), and their mother had already decided to retire them from show business. Therefore, a new actor would be needed. During the month of May, almost two hundred boys were interviewed. None filled the Little Ricky bill.

At about this time, bandleader Horace Heidt brought his *Youth Opportunity* show to town (you will recall that *I Love Lucy* replaced Heidt in the 9–9:30 P.M. Monday-night time slot in October 1951). One of the acts, featured under the billing "The World's Tiniest Professional Drummer," was little, five-year-old Keith Thibodeaux, a native of Lafayette, Louisiana. Heidt called his prodigy "pound for pound, the greatest drummer around."

A friend of Keith's father happened to mention that Desilu was searching for a little boy for one of its television shows. The elder Thibodeaux, an insurance agent, took his drummer boy to the casting department at Motion Picture Center, not really expecting a job to materialize, but anxious to get a firsthand look at the lot where his favorite TV show, *I Love Lucy,* was made.

Desi took one look at young Keith (born December 1, 1950), and signed him to a seven-year contract at a beginning salary of $300 a week, saying: "He's a remarkably talented youngster, and there will be plenty for him to do besides *Lucy*—if the show doesn't last that long." Aside from his incredible drumming facility, Keith actually looked like a miniature Desi Arnaz. Arnaz immediately ordered basic Spanish lessons for the young boy of French extraction whose name was then Americanized to Richard (Ricky) Keith.

Keith's first *Lucy* episode was "Lucy Meets Bob Hope," shot in June 1956, and used as the 1956–1957 season premiere show, aired October 1. The five-and-a-half-year-old was used sparingly at first. His appearance, for instance, in the Bob Hope show was confined to a short sequence set in the Yankee Stadium bleachers. The boy proved he was a competent performer when given the chance to display his acting and drumming abilities in two delightful *Lucy* shows, "Little Ricky Learns to Play the Drums" and "Little Ricky Gets Stage Fright."

There were other changes in the basic *Lucy* format that season. Writer Bob Carroll pointed out, "Ricky doesn't play tourist traps anymore. He owns his own nightclub [Club Babalu]. He is moving to the suburbs [Westport, Connecticut], and makes about twenty thousand clams a year. If he wasn't any better off than he was six years ago, people would say, 'What kind of a no-talent bandleader is this—never gets a raise?' "

During the June 1956 filming of "Lucy Meets Bob Hope," Desi Arnaz was injured. In one scene Lucy was thrown into the air by Arnaz and Hope. When she came down, she leaned too heavily on Desi, tearing the ligaments in his back. Desi kidded that Lucy must be gaining weight; she retorted that maybe he wasn't as strong as he used to be.

Other sixth-season episodes made use of guest stars: Orson Welles popped up in the October 15, 1956, segment that also featured *The Waltons'* Ellen Corby. The show was supposed to have Vivian Vance playing Cleopatra to Mr. Welles's Julius Caesar, but the scenes didn't work well enough to include in the final version. The sequences featuring Lucy mixing Shakespeare with

Orson's magic act proved sufficient to carry the comedic climax.

In the "Visitor from Italy" show, Jay Novello played Mario Orsatti, a Venetian gondolier whom the Ricardos supposedly encountered while in Italy the year before. This was Novello's third *I Love Lucy* appearance ("The Seance" and "The Sublease" were the others). Elsa Lanchester turned in a bravura performance as Mrs. Grundy, a health-food fanatic who gave Lucy and Ethel a ride to Florida in her convertible in "Off to Florida."

In "The Ricardos Visit Cuba," originally telecast December 3, 1956, Richard Keith had the opportunity to do a conga drum duet with his TV-dad, Desi. They did a beautiful rendition of "Babalu." Young Keith once again had proved himself to be a real trouper.

Desi Arnaz, Jr., whom, in a way, Keith was portraying, reacts to his past "competition": "I can still remember watching the show when I was about three and wondering who was the baby with Mommy and Daddy. When my parents said it was me, I was confused because I knew it wasn't.

"So I had this identity problem, and it wasn't helped any by people calling me Little Ricky, a name I learned to despise. I remember wanting rather desperately to be better at something—anything—than the boy who played Little Ricky, Keith Thibodeaux. Although he was two years older than I, we became close friends. One of the things he did was play the drums, and that's what really got me interested in music. I studied percussion because I wanted to drum better than Keith did—and I'll always be grateful to him for that."

Jay Sandrich also joined the *I Love Lucy* company that season, first as second assistant director. He was upped to first assistant status in a few weeks, and today is one of the most sought-after sitcom directors in the industry, with numerous Emmys to his credit. Son of the late director Mark Sandrich (*The Gay Divorcee* and *Top Hat*), Jay learned the three-camera technique from Jerry Thorpe and Jack Aldworth who had preceded him as first assistant.

"The basic thing in comedy for three cameras is that you have much more flexibility in finding ways to work the comedy," Sandrich explains. "You have, in essence, five days to make a show work and you're constantly aware that you're going to do it for an audience—not for a laugh machine and not for three people sitting at home. You're really going to do it for people out there, and it had better work; you can't fool yourself. You don't ever get a chance to become complacent, because maybe last week's show was wonderful but you've got a trouble show this week, *or* you read a script for two weeks from now and that needs work. So you're never able to sit back and relax," Sandrich concludes.

Desi Arnaz found that out, too. His work pace, which included acting in and producing *I Love Lucy,* as well as running Desilu Productions, had got out of hand.

"I noticed the change in Desi," Lucille Ball revealed. "When I felt fatigued, I could relax at home with the children. Now I could see the evidence of overwork in Desi. There were weekends when he stayed at home with us and seemed to enjoy it, but not enough of them to build up his physical reserve. When he found he couldn't relax, he would go out on the town. Desi had a tendency to play even harder than he worked.

"At the beginning, he would go off on long fishing trips, which were perfectly all right with me. I understood a man's need to be alone occasionally. But then it dawned on me that Desi was seeking more than solitude."

Years later Lucy confided, "It was a horrifying experience to watch someone you love, someone you think you know, turning into a stranger. We saw it happen. Then we hardly saw him anymore."

At the Ninth Annual Emmy Awards ceremony, telecast over NBC from its Burbank studios on March 16, 1957, the series garnered three acting nominations, but no awards. Lucille lost to Nanette Fabray in the "Best Continuing Performance by a Comedienne in a Series" category, Bill Frawley lost to Carl Reiner, and Vivian Vance lost to Pat Carroll.

Shortly thereafter, Desi flew to New York to huddle with CBS chieftain William S. Paley at his corporate headquarters on Madison Avenue. Arnaz's decision regarding the future of *I Love Lucy?* No more half-hour episodes. Paley was furious with the Cuban: How could he give up the Number One show on television? Had Paley taken the time to look at the lines on the forty-year-old producer's face, he would have had his answer.

On April 8, 1957, at the Conrad Hilton Hotel convention headquarters of the National Association of Radio and Television

Broadcasters, Hubbell Robinson, Jr., executive vice-president in charge of CBS television programs, made the important announcement to a gathering of network affiliates: "Lucille Ball and Desi Arnaz have decided to discontinue *I Love Lucy* after this season. As you all know, they had threatened some time ago not to make any more half-hour *Lucy* films. They want to do a one-hour program once a month next season, but we have not made a commitment on this show as yet."

Simultaneously, *TV Guide* ran this blurb: "Though contracts have not been signed at this writing, it is virtually a foregone conclusion that next year's *I Love Lucy* will be a monthly hour-long show, a format Desi Arnaz has wanted for two seasons now. If plan goes, *Adventures of a Model* and *December Bride* would run three weeks out of four in the Monday, 9–10 P.M. period."

A week later, the same publication suggested, "Current plan for *I Love Lucy* is to alternate an hour version of the show with the *Perry Mason* series on an every-other-week basis." Obviously, plans for the 1957–1958 season still were unresolved.

As you can imagine, the Arnazes were flooded with mail from admiring *Lucy* fans who did not want the series discontinued in its present form. These outraged cries sent newspaper and magazine reporters to Desilu's Cahuenga Boulevard headquarters for answers.

"We've loved our work and we've loved being pioneers," said Lucille Ball after completing her one hundred eightieth *I Love Lucy* segment, "but the time has come to let somebody else 'enjoy' it. We're a little brain-weary, you know. How do you make people understand that? In letters, viewers tell us they're sad because of our plans, but I don't think they understand.

"As I say in the return correspondence, we're not exactly quitting. There'll actually be as much of *Lucy* around next season as they'll want to see. Even the kids will be able to see us next year."

Desi negotiated an outright sale of the entire *I Love Lucy* catalog of episodes to CBS Films, Inc. (the asking price: $5 million). The network made plans, with Glass Wax as the sponsor, to air the reruns of the classic half-hour films every Wednesday evening at 7:30 (ET), beginning September 11, 1957.

When the current season ended, the Ricardos and Mertzes were living in the suburbs, away from the congestion of New York

City. The four *Lucy* writers—Bob Carroll, Jr., Madelyn Martin (she had married producer Quinn Martin that year), Bob Schiller, and Bob Weiskopf—capitalized on the living-in-suburbia syndrome that had become widespread in the 1950s. A total of thirteen segments—the final batch of *I Love Lucy*s—used this story-line approach. A new set of neighbors was fashioned to lend support to the existing ensemble: Betty and Ralph Ramsey and their young son Bruce. *Lucy* veteran Frank Nelson played the husband, Mary Jane Croft (who had been seen most recently in "Return Home from Europe") portrayed his wife, and Ray Ferrell took the part of the son. Even Bill Asher who had directed *I Love Lucy* through three seasons (1952–1955) returned for these episodes to take over direction from the departing James V. Kern.

It was during this story period, which ran from January 28, 1957, to May 6, 1957, that *I Love Lucy* recorded the longest laugh in its six-year history. The show was "Lucy Does the Tango," and it involved Lucy's attempt to hide from Ricky the fact that she had bought five-dozen eggs to make it appear their new laying hens were laying . . . when they really weren't.

"I had sixty eggs tucked away in my blouse," Lucille recalls. "I had to do a dance, and they got jostled. The laugh went on so long [sixty-five seconds] that we had to cut the laugh track in half."

One *I Love Lucy* episode, shot that sixth season, was not very funny and hasn't been aired since December 24, 1956, when it was originally broadcast. Details are sketchy but it was a yuletide-themed half hour that *TV Guide* described: "It's Christmas and Fred Mertz grudgingly buys a tree for Little Ricky [shades of Dickens's *A Christmas Carol*], then Lucy decides to improve on its looks by cutting off branches here and there." Nothing further is known about the episode, which was sandwiched between "Little Ricky's School Pageant" and "Lucy and the Loving Cup," except that St. Nicholas was played by actor Cameron Grant.

"The Ricardos Dedicate a Statue" was the last half-hour *Lucy* ever filmed. The episode made typical use of Lucille Ball's many talents. The final show ironically played host, for the first and only time, to the real Arnaz children—Lucie, five and a half, and Desi IV, four. They were featured in the dedication ceremony crowd scene in the second act.

Six years before, *Daily Variety* had warned that *I Love*

138

Lucy was "not to be taken seriously . . . as story-line comedies go. . . ." One hundred eighty episodes later, Lucille Ball and Desi Arnaz were TV's most successful couple, owning the busiest television production company in Hollywood.

10

"For three years now, I wanted to turn *I Love Lucy* into an hour-long show on maybe a once-a-month basis," said Desi Arnaz in the spring of 1957 after firming up a deal with the Ford Motor Company to sponsor five Lucy-Desi specials. "Two years ago, when I first suggested it, CBS wouldn't listen. Last year again, they talked me into continuing with the weekly half hour. But this time I made up my mind."

It was not an easy decision to come by. When Arnaz first revealed his plans to Paley, CBS made the Cuban an unprecedented offer: They proposed to pay Desilu $80,000 per *Lucy* half hour and $30,000 for each repeat. (The average cost of a top quality half-hour sitcom in 1957 was $48,000.)

"When I turned that down," Desi continues, "they finally realized I wasn't kidding."

The original plan called for eight one-hour Lucy-Desi specials, each budgeted at $350,000, for the 1957–1958 season. With a $4 million price tag, the proposal found no takers among prospective sponsors. Finally Desi took his idea to Ford; he had done business with the automobile manufacturer earlier in the season when he agreed to preview the first retractable hardtop on the March 4, 1957, *I Love Lucy* installment ("The newest kind of Ford. It's the bright new star of *I Love Lucy*," read the ads). After month-long negotiations, the company agreed to underwrite five color specials, the first of which would star Ann Sothern.

The $350,000-budget specials were a far cry from the original *Lucy* films, which were brought in for less than $25,000 each six years before. "They not only have to be good," Arnaz confided to one of his staffers when the deal was being finalized, "they have to be great. We're going to be in an awful spot with these shows; they've *got* to be good."

Why did Desi want to abandon the reliable *I Love Lucy* half-hour format in favor of the untried, the untested? "You've got to change in this business. You can't afford to stand still," he once said incisively. "I would rather make a big change while we are still ahead. It would be ridiculous for us to wait until people got sick and tired of the regular half hour every Monday night. We have been the luckiest show on the air, but we've worked for it. I have never worked so hard in my life. And while I suppose it's not really for me to say, I think I can honestly say that we have never done a really bad show in six years. We threw out only two scripts that whole time and started over again. What other program ever had writers with a record like that?"

The general form of the hour specials placed guest stars into the old *I Love Lucy* format. For the first show, Desi and producer Bert Granet lined up, besides Ann Sothern, Hedda Hopper, Cesar Romero, and Rudy Vallee. The writers—the "Three Bobs and a Babe"—dreamed up an excellent tale that they titled "Lucy Takes a Cruise to Havana."

The opening scene is set in the Ricardos' Westport, Connecticut, living room where Hollywood gossip columnist Hedda Hopper is querying the couple on how their romance started sixteen years ago. A flashback transports us on a cruise to Cuba where Lucille MacGillicuddy and Susie MacNamara (Ann Sothern's *Private Secretary* role), are two stenographers on vacation. On board the ship, they meet newlyweds Fred and Ethel Mertz (he with hair) and Rudy Vallee. On arrival in Havana, the girls encounter two local gentlemen who run a taxi-sightseeing service—Ricky Ricardo and his buddy Carlos (Cesar Romero). They soon discover that Ricky's real wish is to become a musical entertainer. The story goes on to relate Lucy's madcap escapades and whirlwind romance. Songwriter Arthur Hamilton wrote two original songs for the hour special—"Our Ship Is Coming In," sung by Ricky and Carlos, and

"That Means I Love You" with Ricky singing to Lucy's drum accompaniment. It was a terrific writing job, all agreed.

Shot before a live audience at Motion Picture Center in June 1957, with Jerry Thorpe directing and Sid Hickox in charge of the four cameras, "Lucy Takes a Cruise to Havana" was an absolute tour de force. The enlarged budget was obvious—the sets were sumptuous and the costumes were a period delight. The latter element particularly pleased Vivian Vance. Remembers one observer, "Viv had no desire to continue in the hour shows. She had gotten pretty fed up with her treatment in the old *I Love Lucy,* particularly having to wear all those frumpy clothes. Her new contract with Desilu for the Lucy-Desi specials included a clause calling for better costumes. This, more than anything, pleased her. She was always very conscious of how she looked."

That first segment was a first in many ways—it was TV's first hour show that ran seventy-five minutes. Lucy explains: "In the middle of rehearsals, everything went like this," she indicated, snapping her fingers in rhythm. "But suddenly Desi slowed down. I thought, 'This man has finally forgotten a line after seven years.' [Arnaz was well known for memorizing his lines after only one reading.] But, no, he had suddenly gotten the idea the script was so good it had to be extended another fifteen minutes!"

CBS refused to run a segment of seventy-five minutes, demanding that Arnaz either shorten it by fifteen minutes or pad it with an additional fifteen minutes of material. Desi balked on both counts, claiming it would spoil and weaken the total effect.

Bill Paley told Arnaz that CBS did half-hour shows, hour shows, and hour-and-a-half shows. There was, he said, no such thing as an hour-and-fifteen-minute show!

Desi suggested to the CBS head that *The United States Steel Hour,* which would follow the Lucy-Desi special come Wednesday, November 6, 1957, be shortened fifteen minutes, just that one week. Paley flatly refused.

Well known in the industry for solving problems his *own* way, Arnaz went over Paley's head and called the head of U. S. Steel. He assured the magnate that with the Lucy-Desi special as a lead-in, *The United States Steel Hour,* which wasn't doing that well at the time, would probably double its rating. U. S. Steel gave Desi permission to use the first fifteen minutes of its weekly hour, provided the Ford Motor Company picked up the tab for the extra quarter hour.

The result, when the ratings were issued in late November, was a high rating for the first Lucy-Desi effort and the *highest* rating *The United States Steel Hour* ever garnered.

"We're trying to get Gary Cooper for another show," Desi hinted, following filming of the first *Lucille Ball-Desi Arnaz Show*. "Maybe Bill Holden for another. He was so wonderful that first time he worked with us ["L.A. at Last"]. We'll be able to move around more and won't have to keep up that weekly continuity. We hope to do location stuff, too. Each show can be a complete and different story without having to worry about being in that apartment every week or in a home or all that."

Planning the second Lucy-Desi show proved a problem. Desi signed Bette Davis in early June 1957 to guest star in "The Celebrity Next Door," which would be filmed in September and aired in a yet undisclosed time slot (the first season of Lucy-Desi specials had no regular time period) sometime in December. Miss Davis was once a classmate of Lucille's when the two were students at the John Murray Anderson-Robert Milton Dramatics School in New York City in the mid-1920s.

Davis was not easy to deal with. She demanded an enormous salary of $20,000 for a twelve-day rehearsal and shooting stint *and* equal billing to Lucy and Desi. The Arnazes graciously agreed on both counts. She also wanted a clause added to her contract that stipulated that Desilu pay her plane fare home to Maine if she left within ten days after her assignment.

As most readers probably know, Bette Davis never did "The Celebrity Next Door." On June 23, 1957, she suffered a fall in a rented Los Angeles house at 641 Bundy Drive and cracked her vertebra. This was only two weeks after she filed for divorce after seven years of marriage to Gary Merrill in Santa Monica Superior Court. By month's end, she was thrown from a horse and broke her arm. Obviously, she was in no shape to be a "Celebrity Next Door" (unless she was next door to Marcus Welby).

The search for her replacement, which also required a rewrite of the Martin-Carroll-Schiller-Weiskopf teleplay, got under way immediately. A half-dozen famous movie actresses were considered, until, finally, Desi decided on Tallulah Bankhead. One of

143

Lucy's favorite actresses (Ball often amused her friends with a Bankhead impression), Tallulah agreed to fly in from the East to begin rehearsals on September 15, 1957.

The next ten days were a nightmare. "Tallulah was half bombed everyday," remembers one assistant director. "She wouldn't cooperate with Jerry Thorpe, the director, and this infuriated Lucille who's a stickler for rehearsals. There were a lot of battles on the set, let me tell you. Lucy and Desi were sorry they ever hired her."

When Miss Bankhead was questioned about the rumors that "fur flew" during her *Lucy* guest stint, she bristled. "Never. Unequivocally never! I've got not even one picayune derogatory thing to say about those wonderful people," Tallulah began.

"Of course, I *did* have pneumonia at the time. And someone nearly blinded me one day at rehearsals with hair spray. But Lucy? She's *divine* to work with! And Desi? He's brilliant! He *has* a temper, however. But that's because he's fat. It worries him.

"I rehearsed ten days for them. I was there every morning at ten. We left at five, and I returned to my bungalow at the Beverly Hills Hotel, exhausted. I broke a tooth. I broke the cap they put on the tooth. I broke my nails. I had pneumonia," Tallulah lamented.

About "The Celebrity Next Door" script, Bankhead explained foggily, "They had this plot, darling. They were living in Connecticut, or somewhere, and rehearsing a play for the PTA, whatever *that* is. In one scene I sat down in wet paint. In another, I said to Lucy, 'Remove yourself before I pull out that pink hair and expose the black roots underneath!' Then I locked her inside an iron maiden while she was smoking a cigarette. But when they wanted to paint a moustache on me, I drew the line!"

Desi confirms the disagreements with Miss Bankhead. "She would arrive on the set at 9:30 in the morning. But she wouldn't really wake up until eleven. Between eleven and twelve, she was fine. But at 1 A.M., right after lunch, we'd lose her again. Regarding the moustache incident, I finally had to drop the good manners and lay it on the line to her. I told her we were paying her good money and we expected her to do her best.

"The night we did the actual filming [September 27, 1957], I was terrified. I kissed her quickly, wished her luck, and walked

144

away, hoping against hope. What happened? She came through and was nothing short of magnificent," Arnaz recalled.

The episode contained a deceptively simple plot: Tallulah Bankhead moves into the house next door to the Ricardos. Lucy invites the actress to dinner (Fred and Ethel pose as the Ricardos' butler and maid) with two ulterior motives in mind. She wants to impress the actress and persuade her to appear in a PTA benefit show. Suddenly disenchanted with each other during rehearsals, Lucy and Tallulah resort to some unbelievable chicanery to upstage one another. The result is sheer pandemonium, brilliantly turned.

If the Tallulah upsets weren't enough to tax Desi's stamina, he was in the throes of negotiating a deal to buy RKO studios from General Tire & Rubber Company, which had bought the movie-making property two years before from Howard Hughes for $25 million.

After several days of haggling, Desi made General Tire an offer—$6,150,000 for RKO's fifteen-stage, fourteen-acre lot in Hollywood (where Lucy and Desi met in 1940), its Culver City complex (RKO-Pathe, formerly David Selznick's studio where *Gone with the Wind* was made) with eleven sound stages and a twenty-nine-acre backlot, and its valuable library of stock film footage. This would give the Ball-Arnaz TV empire, with its already owned Motion Picture Center, a total of thirty-three sound stages—four more than M-G-M and eleven more than Twentieth Century-Fox boasted in 1957. Though the deal was finalized the very night of the Tallulah Bankhead filming, due to tax reasons, title was not transferred until January 1958.

"When Desi decided to buy the RKO studios [he never consulted Lucy beforehand] for Desilu's expanding business, I knew this would mean more pressure on him than ever before," Lucy notes. "Some columnists wrote that both of us had been fired from RKO in years past and we were now taking revenge. That was ridiculous. Neither of us was fired from RKO; our association had been peaceful. I, for one, certainly never thought of buying the studio. In fact, I never dreamed of owning anything. I never had such high aspirations.

"Desi had high aspirations, but I can't believe they included *buying* RKO. It just happened. We needed more space and it was

145

Some celebrities appear on the show.

available there. Someone asked, 'Why don't you buy RKO?' and he said, as usual, 'Well, why not? How much do they want for it?' He went to the bank [Bank of America] and said, 'Can I buy a studio for six million one hundred thousand dollars?' and they said, 'Yes. You have excellent credit.' Neither of us decided many years ago, 'Someday we'll own this place!' "

Later that fall the company filmed its first Lucy-Desi show on location; guest starring Fred MacMurray and his wife, June Haver, it was titled "Lucy Hunts Uranium." Only a handful of *I Love Lucy* shows had been done on location, and these usually consisted only of short scenes, *sans* sound. The first time had been for "First Stop," an episode in the 1954–1955 season. A second-unit team shot footage of the Ricardos and Mertzes riding in the 1955 Pontiac, but the major portion of the episode, of course, was filmed at Motion Picture Center. A few other fourth-season shows used location footage ("The Tour," for example), but that was about the extent of away-from-studio filming. Costs were too prohibitive.

Now with $350,000 being spent on each Lucy-Desi special, location filming became more feasible. The Fred MacMurray hour was set in Las Vegas, and that's where the Desilu cast and crew went to film a number of outdoor scenes. It was November 1957.

The script called for a stunt man, doubling for MacMurray, to drive a Thunderbird down a hill at top speed and plow into a newly blacktopped road, skidding sideways. Every time the stunt was performed, the sports car careened out of camera range, making expansive retakes necessary.

"This is costing us money," complained Desi, who, as producer, had to pay the bills for such extra costs. "Besides, it don't look so damned hard to do."

Pushing the stuntman aside, Desi climbed into the driver's seat, gunned the motor, and barreled down the Las Vegas hill toward the grimy blacktop. The car finally came to a perfect stop directly in front of the camera. It was a flawless take, except for one small problem. The cameras weren't rolling.

Told by director Jerry Thorpe that it was a wasted effort, Arnaz cursed out the camera crew and walked away fuming. Standing on the sidelines were Lucy, Vivian, Bill, and several dozen members of the crew—dissolved in laughter.

Working without a studio audience was a new experience for the regular *Lucy* cast who had become accustomed to instant reaction. "It's very important to me to have an audience there because I can always tell . . ." Lucille Ball maintains. "They're an immediate barometer, and they're a cross section of America."

Therefore, the next *Lucille Ball-Desi Arnaz Show* was shot at the studio on Cahuenga Boulevard. Lucy was delighted and so were her guests for the hour, Betty Grable and Harry James. Titled "Lucy Wins a Racehorse," the hour centered around the fact that Little Ricky, played for the second season by Richard Keith, wanted a horse. For the one hundred eighty-fourth time, it was Ricky *vs.* Lucy; he was against the idea and Lucy was for it. She entered a "Name the Horse" contest, sponsored by a breakfast cereal company, and won Tony, a love-starved horse.

The animal, one of the best-trained horses in Hollywood, had been taught to do his tricks whenever he heard the word *action*. The horse was trained so meticulously that he would respond even if the command was whispered.

In one scene involving Lucy and Betty Grable, the horse stood in the wings waiting for his cue. Each time Jerry Thorpe called for action, Tony jerked to attention, playfully bared his teeth, and pranced before the cameras. He would perform his bits perfectly, including planting a big kiss on Lucy's cheek.

To break the monotony, Thorpe huddled with cast and crew and mapped out a plan to spell the word *action* rather than speak it. Everyone returned to his place, and orders for silence were issued by an assistant director. Then Jerry carefully enunciated each letter of the word. As he finished, Tony trotted into the scene, reared up on his hind legs, did a dance step or two, and gave Lucy another kiss.

"My God," Thorpe gasped seriously. "The horse is a genius. He can spell!"

What Thorpe didn't know was that when he had finished mouthing the word, Bill Frawley had whispered "action" into Tony's ear, starting him off again.

On January 6, 1958, less than a month before the Grable/ James episode was to be aired, Jerry Thorpe and producer of the thirteen, hour Desi-Lucy specials, Bert Granet, drove out to Palm Springs in an official Desilu station wagon with a few assistants

149

to show the Arnazes, who were enjoying the holidays in their sprawling desert ranch house, a "rough cut" of "Lucy Wins a Racehorse."

"We carried a projector, screen, and several cans of film into the house," remembers one of the assistants, "and set it up in Lucy and Desi's bedroom. When we were ready to show the film, in came Lucy, Desi, the two kids, and three poodles. Lucy pulled her chair next to a lamp table and put a bottle of red nail polish on it. Desi took his place on a chair near the screen. He had just returned from a round of golf at the Thunderbird Country Club. The kids sat on the floor close to their father, and the rest of us sat on the beds or on the long bench in front of the windows.

"The projector was stopped whenever Desi, Jerry, or Bert disagreed over the best way to sharpen a scene, rerunning the parts in dispute so that one or the other, but mostly Desi, could demonstrate the rightness of his solution. Lucy was busy painting her fingernails, seemingly uninterested in the various arguments. Sometimes without even looking up from her nails, she'd say something and the contradicting would stop because the others all said that was just what they meant."

The finished product aired on Monday, February 3, 1958, from eight to nine o'clock. An estimated 50 million people watched the special, which placed fifth in the ARB race for the month behind *Perry Mason, Person to Person, Gunsmoke,* and *Playhouse 90.*

Almost a year before, Desi had begun speculating on what would eventually become the basis of the upcoming, 1958–1959 season. "I would like to do a series of hour shows I'd call *Desilu Playhouse,*" Arnaz told a reporter. "It would be *I Love Lucy* alternating with three others, all of them comedies. Maybe Lucy herself would play opposite somebody else in a one-shot. Maybe I would play opposite some young blond or something. I don't know."

By February 1958 the plan was in the works. It called for thirty-seven hour-long shows to be aired under the "umbrella" title *Desilu Playhouse;* Lucille and Desi would "appear in five or six of them." The budget: a cool $7.5 million.

Ford had decided to withdraw as sponsor, after the initial five Lucy-Desi shows of the 1957–1958 season. "This time we're going to do the shows first and then go looking for a sponsor," Arnaz revealed.

It wasn't that easy. Amid the filming of *The Lucille Ball-Desi Arnaz Show* (number five) with guest star Fernando Lamas, Desi and his creative staff put together a lengthy proposal. He proposed a series of weekly dramas, comedies, and musicals, plus a few undisclosed spectaculars and six Lucy-Desi shows. "No violence, no psychopaths, no dirtiness. [Arnaz had made no plans to produce *The Untouchables* when he made the above statement.] There will never be any need to send the kids to bed when we come on."

When "Lucy Goes to Sun Valley" wrapped up production in early March (part of it was shot on location in the resort town), Desi flew to Pittsburgh to meet with the president of Westinghouse, Mark Cresap, Jr., to present his *Playhouse* proposal. At the time, Westinghouse was sponsoring the distinguished *Studio One,* a CBS anthology series, with an advertising price tag of about $6 million.

"Desi came into town feeling pretty confident," recalls an aide to Cresap. "He was very flashy and very persuasive. Mr. Cresap liked him and was a fan of *I Love Lucy.* But when Desi revealed the proposed budget of his venture—$12 million—Mark was taken back. This was a lot of money then, and business wasn't that hot. In fact, it was lousy."

That's all Desi had to hear. Using his charm and powers of persuasion, he promised the Westinghouse mogul that business would double within a year if the company agreed to underwrite *Desilu Playhouse.*

"Mark took the idea to the board of directors," the company aide continues, "and they approved the twelve-million-dollar outlay just like that."

Upon the Cuban's return to Hollywood to oversee Desilu's official takeover of the RKO facilities, *TV Guide* reported in its May 24, 1958, edition: "Desi Arnaz swung his record-breaking $12 million Westinghouse *Desilu Playhouse* deal which calls for forty-eight hour-long films, including seven new Lucy-Desi shows, thirty-six dramas, comedies, and musicals, five repeats of this season's Lucy-Desi hours—all without a single test film, no scripts, no guest stars—just the Desilu track record."

151

Then Arnaz was hit with a bombshell. Bob Carroll and Madelyn Martin, writers of *Lucy* since the very beginning in 1951, wanted to quit, even though they had signed new three-year contracts a year or so before. It was their contention that they had run dry, had exhausted every imaginable *Lucy* premise.

Desi knew he couldn't force them to write. Perhaps you can coax a bricklayer to lay more bricks, but you can't needle the creative process in the same way. As an incentive to remain, Desi offered to pay for a European vacation Bob wanted to take, and build a nursery on to Madelyn and Quinn Martin's house for their newborn son. Despite these gestures of good faith—some observers labeled them bribes—Bob and Madelyn took leaves of absence for what would be an undetermined length of time.

With only a month in which to fashion a one-hour teleplay for the opening Lucy-Desi special for the new season (filming in June with guest star Maurice Chevalier), Arnaz had to do some fast thinking. Schiller and Weiskopf, competent enough *Lucy* scribes with three years experience in the genre, needed some help, particularly with a script as important to Desilu and Westinghouse as this one.

Desi approached Everett Freeman, a veteran M-G-M comedy screenwriter who has since created innumerable TV pilots, with an offer to collaborate with the two Bobs on a Lucy-Desi script for Maurice Chevalier. Freeman dreamed up "Lucy Goes to Mexico" in time for the late-spring filming. According to Viacom, the company that syndicates these specials as well as the 179 original *I Love Lucy* episodes, Freeman was not credited for his creative contribution. Schiller and Weiskopf have the "written by" credit and, surprisingly enough, Bob Carroll, Jr., and Madelyn Martin retain their "story consultants" title even though they did not work on the script.

The pair, however, did contribute to the next Lucy-Desi outing, "Lucy Makes Room for Danny," which they proceeded to write in their new Desilu-Gower (the new name of RKO's Hollywood plant) offices even before the Chevalier show went before the cameras. After seven years with *Lucy,* they were lost without her.

11

"We're planning preview parties in twenty-two cities," Desi Arnaz explained before the premiere episode of *Desilu Playhouse.* "A helicopter will fly over, showing our three studios, and we'll tell about our various activities and two thousand employees."

The first *Westinghouse Lucille Ball-Desi Arnaz Show,* "Lucy Goes to Mexico," aired Monday, October 6, 1958, at 10 P.M. This was the Maurice Chevalier outing, considered by Desi to be his real coup. The Cuban had tried unsuccesfully for three years to get the Frenchman to appear on a *Lucy* show. He had met Chevalier in San Francisco in 1947 and was a great admirer of his talents and charm.

Filming of the special at the Desilu-Cahuenga studios (formerly Motion Picture Center) was completed by mid-June 1958. The plot, devised by Everett Freeman with Schiller and Weiskopf, was deceptively simple—Lucy gets involved with U.S. Customs officials in Tijuana, Mexico, while Ricky is rehearsing with Chevalier for a show aboard a navy aircraft carrier (*Yorktown*) in San Diego harbor.

The script included a bullfight sequence that called for Lucille to work with a live bull that had foot-long horns. Trained carefully, the animal was guaranteed to be docile. Lucy was, nevertheless, dubious, especially since she had to approach the snorting bull and wave a perfume-soaked handkerchief at him. The smell was supposed to stop the bull in his tracks.

During the rehearsal break, a prop man asked Lucy, "What kind of perfume have you got on that hanky?"

Miss Ball, always the kidder, cracked, "Eau de hamburger. That oughta keep him in line."

The wisecrack broke up everyone within earshot and was so hilariously appropriate it was written into the script and subsequently used.

One of the bullfight scenes, however, caused Lucille some less than hilarious anguish. "They had mounted a bull's head on the camera and rolled straight toward me at high speed. And would you believe, I was gored . . . just as if it had been a real bull!"

Even before the premiere, N. W. Ayer & Company, a leading ad agency known for its TV-ratings predictions, speculated that *Desilu Playhouse* would be among the top shows of the season, ranking high with Danny Thomas, *Gunsmoke, Wagon Train, The Ann Sothern Show* (a Desilu series), and *Restless Gun* (a Western bomb starring John Payne). Desi admitted that *Playhouse* was his most important concern that year. "It's my Number One baby," he said.

A Lucy-Desi special featuring Danny Thomas and his TV family, the Williamses, followed the Chevalier show on December 1, 1958. The script by Schiller and Weiskopf was story-edited by Bob Carroll and Madelyn Martin who had returned with a lessened workload to their writing posts at Desilu. The breakneck schedule they had pursued during the preceding seven years (writing as many as sixty pages of *Lucy* script a week) was a thing of the past. For Madelyn, Desi built a nursery adjacent to her office at Desilu-Gower, so she could bring her infant son to work and care for him at the same time.

For the third Westinghouse Lucy-Desi hour, the company went on location to Lake Arrowhead, a mile-high resort area two hours from Los Angeles, to film a sequence simulating the frozen wastelands of Alaska, not yet our forty-ninth state. Guest starring Red Skelton, the show aired February 9, 1959, just a month after Alaska was admitted officially into the Union.

The highlight of the show was Lucille Ball's teaming with Skelton for a ten-minute "Freddie the Freeloader" sketch, entitled "Dining at the Waldorf."

In late 1958 Vivian Vance, who had achieved an enormous popularity due to her hundreds of *Lucy* appearances, was tapped to play the lead role in an ABC comedy pilot based on the Patrick Dennis novel *Guestward Ho!* Ralph Levy, the director of the original *I Love Lucy* pilot, was signed to supervise the production as well as direct the test film.

"On the first take, I yelled 'action' and Vivian just stood there frozen," Levy points out. "On the second take, the same thing happened. And again with the third. I went up to her to find out if she was all right and Viv said, 'This is the first time in eight years I've been in my own light,' meaning, of course, that after being in the shadows of Lucille all that time, she was finding it a little difficult going it alone. It was a big change for her."

The pilot did not sell, which meant that Miss Vance would remain with Lucy and Desi for an upcoming ninth season. To make matters worse for the Kansas-born actress, she was sued for divorce on March 30, 1959. In the divorce action, Philip N. Ober, then fifty (Vivian was forty-six), said that his wife was cruel to him. (Ethel Mertz . . . cruel?) She said in rebuttal that they "could never agree on how to handle my success." She also revealed that he was "extravagant and did not believe in savings."

They divided property valued at more than $160,000, which included their California home at 629 Frontera Drive in Pacific Palisades; the Cubero, New Mexico, property; and some stocks and bonds.

Vivian's divorce was not the only example of marital discord on the *Lucy* set. By the beginning of 1959, Ed Sullivan, in a blind item in his syndicated newspaper column, hinted of the divorce of "TV's famous husband and wife team." There weren't that many such teams, but, coincidentally, one of them made a guest appearance on the last Lucy-Desi special of the 1958–1959 season. Howard Duff and Ida Lupino, then starring in their own CBS sitcom, *Mr. Adams and Eve,* appeared in the June 8, 1959, telecast of "Lucy's Summer Vacation." Jerry Thorpe directed the script by Schiller and Weiskopf in mid-April. The result was a delightful romp, set in a mountain lodge in Vermont, although filmed on Stage 9 at Desilu-Cahuenga.

Following filming, Lucille and Desi escaped the rigors of their studio existence. It had been a busy and demanding year that saw

155

Desilu go public and offer half of its stock, or 565,600 shares, on the American Stock Exchange on December 3, 1958. To save her faltering marriage, Lucy planned a trip to Europe aboard the French ocean liner, the *Liberté*. Despite the warning of close friends, she decided to bring the children along.

While in Europe, they visited Maurice Chevalier at his home, about twenty minutes outside Paris. It was a wonderful reunion, which took the edge off the negative aspects of the vacation: When the Arnazes returned to the States, they were scarcely speaking to each other. Desi was weary from his overwork and also resented the presence of his children, even though he was a doting Daddy. The pair's anxieties toward each other touched off one quarrel after another.

In July 1959, Desilu announced that its gross for the year just ended was $20,470,361 in contrast to the 1954 gross of $4,668,660. Its profit for 1959 was $249,566; the net for 1958 was only $92,336. Business was good, even though the marriage—from which Desilu was created—wasn't. Tensions built steadily. In fact, Desi was no longer sleeping in the master bedroom of the couple's mansion on Roxbury Drive in Beverly Hills.

At the studio, they had to put up a front. In late June, upon their return from the European cruise, Lucy and Desi started production on the eleventh one-hour *Lucy* special, which would open the 1959–1960 season of *Desilu Playhouse* on September 25. Their guest star was Mr. Television himself, Milton Berle. He agreed to appear only if the Arnazes reciprocated by costarring with him in an NBC special the next season. They acquiesced, although the venture never came off.

Because Jerry Thorpe was busy directing another Desilu show that would premiere in the fall, Desi himself took on the added burden of directing the "Lucy Meets Milton Berle" show. By this time, the company had all but totally abandoned its technique of filming before a live audience. Production problems inherent in many of the hour specials precluded bringing in guests. The system of using multiple cameras shooting simultaneously was, however, retained.

On and off the set, and despite persistent rumors in the press, Lucy and Desi tried desperately to maintain a friendly relationship, especially around Milton Berle. A number of times during rehearsal, tempers—particularly Desi's—flared.

"What do I say here?" Lucy asked director Desi, interrupting a run-through.

"You say, 'I can't.' "

Desi's accent is as thick off camera as it is on. "Can?" queried Lucy.

"Can't!" replied Desi brusquely.

"Are you saying 'can' or 'can't'?"

"I'm saying *can't,* dammit! Can't!" Desi shouted.

Arnaz was boss. "Nothing goes out of this shop without Desi putting his fine Cuban hand into it," said Howard McClay, once a Desilu executive and now PR director of Lucille Ball Productions, Inc. Someone once remarked that if Desi had learned to type in Spanish, he would have written *Lucy* too.

Even Milton Berle, whom some associates have called a tyrant, was in awe of Desi's ability behind the camera: "I was so struck by the way he handled everything on his own show that I asked him to direct a show for me. He's got a tremendous flair for comedy; there's almost nobody like him around. He's a driver, a perfectionist, and he usually knows ninety-five percent of what he wants. I think he can do more serious stuff as well. I have great respect for his ability to handle people and for his knowledge of what plays and what doesn't.

"Look what he did for Lucy," Uncle Miltie continued. "She's the greatest comedienne in the world because she's one of the greatest actresses. He saw that in her and helped to bring it out." That's quite a testimonial coming from a man who once demonstrated to an Irish tenor the proper way to sing "The Wearin' of the Green."

During rehearsals for "Lucy Meets Milton Berle," Desi had the pair play one piece of business five times. It was a bit that would last no more than thirty seconds on the screen, but the rehearsals alone took a half hour. At the end of the repetitive session, Desi told Lucy and Milton, "Now we go through it one more time."

"Aw, come on, Des," Berle whined.

"No," Lucy said flatly. "We'll *not* do it again!"

"Come on," Desi insisted. "We do it one more time."

They did it one more time.

If Desi was manic in rehearsal, he became downright frantic when it came time to shoot. He used his usual three cameras, but sometimes ordered a fourth and even a fifth. His day was one solid block of work. When the cast and crew knocked off for lunch, Desi raced back to his office to dispose of other business demands.

"You want to eat, dear?" Lucy asked him.

"No. No time." There was almost hostility in his voice. He flung himself away and went back to work.

Inside of fifteen minutes, he had consulted with a script editor, looked through a catalog of performers with a casting director, talked to a prop man about props, conversed with a set designer about sets, and listened to a man who was trying to sell him a new electric golf cart.

Back at Stage 9 after lunch, Desi picked up where he left off. One person who was present during the Milton Berle show preparations recalls, "Desi was all over the set like an unruly school kid, squinting through his viewer, shouting orders at everyone, conferring with the lighting men and other technicians. One instant he was up a ladder; the next, he was on the floor on his hands and knees, showing where we wanted a gravel walkway laid.

"Sometimes he was like a human windmill, his arms flailing wildly. Once, while spreading his arms to show an actor how to do a scene, he accidentally rammed his hand into a running electric fan and shaved the flesh off three fingers.

"Working with the actors, he hopped in and out of the field of action, placing them forcibly in position, showing them where to walk, sometimes even twisting his face into the expressions he wanted theirs to assume," the observer concludes.

Westinghouse had requested in late spring that the *Desilu Playhouse* be moved for the new season to Friday night's 9:00–10:00 time period on CBS. Request granted. The only other second-season change in the show involved Betty Furness who opened the Westinghouse refrigerator doors ("You can be *sure* if it's Westinghouse.") during the 1958–1959 season commercials; she was replaced by a younger woman.

Arnaz also directed the next Lucy-Desi special, which costarred Robert Cummings. Titled "The Ricardos Go to Japan," it was the seventh of a total of eight *I Love Lucy*-type hours contracted with Westinghouse. It was filmed in late September 1959, following a three-month hiatus that Lucy spent working with a new group of young acting hopefuls in her Desilu Workshop.

"I also spent as much time as possible with our children," Lucy confided to a close friend. "I took them to Del Mar a couple of times, to Disneyland, Marineland, and helped them with their French lessons."

Desi went back to Europe after the Bob Cummings show, this time alone. Rumors of Lucy and Desi's separation abounded in Hollywood. Lucy tried to explain them away to inquisitive reporters. "Some people live on rumors," she said. "Desi and I have been in this whole thing long enough to be accustomed to them. We've gotten through the thing before, and we'll get through it again. Maybe it's good for some couples to be separated for a time—maybe it can renew and refresh a relationship."

But the rumors began affecting business on the three Desilu lots. When reporters asked Howard McClay if he thought there was a possibility that Lucy and Desi might split up, he answered, "I don't believe there is. Don't forget, they've got a big vested interest in each other—not just the family, the kids, but this whole thing." His sweeping gesture indicated the huge plant. "No. I don't think so."

Their mutual differences did not escape their own two children, then eight and six and a half. "One night, as I stopped by little Desi's room to tuck him in, I heard him whimpering," recalls Lucille Ball. "Lucie, who was normally a sound sleeper, was tossing and turning in her bed when I looked in on her."

Lucy knew then that she had to tell the children the truth. Daddy was no longer living at home, and there was no use in making excuses for him.

"I took Lucie aside first, because she was oldest. 'Lucie,' I said, 'I have to tell you that Mommy and Daddy are not getting along and I know that the unhappiness you see is affecting you. And I want you to know that it has nothing to do with you. We love you very much. I want you also to know that we are trying to work things out.'

"She said, 'You wouldn't get a divorce, would you?' "

Lucy was dumbfounded by her daughter's naïve frankness.

159

Above left: The divorce was imminent but Lucille and Desi kept face behind the scenes with Ernie Kovacs before filming the very last episode, "Lucy Meets the Moustache" (1960). *Right:* An original costume sketch for *I Love Lucy* by Elois Jenssen. Okayed in the bottom-left-hand corner by Lucille Ball (*Courtesy Elois Jenssen*).

Right: Desi Arnaz directs Lucille's stand-in before filming "Lucy Meets Milton Berle." Note miniature cars used to achieve altitude effect (1959).

Above: Desi Arnaz, Richard Keith, Maurice Chevalier perform "Valentine" (From "Lucy Goes to Mexico," the first *Westinghouse Lucille Ball-Desi Arnaz Show,* 1958). *Below left:* Scene from "Lucy Takes a Cruise to Havana," with guest Ann Sothern playing her *Private Secretary* role, Susie MacNamara (1957). *Below right:* Lucy poses as Ernie Kovacs's chauffeur in "Lucy Meets the Moustache" (1960).

"What do you know about divorce?" she asked the eight-year-old. "What is a divorce?"

Little Lucie stammered, "Well, it's . . . well, you wouldn't get one, would you?"

In reply, Lucy told the child, "I am only planning on being separated from Daddy, and I just want you to know that it has nothing to do with you. We will probably see much more of Daddy, actually."

"I learned pretty early," says twenty-three-year-old Desi Arnaz, Jr., today, "to relate to *I Love Lucy* as a TV show and to my parents as actors in it. There wasn't much relationship between what I saw on TV and what was really going on at home. Those were difficult years—all those funny things happening each week on television to people who looked like my parents, then the same people agonizing through some terrible, unhappy times at home, and each of them trying to convince my sister and me separately that the other was in the wrong."

The fall of 1959 was also a low period for Desi Arnaz, Sr. Problems plaguing a motion-picture production in Europe were constant, sometimes necessitating fifteen-hour workdays. One night in September, he was picked up by Hollywood police on a drunk-driving charge.

What did the people who worked with Desi think of him?

"I'd like to tell you one story about Desi Arnaz which really points up the kind of guy he is," begins one loyal script girl. "In 1957 when he sold the rerun rights of *I Love Lucy* to CBS, he was advised to quit television. He was told that he could pay the government one million dollars in capital gains tax, take the rest free and clear, and live a life of ease and relaxation. You know the answer? He said, 'That's great, but how do I tell all the people who've worked with us in Desilu? How do I tell them, "I've got mine. I'm gonna quit"?'

"Desi couldn't do it," the lady continued. "He went to the Bank of America, borrowed a few more million, and bought RKO so he could expand and put *more* people to work. That's the kind of guy Desi Arnaz is."

Not everyone thought this way. Once, an actor was called in to redo a scene, which under his Desilu contract the studio would have to pay for. The producer asked him to waive the extra payment because of a tight budget problem and, to press home the point, added, "After all, you're one of the regulars here and we're all one big happy family on this lot."

"Some family," the actor cracked. "Daddy's never home."

Daddy, of course, was Desi and he signed the checks. And, of late, Daddy had been neglecting his professional family as well as his real one. Yet the studio and its many projects continued to move forward, thanks to the strange devotion both Desi and Lucy seemed to have generated among their professional "family."

Such dedication is difficult to decipher. With one of the regular actors, now deceased, the reason was simple: He and Desi once worked together in a band many years ago; subsequently, the actor fell on hard times and when Desi hit it big, he took him in.

"Desi liked to play the part of Big Daddy," says one former member of the family. "And Lucy, God bless her, liked to play Baby Snooks."

Lucy and Desi differed in their attitudes toward the huge complex of studios they owned. To Desi, contends one associate, it was an opportunity for a former bandleader and actor to show what "a shrewd cookie he was as an executive." To Lucy, it was the "world's biggest sandpile."

One insider to the many Desilu machinations points out: "Success went to their pocketbooks. Desi had made so much money that success became very dull and monotonous."

But despite the so-called monotony, Desilu continued to flourish as a multimillion-dollar business enterprise. In early October 1959 Desi again took off for Europe, leaving Lucy alone. Since they were no longer living in the same house, she hardly missed him. Professionally, Lucille was working with her acting workshop, getting ready to stage a revue that would constitute the Christmas Day *Desilu Playhouse* installment. Without her Cuban compass, Lucy found the going rough.

"Lucy asked me to appear on the Christmas show," Hedda Hopper once wrote. "She was making her bow as director, coaching a dozen or so young players she had been training in her school for over a year. Desi had just returned from a solo trip to Europe.

"During rehearsals, Vivian Vance and Bill Frawley wanted to take cover with me to avoid the storms between Lucy and Desi. It was dreadful. 'You can't insult him before the entire company,'

163

I warned her in her dressing room. 'You're partly responsible for this show, too, you know.'

"It seemed we were doomed to have a flop on our hands. As director, Lucy was lost without Desi, too mad to see straight, and the show was going to pieces. In dress rehearsal Desi said, 'Lucy, dear, will you let me see if I can pull this thing together for you?'

"Lucy snapped back at him with blood in her eye, 'Okay, try it!' In ten minutes, he had the revue ticking like a fine clock," Hedda concluded.

Besides Miss Hopper, Vivian, and Bill, the show, which was called "The Desilu Revue," featured cameo appearances by Ann Sothern, Hugh O'Brian, Spring Byington, and Lassie—all Desilu performers. With a script by Bob Schiller and Bob Weiskopf, the hour-long special spotlighted twenty-two talented newcomers who were personally selected by Lucy from the total enrollment of her Desilu Workshop Theatre.

With the revue behind her, Lucy decided to abandon the workshop completely. "Sure, I'll miss it," she said. "It's a satisfying thing. But I've given two years of my time and my heart to the kids, and you can't do everything for them. The objective of the workshop was to provide a stepping-stone for young, talented performers. I think we achieved this. However, I found myself caring about each one. They took two years out of my life as a lay psychiatrist. That's over now, because they drained me dry. I figured if I ever wanted to work again I'd better conclude it."

The workshop was not the only venture Lucille wanted to discontinue. Before the year (1959) was out, she wanted to sue Desi for divorce.

"You can't," a close confidante told her. "You and Desi both signed the Westinghouse contract as partners. If you walk out now, they could cancel and sue you."

The Westinghouse deal did have several months to run, so Lucy decided to wait until the propitious moment before making her long-awaited move. Desi was already aware of her intentions. In fact, they had worked out the details some time ago.

Their most difficult task during the final few months of their stormy marriage was telling the children of their plans.

"We drove to our home in Palm Springs, specifically for the

purpose," Miss Ball recounts. "And Desi told them while I just sat there."

He began by telling them that Mommy and Daddy weren't getting along. That's when little Lucie looked up, "But you won't get a divorce?"

Lucy continues: "Desi explained that perhaps we would. The kids got very quiet, put their heads down, and didn't want to look at us. Desi told them he loved them very much.

"Finally, little Desi looked up and said, 'But, Daddy, a divorce? Isn't there some way you can take it all back?' That was almost more than we could take," says Lucille retrospectively.

It now came time to perform as Mr. and Mrs. Ricky Ricardo for the last time. It was their most difficult assignment in the eight and a half years playing the parts.

The atmosphere around the set was different. "There was no sign of unpleasantness," one witness maintains. "At the studio they acted with deference and courtesy to each other. In the old days, their relationship had been marked by an easy give and take. They used to kid each other unmercifully. Now they were being *too* nice to each other. We all knew something was really wrong."

The last Lucy-Desi outing was titled "Lucy Meets the Moustache" and co-starred the late comedian Ernie Kovacs and his wife, Edie Adams. It was the thirteenth hour-long special in the three-year period. It was the one hundred ninety-third Lucy/Ricky/Fred/Ethel plot since 1951.

"Every time they wanted to film a funny scene," Miss Adams recalls, "Lucy would break down and cry. Nobody could stand to watch it."

Ironically, the last scene Lucy and Desi ever played together seemed to explain their marital problems in just a few Schiller-Weiskopf lines:

LUCY: Honest, honey, I just wanted to help.
RICKY: From now on, you can help me by not trying to help me. But thanks, anyway.

As per the script, they embraced and kissed. But before the kiss, Lucy removed the moustache she was wearing to impersonate

Kovac's chauffeur. The audience laughed appropriately . . . for the last time.

Backstage, there was no laughter, nor were there any smiles. A heavy air of melancholy invaded the huge sound stage as good-byes were said, kisses exchanged. Vivian Vance was teary-eyed, and so was gruff old Bill Frawley. They, more than anyone else, had labored the longest with Lucy and Desi.

"I filed for divorce the day after I finished my last piece of film under the Westinghouse contract," Lucille Ball admits. On Thursday, March 3, 1960—a day after Desi's forty-third birthday —Lucy filed papers in Santa Monica Superior Court, claiming married life to Desi was "a nightmare," nothing at all like it appeared on *I Love Lucy.*

By the time the public saw the last *Lucy* episode on April 1, 1960, their divorce was already old news, and Lucy and Desi's nine-year reign as "TV's favorite couple" had officially ended.

12

"It wasn't the industry and our working together that broke us up," claims Lucille Ball of her nineteen-year marriage to Desi Arnaz. "The pressure had a lot to do with it. He was a very sick man. I was living with hope for many years.

"When the children got to an age when they were noticing the unhappiness, it was time to move away. That helped me make up my mind . . . that, and the end of our performing commitments together.

"For years and years I wore blinders where he was concerned. I saw only his good points. But somehow I couldn't help myself. I'm very sensitive," the redhead continued. "I stored up all the hurts and humiliations, not the hurts of a day or a week, but the hurts of years. Then some little thing comes along. It opens up the dam; all the resentment rushes out."

When Lucy won her default divorce from Desi on May 4, 1960 —a little more than a month after CBS canceled *Desilu Playhouse,* the last vestige of the *I Love Lucy* legend—she admitted to the press, "It's very difficult to work the way he worked for the last nine years. Mostly, I think it's bad for the children. It's much better for us to be apart."

In truth, the marriage shattered five years before it was officially terminated by divorce. "Those last five years were sheer, unadulterated hell," Lucy confirms today. "I'm afraid I didn't cope too well. We both knew it was over. But we had commitments to fill.

So we stayed together. I was hoping in my heart that maybe everything might change, a miracle might happen, maybe, maybe, maybe. But people don't really change.

"Desi drank and I knew he went out with other women, but I didn't worry about it soon enough. The last five years were the same old booze and broads, the only change being that he was rarely at home anymore. And that was a blessing, because we didn't yell at each other when we didn't see each other."

Superior Court Judge Orlando H. Rhodes listened to Lucy's teary-eyed testimony, then awarded her an uncontested divorce. She was awarded half of the $20 million television empire built on the success of their TV marriage as the happy-go-lucky Ricky Ricardos, as well as the Beverly Hills mansion, two station wagons, and a cemetery plot at Forest Lawn. Desi retained the other half of the Desilu fortune, a golf cart, a membership in the Thunderbird Country Club in Palm Springs, a truck, eleven racehorses, and the ranch at Riverside.

Desi issued a formal statement soon after: "We deeply regret that after long and serious consideration we have not been able to work out our problems and have decided to separate. Our divorce will be completely amicable and there will be no contest. Lucy will pursue her career on television and I will continue my work as head of Desilu Productions."

Following the divorce proceedings, Lucy did not pursue her television career. Instead, she immediately plunged into a motion picture with Bob Hope, *The Facts of Life*. When production ended, she packed up the kids and went off to New York, ensconced herself in a twenty-third-floor luxury apartment in the East Sixties, and began rehearsals for her first Broadway play. This was something that was in the offing for over a year; in fact, the previous summer, she had made a verbal commitment to producers Kermit Bloomgarten and Morton DaCosta to star in a stage play adaptation of a Dorothy Parker short story, *Big Blonde*. The deal never came off (the play was too maudlin for Lucy), so Miss Ball jumped at the chance to headline a new musical, *Wildcat!*, which had music by Cy Coleman (*Sweet Charity*) and a book by N. Richard Nash (*The Rainmaker*). The play, bankrolled by Desilu Productions, opened in December 1960. It was a hit only because Lucille Ball was the star; when she withdrew some months later because of "ill health," the show posted its closing notice.

Desi flew to New York regularly to visit his two children whom he missed immensely. His workload, running the massive Desilu operation, was still a formidable situation. Desi, Jr., contends that his father aged ten years because of the pressure of the television industry. "The major operations he underwent in the 1970s didn't help either," the young actor adds.

Bill Frawley wasted no time in securing another acting assignment when the nine-year *Lucy* stint folded. Even though his Desilu contract ran until June 1, 1960, Frawley accepted an offer in the spring from TV producer Don Fedderson to costar with Fred MacMurray in a new situation comedy that would premiere on the ABC Television Network in the fall, *My Three Sons*.

"Desi was a little irate about my accepting another job while I was under contract to him," Frawley once admitted.

His *My Three Sons* role, that of Michael Francis O'Casey, or "Bub" as he was more commonly called, was similar in attitude to the Fred Mertz character he portrayed for so long. "While doing *My Three Sons,* I've been getting residual checks from the reruns of *Lucy,*" said Frawley. "And, I must say, they look beautiful."

When *Lucy* ended its first-run engagement on April 1, 1960, the series was still enjoying enormous popularity in the daytime. Since January 5, 1959, the original half-hour films were being broadcast Monday through Friday at eleven o'clock in the morning (ET). And beginning July 13, 1960, CBS—which now owned the 179 films outright—retitled the series *Lucy in Connecticut* and beamed it every Sunday night in prime time for the duration of the summer.

At first, network bigwigs were worried that the Arnaz divorce would dissipate the value of the *I Love Lucy* films for which they had paid millions. Would the public still accept the pair as a married couple? Today, sixteen years later, that seems like a silly question.

Frawley continued in his *My Three Sons* role for five years before poor health forced him to retire. A short time later, while strolling down Hollywood Boulevard after seeing a movie one night, he died suddenly of a heart attack on March 3, 1966, just

169

a week after his seventy-ninth birthday. He collapsed near the Hollywood Knickerbocker Hotel where he had lived for many years before moving to an apartment at 450 North Rossmore in Hollywood. His male nurse, a constant companion since Frawley's prostate surgery in 1965, dragged him into the hotel lobby to try to revive him. It was too late. The actor was rushed to nearby Hollywood Receiving Hospital where he was pronounced dead.

Upon hearing of his passing, Lucille Ball remarked, "Oh, I'm terribly sorry. I've lost one of my dearest friends and show business has lost one of the greatest character actors of all time. Those of us who knew him and loved him will miss him."

Ironically, Bill's last video appearance was in a segment of *The Lucy Show,* telecast October 25, 1965. "I love that girl," Frawley told a reporter before his death. "I've loved her since she was a star-struck kid at RKO. I get along all right with Desi, too."

Arnaz's affection for the crusty old curmudgeon was demonstrated the day of Frawley's burial at San Fernando Mission Cemetery. Besides acting as one of the pallbearers, Desi took out and paid for a full-page ad in the Hollywood *Reporter.* The layout featured a photograph of Frawley with the dates of his life (February 26, 1887, to March 3, 1966) underneath and the inscription *"¡Buenas Noches, Amigo!"*

What happened to Frawley's TV wife after the demise of *I Love Lucy?* Vivian Vance did not go back to work like Frawley. When her *Guestward Ho!* pilot failed to sell in 1959, Desilu decided to film a new version for possible airing in 1960. Director Ralph Levy wanted Vivian to reprise her role as Babs Hooten in the second attempt, but not everyone agreed. When the revamped version went before the cameras in March 1960, Joanne Dru had inherited Vivian's part. (*Guestward Ho!* premiered September 29, 1960, on ABC and lasted only one season.)

This didn't bother the forty-eight-year-old actress in the least. She had successfully shaken off the trauma of her 1959 divorce from Phil Ober and had met a charming man that same summer at a Santa Fe, New Mexico, party. Seven years her junior, John Dodds, a successful literary agent from the East, proposed to Vivian shortly thereafter. They were married on Monday, January 16, 1961, at the sight of their first encounter, the home of author Babs Hooten and her husband. Vivian was given away by John

Emery, Tallulah Bankhead's ex-husband, who himself had made a number of *I Love Lucy* appearances. The Dodds set up residence in Stamford, Connecticut, an easy commute to Manhattan where John maintained offices. Vivian became active in the Connecticut Association for Mental Health and received a well-deserved award for her dedication. She was a happy lady, satisfied with her new life.

Lucille, too, met a new man and married him that year. "I didn't want to get married again," said Lucy. "I didn't think I would find a mature, adult person like Gary [Morton], a really understanding guy who is wonderful to be around and uncomplicated. He has none of the worrisome characteristics I lived with. I learned from experience. I wasn't going to walk into the same trap.

"One night when I was in *Wildcat!,* Jack Carter and his wife, Paula, said they wanted me to meet a friend. I put it off two or three times . . . I was too tired, I said. Finally one night I was hungry and I said, 'Well, I'll go for something to eat,' and I met Gary. We had fun. He was going away for a couple of weeks. When he came back we started seeing each other after the theater.

"I found out he was, as I said, uncomplicated, good, sweet, hip, funny, and he appreciated a home, not just the trappings. He knew how to enjoy himself in a home. I got sick during the run of *Wildcat!* Maybe it was emotional, I don't know. I came to the Coast to sell my house and go to Switzerland or somewhere, and he followed me. My friends met him. He knew more people than I did.

"By the time he was here for a while everybody was saying, 'My lord, why don't you marry this guy?' Finally I said, 'Yes.' "

Lucille Ball and Gary Morton were married November 19, 1961. She credits him with gently coaxing her back into television the following year.

"In early 1962, Lucy came East for a visit," says Vivian Vance Dodds. "She told me she had a script for a new TV series in her purse. I said, 'Lucy, don't take it out. I won't read it.' "

Six months later, Vivian Vance was in Hollywood, making the first episodes of the new *The Lucy Show.*

"I don't believe I'd have started the show without Vivian," contends Lucy. "And I really didn't know how I could start it *with*

171

her. After all, she had settled into a new way of life since we last worked together. She'd gotten married, she had a home in Connecticut, her garden, her pets, her new interests—all the things she loves. She was willing to come back if it was okay with John, and even though it would involve five years of long-distance commuting, he agreed. John felt it was doing him a favor because it made Vivian happy."

Desi Arnaz produced *The Lucy Show* for Desilu Productions. When rehearsals for the first show commenced one summer morning, Desi was present on the set. He gave Lucy a kiss on the cheek and a good luck emblem, a tiny four-leaf clover made out of antique emerald jade.

"Lucy, dear," he said, "I wish you all the luck in the whole ever-loving world. You really deserve it, kid."

"Oh, Desi," she said smiling. "How thoughtful."

She returned a sincere embrace, then went back to her rehearsing. Desi made his way up a few steps to one of the catwalks that service the overhead lighting. Leaning on the wooden guardrail, he gazed down at Lucy as she practiced a complicated telephone scene. Suddenly his eyes filled with tears and he broke down crying.

As he dried his face with a handkerchief, he turned and discovered that Vivian Vance had climbed to the catwalk and was standing beside him. She, too, was crying. He put his arm around the actress, the same girl whom eleven years ago he had discovered at the La Jolla Playhouse and cast as Ethel Mertz.

"Oh, Desi," Vivian cried. "It isn't the same, is it?"

Vivian knew exactly why Desi was crying. "Like me, he was thinking back to when we all started in on *I Love Lucy*—him and Lucy and William Frawley and me, and how it was then. All the newness . . . all the anticipation and the hope . . . and the fun. And here we were, starting again, only this time he was on the outside looking in and it wasn't fun anymore. He wasn't acting. He was divorced. I'd been divorced, but I was married again. And Lucy was married again. So much had happened to so many people, but most of all to Desi, leaving him alone and a little sad, although he tried to hide it," Miss Vance explains.

The Lucy Show was a good situation comedy. It lasted six years on CBS, occupying the *I Love Lucy* time slot, Monday at nine o'clock. But it never came up to the standards of its incredible predecessor. Something was missing.

Critic Edith Efron once wrote: "Encountering America's favorite zany in a new habitat, with a new last name (Carmichael), with unknown young children, and without her dashing Desi, is an odd experience. A decade of *I Love Lucy* shows has so indissolubly wedded the images of Lucy and Desi Arnaz that to discover a Desi-less Lucy on the screen is like finding a revised edition of *Gone with the Wind* in which Scarlett O'Hara appears without Rhett Butler."

Bob Carroll, Jr., and Madelyn Pugh Martin, after two *Lucy*-less seasons, were back as head writers on *The Lucy Show*. After *The Lucille Ball-Desi Arnaz Show* went off the air in the spring of 1960, the pair created *The Tom Ewell Show,* a CBS sitcom from the Four Star Entertainment factory. Though it had an unusual premise—a man surrounded by women: wife, three daughters, and mother-in-law—it lasted only one season.

Bob and Madelyn's ex-writing cohort, Jess Oppenheimer, fared no better that season. Having left his NBC network post to return to active television production, which he preferred, Oppenheimer put together another CBS sitcom, *Angel*. In a way, *Angel* was *I Love Lucy* in reverse. A young American architect, Johnny Smith (played by Marshall Thompson), marries a foreign girl, Angel (portrayed by Annie Fargé). Slotted at eight o'clock every Thursday evening, *Angel* boasted some *I Love Lucy* alumni, namely Doris Singleton (Caroline Appleby on *Lucy*) and Maurice Marsac. Unfortunately, *Angel* added up to zero and was canceled during its first season, after a number of futile time-slot changes failed to bolster the sagging ratings.

In 1964, Bob and Madelyn "quit" television. With two seasons of *The Lucy Show* behind them, they decided to explore new areas. Bob wanted to write movies, and Madelyn was getting married again.

Lucille Ball contends, "They got a little too rich for a while and they quit. Seriously. You see, outside of my show, all my money goes back into my business. The big thing in this business is residuals, and these people became millionaires very quickly."

The writing team soon became bored with their "retirement"

and returned to their respective typewriters (the female half as Madelyn Davis) to pen sitcom scripts for other series like *The Cara Williams Show,* and *The Debbie Reynolds Show,* which Jess Oppenheimer created and produced in 1969.

Vivian Vance left the *Lucy Show* cast after three seasons. Commuting from one coast to another for more than six months a year grew to be a burden on her and her marriage. However, every year or so, she returned to California to guest star in Lucy's sitcoms, ostensibly for old times' sake. Today, Vivian Vance enjoys her life with John Dodds, now a publishing executive. They travel a good deal, and Vivian works only when she wants to. A seasoned lecturer on the college circuit, Vance looks back on her years with Lucy. "For years I've heard from my family and friends, 'Don't make a fool of yourself, Vivian.' And look how rich I got making a fool of myself!"

Shortly after the premiere of *The Lucy Show* in 1962, Desi Arnaz asked his ex-wife if she was interested in buying him out—his half-interest in Desilu Productions, Inc., that is. With a little help from the City National Bank of Beverly Hills, Lucille Ball paid her ex-husband $2,552,975, the price for buying out his 300,350 shares of Desilu stock, pegged at the time at $8.50 per share.

Arnaz retired to his horse-breeding ranch in nearby Corona. The following year, he married Edith Mack Hirsch, the redheaded ex-wife of a millionaire sportsman, in Las Vegas. He returned to the business he once called a "monster"—television—several years later as an independent producer. Doing business as Desi Arnaz Productions, he bankrolled a number of promising TV pilots. The one that sold, *The Mothers-in-Law* in 1967, was created by Bob and Madelyn and ran two seasons on NBC with Eve Arden and Kaye Ballard as the stars. Desi rented his studio space at Desilu-Cahuenga. His landlord, at least for a short time, was Lucille Ball.

Desi continued to use the three-camera filming technique on *The Mothers-in-Law,* the same system he had developed with Karl Freund sixteen years before for a new situation comedy, *I Love Lucy.* Twenty-five years later, today, when you see "filmed before a live audience" in the closing credits of your favorite sitcom, think of Desi Arnaz. It was his brainchild.

"Let's look at it objectively," Desi once observed. "We were lucky. We got in first with a basically good idea and we had one of the great comediennes of all time—Lucille Ball. And, as far as I'm concerned, we had the best comedy writers in the business—Jess Oppenheimer, Bob Carroll, Jr., and Madelyn Pugh. We had the best cameraman in Hollywood—"Papa" Freund. We filmed our shows honestly, in front of an audience. There was no phony laughing. You saw exactly what the studio audience saw, and, hopefully, you reacted the way they did. You add all that up and throw in two magnificent troupers like Vivian Vance and Bill Frawley, and you're the luckiest sonofabitch in the whole business!"

At about the time *I Love Lucy* went off the prime-time schedules in 1960, the Bureau of Applied Social Research at Columbia University conducted a survey of TV-viewing habits. One of the questions was, "Are there any programs that you'd like to see put back on the air? I don't mean reruns; I mean new versions. If 'yes,' which one(s)?" The overwhelming favorite—*I Love Lucy*.

Why? A British anthropologist once endeavored to determine what "sends" the American people when it comes to television entertainment. He reported, tongue firmly in cheek, "Lucy and Ricky and their friends Fred and Ethel are the typical American middle class, in a typical American middle-class environment. But with one significant difference: Instead of sitting around waiting for things to happen, they *make* things happen. They and their audience are so alike, the audience comes to believe that it is *it* that makes things happen. Pure mass hypnosis, or if I may say so, twaddle. But awfully clever."

No format appeared so unlikely to succeed as the adventures of a carrot-top clown and a Cuban bandleader with an accent so thick you could cut it with a cleaver; yet for nine happy years the lives of millions of Americans, and countless more worldwide, ran on one tether with the Ricardos. They and the Mertzes became America's favorite foursome; they were faces that launched a million laughs, and the laughs have gone on, uninterrupted, for twenty-five years.

Jack Gould of the *New York Times* summed up his feelings about the success of *I Love Lucy* by saying, "*I Love Lucy* is very human—and so are we."

A French actor explained his addiction to the sitcom: "It has the reality of *l'amour* or as you say, 'sex.' While it is possible to believe that other husband and wife comedy teams share the same bedrooms, it is not possible to believe that they do so with pleasure. Lucy and Ricky Ricardo skirmish in the daytime so they can 'reconcile' at night."

Like the foreign actor, there are countless *Lucy* addicts out there. The popularity of the classic television series knows no age barrier. Children adore it as much as their adult counterparts. Ask any fan why he is "hooked" on *I Love Lucy,* and nine chances out of ten, he will respond simply, "It's funny." What better reason is there to explain the appeal of a comedy?

In her wildest imagination, did Lucille Ball ever expect *I Love Lucy* to become a hit?

"No, of course, not," she admits readily. "But TV was in its infancy, and I figured it would go for a year. We had like a two-, three-year plan, but we figured if it went for a year. . . . The parts all happened to come together: the people, the writers, the producers. The combination worked. Hell, we're still on the air today! I guess it did."

THE *I Love Lucy* LOG

Lucy demonstrates her good manners for Edward Everett Horton (Episode #1050/15).

Cast with Maurice Marsac (Episode #1050/35).

Left: Lucy plays "Glow Worm" (Episode #1050/40). *Right:* Lucy and Ethel hear some shocking news through "snooper's helper" (Episode #1050/36). *Below:* Gloria Blondell (*center*) as neighbor Grace Foster (Episode #1050/36).

Left: Lucy suffers the consequences when she "tells the truth" (Episode #1050/72). *Right:* "Wicked city woman," Lucy, "vamps" Tennessee Ernie Ford (Episode #1050/94).

Lucy and Ethel in Martian drag; with Herb Vigran (*left*) Episode #1050/89).

Lucy poses as Marilyn Monroe (Episode #1050/103).

Left: Golf widows Lucy and Ethel retaliate (Episode #1050/96).
Right: Ricky fools Lucy . . . for a change (Episode #1050/65).

It's "California, Here We Come!" as the group crosses the George Washington Bridge on way to Hollywood (Episode #1050/110).

A harrowing night in a rickety motel near Cincinnati (Episode #1050/111).

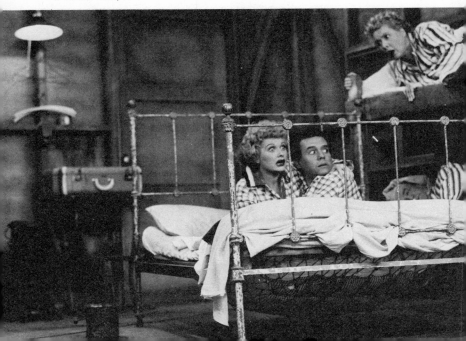

Pianist Marco Rizo
gets a kiss from Lucille
between acts of
"Lucy Gets in Pictures"
(Episode #1050/116).

Trapped in Richard Widmark's trophy room, Lucy disguises herself
(Episode #1050/127).

Lucy nearly drowned when Teresa Tirelli got carried away in this classic scene (Episode #1050/150).

Left: Lucy: "Waiter, there are snails in this food!"; Maurice Marsac plays waiter (Episode #1050/145). *Right:* Charles Boyer gets the standard Lucy treatment (Episode #1050/146).

Orson Welles levitates mysterious Princess Loo-Cee (Episode #1050/155).

Chaos in the Ricardos' Connecticut living room (Episode #1050/171).

Another of Lucy's harebrained schemes in the making (Episode #1050/176).

Maurice Chevalier and Charles Lane are no match for Lucy.

From hour-long "Lucy Goes to Mexico."

Lucy tangles with a bull
. . . or vice versa.

From October 15, 1951, until May 6, 1957, the Ricardos and Mertzes romped through 179 half-hour episodes of *I Love Lucy* on the CBS Television Network. Here is the definitive filmography of them all—with script titles, official Viacom episode numbers, original air dates, players' names, plots, and trivia for *Lucy* aficionados everywhere.

1951–1952

"The Girls Want to Go to a Night Club"; #1050/02; October 15, 1951.

It's the Mertzes' eighteenth wedding anniversary, and Ethel wants to celebrate by going to the Copacabana, while Fred itches to attend the fights. An argument ensues, culminating with Ethel and Lucy informing Fred and Ricky that they'll go nightclubbing by themselves, with dates. Not to be intimidated, the men counter by telling their wives they'll go to the fights with their own dates that Ginny Jones of the Starlight Room can easily arrange. Lucy intercedes, scheming to impersonate the boys' female fight companions. Dressed as country bumpkins, Lucy and Ethel arrive at the Ricardo apartment. After Ricky sings a chorus of "Guadalajara," some funny hillbilly schtick unfolds until he realizes the dates are actually Lucy and Ethel. In the end, the men prevail and it's a night at the fights for an anniversary celebration.

"Be a Pal"; #1050/03; October 22, 1951.

Lucy thinks Ricky is losing interest in her. Ethel suggests the book-of-the-week selection by Dr. Humphreys, *How to Keep Your Honey-*

moon from Ending. Chapter one suggests that the wife dress up for breakfast. But even with Lucy in her most profound feminine attire, Ricky barely looks up from his newspaper. Chapter two—"The Be a Pal System"—prompts Lucy to join Ricky and Fred, and two other men (Dick Reeves and Tony Michaels), in a poker game. She beats them badly, which only serves to stimulate the marital discord. Chapter three proposes that the wife surround her husband "with things that remind him of his childhood." Naturally, Lucy takes the suggestion a step too far, decorating the apartment like Cuba, with palm trees, sombreros, a flock of chickens, and even a mule. A funny sequence finds Lucy lip-syncing to a Carmen Miranda record, moments before Ricky confirms his eternal love for Lucy with a finale kiss.

"The Diet"; #1050/04; October 29, 1951; with Marco Rizo.

To her dismay, Lucy discovers she's put on twenty-two pounds since marrying Ricky. Ethel: "On behalf of the tubby trio, I welcome you to our flabby foursome." A phone call from Ricky's agent reveals that Joanne, a singer featured in Ricky's Tropicana nightclub act, is getting married and will be quitting the show. Needless to say, Lucy wants the job. At auditions the next day, Lucille MacGillicuddy (Lucy Ricardo) can have the part provided she loses twelve pounds in four days to fit into the ex-singer's size-twelve gown. Lucy tries jogging ("the fourth-floor dash"), but loses only five ounces. At dinner, she munches celery while Ricky and the Mertzes dine on steak and potatoes. In a funny scene, Lucy wrestles the Mertzes' dog Butch for a scrap of meat. With only five hours left to lose five more pounds, Lucy resorts to a "human pressure cooker" (steam cabinet), finally weighing in at the required 120 pounds. Hours later in the nightclub act, Ricky sings "Cuban Pete" and Lucy warbles "Sally Sweet." After the show, she collapses, suffering from malnutrition.
(Note: The songs were featured in the Arnazes' 1950 vaudeville tour and the subsequent *I Love Lucy* pilot.)

"Lucy Thinks Ricky Is Trying to Do Away with Her"; #1050/01; November 5, 1951.

Engrossed in a new whodunit, *The Mockingbird Murder Mystery,* Lucy is a nail-biting wreck. Adding to her problems, Ethel, using her infallible fortune-telling playing cards, reveals Lucy's imminent death. To make matters worse, Lucy overhears a phone call from Ricky's agent Jerry (Jerry Hausner) and misinterprets the names of dogs in a new act for Ricky's girl friends. When Jerry routinely asks Ricky about Marilyn, a singer, Ricky responds: "I've decided to get rid of her . . . I'll probably miss her some, but in a couple of weeks I can get a new one." Naturally, Lucy thinks Ricky is referring to her. Panic-stricken (Lucy: "I'm not even cold yet, and Ricky is already lining up girls to take my place!"), she intends to take action. She outfits herself with a bulletproof skillet, certain that Ricky is out to kill her. Her strange behavior causes Ricky to worry, and he tries to slip her some sleeping powder, which Lucy thinks is poison. Lucy: "I got a mickey from Ricky!" She hastens to the Tropicana and confronts Ricky with a gun. There she sees the dog act made up of Ann, Mary, Helen, Cynthia, Alice, and . . . Theodore, and finally realizes Ricky has no plans to do away with her.

"The Quiz Show"; #1050/05; November 12, 1951.

Lucy's careless accounting habits force Ricky to cut off her allowance and charge accounts. When Ethel enters with tickets for a radio quiz show that awards $1,000 cash prizes, Lucy jumps at the chance to attend. After her qualifying round on *Females Are Fabulous,* "based on the theory that any woman is willing to make an idiot out of herself to make money," host Freddie Fillmore (Frank Nelson) tells Lucy of her money-winning stunt. She will have to introduce Ricky to her "long-lost first husband." That night Lucy is a bundle of nerves as she awaits the arrival of the bogus spouse. Meanwhile, a tramp (John Emery) appears at the door and Lucy assumes he is the "long-lost husband." When she discovers her mistake and throws him out, a second "first" husband arrives on the scene (Phil Ober) whom Lucy introduces to Ricky as per the radio show requirement. Alas, she wins the $1,000, but after paying all her overdue bills, is left with only twenty-five cents.

"The Audition"; #1050/06; November 19, 1951.

When Lucy learns that a talent scout from a television network is going to catch Ricky's nightclub act, she hounds her husband for a chance to be in the show. Lucy: "George Burns uses his wife on TV." Mrs. Ricardo parades around the apartment with a lampshade on her head, humming "A Pretty Girl Is Like a Melody" and imitating a Ziegfeld girl. When Boffo the Clown has an accident at a rehearsal, Ricky sends him to the Ricardo apartment to rest up, and Lucy connives to take his place in the show. As network officials watch Ricky sing "Babalu," Lucy meanders onstage as "The Professor," wearing a broken-down tuxedo and carrying a "loaded" cello, looking for a "Risky Riskadoo." She performs some funny bits with the instrument, then impersonates a seal by playing a motley group of horns. The TV bigwigs are so impressed, they offer *her* a contract. In the end, Lucy agrees to remain a wife and give up show business (this week).
(NOTE: One third of this episode was the original *I Love Lucy* pilot. . . . The TV network representatives were played by producer Jess Oppenheimer and Harry Ackerman, a CBS vice-president.)

"The Seance"; #1050/07; November 26, 1951.

Preoccupied with numerology and horoscopes, Lucy assures Ricky that it's a "yes day" until realizing she had consulted yesterday's newspaper. A Gemini, Ricky was advised "to climb in a hole and pull the hole in after you." Consequently, when Mr. Meriweather, a theatrical producer (Jay Novello), phones, Lucy immediately says no, without even listening to what the man said. This infuriates Ricky, so to get back in his good graces, Lucy goes to see Meriweather at his office, only to discover that he, too, is a horoscope/Ouija board/numerology nut. She tells him they're conducting a seance that evening and he might be able to contact his long-departed Tillie. Ethel portrays the medium Raya (Fred: "Well done, medium Raya."), or, as she is more commonly called, Madame Ethel Mertzola, complete with deluxe crystal ball. They contact Tillie, Meriweather's cocker spaniel, and the man's late wife, Adelaide. The producer is so pleased with the results of the seance that he hires Ricky for a new show.

"Men Are Messy"; #1050/08; December 3, 1951.

"Men are nothing but a bunch of messcats," complains Lucy Ricardo while Ricky insists, "A man's home is his castle." To make a point, Lucy divides the apartment into two equal halves. If Ricky wants to be a slob in his half, it's fine with Lucy. When Ricky's press agent, Kenny Morgan, lines up a publicity spread in *Halfbeat* magazine, Lucy decides to teach her sloppy husband a lesson. Jim White, the photographer, arrives at the Ricardos and finds it looking like Tobacco Road. Ricky: "It's a regular pigpen!" Lucy: "It's not a *regular* one, but it'll do." Lucy playfully poses for photographs amid the pile of junk, until she realizes the cameraman is from *Look,* not the musicians' journal.

(NOTE: Kenny Morgan, Desilu's PR head, appeared as himself.)

"The Fur Coat"; #1050/10; December 10, 1951.

Ricky arrives home with a $3,500 mink coat that he has rented for an act at the club. Lucy immediately jumps to the conclusion that it's her anniversary gift and showers her man with grateful kisses. Thrilled, Lucy wears the coat night and day, and even does the dishes in it. Ricky implores Fred to dress as a burglar and "steal" the coat at gunpoint. But before Mertz appears, a *real* thief (Ben Weldon) arrives and almost makes off with the fur. When Lucy learns from Ethel of Ricky's nefarious ploy, she plots to teach him a lesson by buying a cheap imitation fur coat and, in full view of Ricky, proceeds to "restyle" it. She cuts it in half and removes the sleeves, saying, "Congratulations, Ethel. You're the first woman ever to wear a mink T-shirt." Ricky promptly collapses, but after being told of the prank, buys Lucy a new hat and dress.

"The Adagio"; #1050/12; December 17, 1951.

Lucy volunteers for Ricky's Parisian apache dance number for an upcoming Tropicana show. Fred offers to teach Lucy the finer points of the terpsichorean art until Ethel manages to produce the real thing, Jean Valjean Raymand (Shepard Menken), who is the nephew of the woman who runs the French hand laundry. The Frenchman has more than dance lessons on his mind, and when Ricky finds him hiding in the hall closet, the fireworks commence. Jean challenges Ricky to a duel with pistols behind Radio City Music Hall, but they finally decide to stage a fake fight in the bedroom to teach Lucy a well-deserved lesson.

"Drafted"; #1050/09; December 24, 1951.

When a letter from the War Department arrives, requesting Ricky to appear at "Fort Dix, Monday at 3 P.M.," Lucy concludes he's been drafted. Actually, Ricky's been invited to the New Jersey camp to entertain. Since Fred knows an appropriate Civil War routine from his vaudeville days, Ricky invites him to go along. Not knowing of these plans, the girls begin knitting their men socks, and also arrange for a going-away party Sunday night with a guest list to include the Sedgwicks, the Orsattis, etc. But now Ricky and Fred determine, based on their wives' knitting, that the girls are expecting babies, and plan a similar party (a shower) that same night.

(NOTE: The Sedgwicks and Orsattis were real-life friends of the Arnazes.)

"Jealous of Girl Singer"; #1050/11; December 31, 1951.

An item in the morning gossip column prompts Lucy to assume that Ricky is seeing another woman, but he assures her that the newspaper piece is merely publicity. To apologize for her lack of wifely faith, Lucy prepares Ricky's favorite dinner, *arroz con pollo,* but her mood changes abruptly when she finds a piece of black lace in Ricky's pocket. He tries to explain that it was torn off accidentally from Tropicana singer Rosemary's gown during the rehearsal of "Jezebel." To keep an eye on Ricky, Lucy manages to wangle her way into the chorus line and upstages Rosemary (Helen Silver) during the number. Later that night at home, Ricky tells Lucy there was a "strange girl" in the chorus—ugly, and a terrible dancer. He knew all along that it was Lucy. They kiss and make up.

(NOTE: *Arroz con pollo* (chicken with rice) was Desi Arnaz's favorite dish.)

"The Benefit"; #1050/13; January 7, 1952.

Ethel wants Ricky to headline a benefit show for her "Middle East Sixty-eighth Street Women's Club," but Lucy refuses to ask him unless she can be on the bill, too. Ethel is not thrilled, especially after hearing Lucy's off-key rendition of "Shine on Harvest Moon," but finally gives in. Only after the posters (ballyhooing Mr. and Mrs. Ricky Ricardo) are printed, Lucy informs Ethel that Ricky refuses to do it. Lucy: "You still have me. After all, what's Ricky got that I haven't got, except a band, a reputation. . . ?" Ethel: ". . . and talent!" After

192

some wheedling, Ricky says he'll do it—an old vaudeville routine known as "Songs and Witty Sayings." Lucy is delighted until she gets a gander at the material—Ricky has all the punchlines. She decides to rewrite the jokes, which are later delivered between choruses of "Under the Bamboo Tree."

"The Amateur Hour"; #1050/14; January 14, 1952; with David Stollery.

After buying a $59.95 dress without Ricky's permission, Lucy insists she'll get a job to pay for it. Unfortunately, Mrs. Ricardo discovers she's unqualified for the jobs listed in the *Times*—stenographer, bookkeeper, cook, lady wrestler. Lucy: "This is terribly unfair . . . Apparently you can't get a job in this town unless you can do something!" A baby-sitting job, paying $5 an hour, sounds perfect, until she discovers that it isn't an infant she'll be sitting with but two rambunctious eight-year-old identical twin boys, Jimmy and Timmy Hudson. Practical jokers, the boys nearly burn Lucy at the stake. When Mrs. Hudson calls from the beauty shop asking if Lucy will take her sons to the Blue Bird Club Amateur Contest that night in her place— Lucy can keep the $100 prize money if they win—she agrees. With Ricky as the MC, Lucy and the twins perform "Ragtime Cowboy Joe" and win the $100.
(NOTE: Lee Scott was credited with the choreography.)

"Lucy Plays Cupid"; #1050/15; January 21, 1952.

The Ricardos' neighbor, Miss Lewis (Bea Benadaret), has fallen for Mr. Ritter (Edward Everett Horton), the local grocery man, claiming he's the "bee's knees," but the spinster's too shy to invite him to dinner herself. Lucy offers to do it for her, but Ritter gets the wrong idea and thinks Lucy is the one who's crazy about him. Mr. Ritter: "I like you, too. You're just my type, Red." In order to throw him off the scent, Lucy plans to deck herself out like a hoyden at dinner that night. Ritter is aghast, especially when he encounters Lucy's twenty-five children (Lucy: "Six are missing."). Finally, Miss Lewis appears—flashing her "come hither" look, which Lucy taught her earlier—and captures the beloved grocer.
(NOTE: The Lucy/Mr. Ritter dinner scene featured the ill-matched pair sitting on crates from a California bottler, not a New York concern.)

"Lucy's Fake Illness"; #1050/16; January 28, 1952.

Contemplating a nervous breakdown because Ricky won't hire her for his new act, Lucy consults a book, *Abnormal Psychology*, for a solution. Three symptoms of her frustration are likely to appear, according to the text: She will assume the identity of a celebrity, develop a hopeless case of amnesia, and revert to her childhood. When

193

Ricky arrives home, he is bombarded with not just one complex, but all three: Lucy impersonates Tallulah Bankhead, can't recognize herself in the mirror, and recklessly rides a tricycle around the living room. Ricky wants to call in psychiatrist Dr. Stevenson to help Lucy, but Fred first warns him that Lucy is faking. Therefore, Ricky decides to enlist the aid of an actor friend, Hal March, to play a phony physician. Doctor: "Just as I feared . . . You've contracted . . . the gobloots. . . . It came into the country on the hind legs of the boo shoo bird. . . . We may have to operate. . . . We'll have to go in and take out your zorch." Lucy believes him and prepares for her death. Ricky finally spills the beans whereupon Lucy insists on being in the nightclub act. Now Ricky is the one feigning amnesia.

"Lucy Writes a Play"; #1050/17; February 4, 1952.

Thwarted by her failure to break into show business as an actress, Lucy takes to the typewriter and pens "a tender, heartwarming story of a Cuban tobacco picker"—*A Tree Grows in Havana*. Naturally she wants Ricky to play the lead when the production premieres at a play competition, but he absolutely refuses, so Lucy has to settle for Fred. Since his Spanish accent leaves something to be desired, Lucy transforms the setting to England and retitles her effort *The Perils of Pamela*. However, when Ricky learns that a big Hollywood producer, Darryl P. Mayer, will be the judge, he wants back in. But what he doesn't know is that the original script has been scrapped. The night of the show, he makes his entrance as per the Cuban version, while Lucy, Fred, and Ethel are doing the English rendition. The result is another maniacal mix-up.

"Break the Lease"; #1050/18; February 11, 1952; with Barbara Pepper.

After a fun evening around the piano singing "Sweet Sue," the Mertzes retire to bed, leaving Lucy and Ricky alone to pursue a short encore. Ethel then phones, demanding quiet. Lucy: "Ethel, you were just up here and said it sounded great." Ethel: "Well, I'm down here now, and it sounds lousy!" One noise leads to another until Ricky threatens to move. The next morning, Ethel informs Lucy that they owe them the next five months rent to pay off their lease. When Ricky hears of this, he decides to break the contract by becoming "the most undesirable tenants" imaginable. After a day of constant racket—the Ricardos even resort to wielding a riveter's hammer against a garbage can lid—they decide to have Ricky's sixteen-piece band rehearse in the apartment. The jam session lasts until 4 A.M., when Lucy suggests the band play "El Breako the Leaso," a special version of "The Mexican Hat Dance." Then Fred and Ethel arrive at the door, covered with plaster, and reluctantly surrender the lease. On moving day, Lucy and Ethel become emotional as they tenderly recall the fun times they've had during the past nine years. Tears are shed and all is forgiven.

"The Ballet"; #1050/19; February 18, 1952.

Ricky is searching for a ballet dancer and a burlesque comic for his new nightclub revue. Lucy, who once played a petunia in a school rendition of *Dance of the Flowers,* wants the ballet job. Enrolling in a dancing school run by the strict Madame Lamond (Mary Wickes), she tries desperately to learn the demanding art. The results are disastrous, and Lucy finally gives up. She next hires a burlesque comic (Frank DeMille) to teach her the "Slowly I Turn" bit. When Lucy is summoned to the club to replace an ill performer, she assumes it was the comic, but it was a ballet dancer they needed. Lucy arrives in her clown getup and while Ricky sings "Martha," she squirts seltzer water at everyone and pitches a custard pie in Ricky's face. To get even with her, Ricky douses her with a bucket of water when she returns home that night.

(NOTE: Lucille Ball ad-libbed brilliantly when her foot accidentally got caught in the ballet practice bar.)

"The Young Fans"; #1050/20; February 25, 1952.

When a teen-age girl, Peggy Dawson (Janet Waldo), drops her steady beau, Arthur Morton (Richard Crenna), for suave Ricky Ricardo, Lucy accepts the dubious challenge of teaching the clumsy schoolboy how to dance. Unfortunately, Arthur gets carried away and proclaims his love for Lucy. To discourage the youthful duo, Mr. and Mrs. Ricardo dress up in old clothes and wire-rimmed glasses, winding up looking like their own great-great grandparents. Ricky barely manages to sing "Babalu" for Peggy, as Lucy comments, "He's baba'ed his last lu." These disconcerting charades prompt the young "fans" to rush out of the Ricardo apartment *together.*

"New Neighbors"; #1050/21; March 3, 1952; with Hayden Rorke, K. T. Stevens.

Lucy and Ethel can't wait to get a closer look at the O'Briens' (new neighbors in the building) belongings, but Ricky makes Lucy promise "not to set foot" in their apartment. Next day, she crawls in ("he didn't say I couldn't set *knees* in"), along with Ethel, to snoop. When the curious pair hears the O'Briens approaching, Lucy quickly hides in the closet. Not realizing the couple are actors rehearsing a play, Lucy jumps to the conclusion that they're going to "do away with the tenants on the upper floor and assume their identities to blow up the Capitol." Panicked, Lucy dons a slipcover, disguising herself as an armchair, and slowly makes her way out of the O'Brien household. Lucy alerts Sergeant Morton (Allen Jenkins) who thinks she's crazy; then barricades their apartment door and takes up arms with Ricky and the Mertzes. The foursome winds up in jail after nearly blowing off the police sergeant's head, and Ricky is despondent over the headlines, "Orchestra Leader Jailed in Shooting Spree."

"Fred and Ethel Fight"; #1050/22; March 10, 1952.

Lucy and Ricky try to patch up the Mertzes' quarrel (Fred: "She said my mother looks like a weasel!") by inviting them each to dinner without the other knowing. They manage to set the couple straight all right, but not without ending up in a squabble of their own, with Ricky moving to the club. To get him back, Ethel suggests Lucy try a subtle sympathy ploy: "Pretend you were hit by a bus." At the same time, Fred encounters Ricky at a local luncheonette, and he urges Ricky to be a hero by saving Lucy "from a burning apartment building." The sight of Lucy, hopelessly covered with bandages, casts, and a splint, trying to escape from the "burning" building is hilarious. But now Fred and Ethel are fighting again, this time over whose fault all this was. This leads Ethel to run home to her mother.

(NOTE: Scene in luncheonette featured a huge advertising sign depicting Johnny, the "Call for Philip Morris" boy; Desilu endeavored to accommodate its sponsor whenever feasible.)

"The Mustache"; #1050/23; March 17, 1952.

When Ricky grows a moustache for a TV role, Lucy takes reciprocal action. She doesn't like kissing a man with a moustache and insists he shave it off at once. Having a little fun with her, Ricky hints he might keep it for good, even after the TV stint. This really annoys Lucy, so she borrows a fake beard from Fred and attaches it to her face with what appears to be spirit gum. When Ricky comes home, she kisses him—to give him a taste of his own medicine. He is amused by her joke, but asks her to remove the false whiskers. She can't. They've been glued on with Bulldog Cement, not mere glue, and Lucy fears she'll have to be a bearded lady for life. But what really makes her distraught is that Ricky is bringing home a talent scout for whom she naturally wants to audition. Her valiant efforts to hide the white mane behind the veil of a harem-girl outfit fail, and Ricky loses out on the TV job.

"The Gossip"; #1050/24; March 24, 1952.

When Lucy is forbidden to gossip, she tapes her mouth shut and, in charades, acts out the latest bit of news for Ethel "about Betty and her husband, Jack." Ricky is disappointed that she didn't keep her word, but at the same time feeds Fred a juicy tidbit "about Joe, the trombone player, and what a wolf he is." Finally, the boys bet the girls they can keep from gossiping longer. The winners are to be served breakfast in bed for a month. Ricky has a surefire plan: He'll talk in his sleep, making up a tantalizing tale about neighbor Grace Foster and the milkman; Lucy is sure to spill it to Ethel. The following day, Lucy blurts out the news to Ethel while Ricky and Fred are listening through the furnace pipes. Fred: "Ethel, this is your conscience. . . . You've been gossiping." Lucy: "Ethel, you have the loudest conscience I have ever heard." Ricky: "Lucy Ricardo, this is your conscience. . . . You've geen gossipin' too." Lucy: "Oh, fine. Mine has an accent." The next scene depicts Lucy serving breakfast to Ricky, with Ethel performing the same deed for Fred. Suddenly, the milkman (Bobby Jellison), followed by Grace Foster's husband, Bill (Dick Reeves), wielding a pistol, rush into the bedroom. The gossip was true after all, and Ricky spilled it first. Seems the tables are turned, so the boys reluctantly head for the kitchen. With Ricky and Fred out of earshot, Lucy quickly thrusts $10 into the milkman's hand with instructions to split the dough with Mr. Foster for their brilliant performance.

"Pioneer Women"; #1050/25; March 31, 1952.

Determining they have washed over 219,000 dishes since being married, Lucy and Ethel demand dishwashers in an effort to rid themselves of dishpan hands—something the Society Matrons League would frown upon. The men insist the women have it too "soft" and bet them $50 that they will "cry uncle" first, after agreeing to live life as it was before the turn of the century, without modern conveniences. Lucy and Ethel take to churning their own butter (costs $23.75 per pound), baking their own bread (Lucy puts in thirteen cakes of yeast, producing a mammoth loaf), and wearing old-fashioned clothes. Ricky complies by riding a horse home from work, bathing in an ancient bathtub, and, along with Fred, wearing period clothing. Unexpectedly, Mrs. Pettybone (Florence Bates) and Mrs. Pomerantz (Ruth Stern) of the Society Matrons League drop in on Lucy and Ethel "to check on them." Lucy tries to explain that Ricky is in show business . . . that the ladies caught them in a rehearsal for a Gay Nineties bit for the Tropicana. When the highfalutin' society women display some reluctance to accept Lucy and Ethel because of their show biz leanings, Lucy becomes irate and informs them she has "no desire to join your phony baloney club." Ricky calls off the bet, and they enjoy homemade bread and butter.

"The Marriage License"; #1050/26; April 7, 1952.

When Lucy discovers that Ricky's name is misspelled (Bicardi) on their marriage license, she concludes their vows are invalid. She returns from City Hall, via East Orange, New Jersey, despondent: "We've been revoked." Now she wants to recreate the entire courtship and ceremony, with plans to go to the Byram River Beagle Club in Greenwich, Connecticut. Against his better judgment, Ricky gets down on his knees to propose, while Lucy feeds him the antedated dialogue. With that out of the way, they head for New England, but run out of gas, whereupon they wander into the Eagle Hotel run by Bert Willoughby (Irving Bacon) and his wife (Elizabeth Patterson). The former just happens to be the town's justice of the peace and can perform the marriage ceremony for them. After his old wife, called

"Mother," sings "I Love You Truly," vows are exchanged, and the Ricardos are married . . . for a second time.

(NOTE: According to ARB, this episode was the first TV show to be seen in 10 million U.S. homes. . . . Lucille Ball and Desi Arnaz really were married in 1940 at the Byram River Beagle Club, and also reenacted their vows in 1949 in a Catholic ceremony.)

"The Kleptomaniac"; #1050/27; April 14, 1952.

When Ricky discovers a large amount of cash in Lucy's purse (Lucy: "It's my mad money." Ricky: "There's two hundred dollars here." Lucy: "I get awfully mad.") and a closetful of silverware and other valuables—unaware that Lucy is collecting items for a club bazaar—he immediately jumps to the conclusion she's a kleptomaniac. At first, Fred finds it hard to believe the heartbreaking news: "She is a poor, sick creature. . . . Hey, that dirty crook just stole my clock!" Ricky's only hope is to call in a psychiatrist, Dr. Tom Robinson (Joseph Kearns), who tries to hypnotize Lucy. What the doctor, Ricky, and Fred don't know is that Lucy is aware of her husband's plan. She puts on quite an act, "reliving" her childhood and telling of her graduation to pickpocketing: "I've picked a peck of pockets!" The climax comes in the form of a baby elephant, which Lucy says she stole from the Clyde Beatty circus.

"Cuban Pals"; #1050/28; April 21, 1952.

Mrs. Lucy Ricardo is at a disadvantage when her husband's Cuban friends Carlos (Robert Morin) and Maria (Lita Baron) visit: Lucy's *español* is a sad sampling of pigeon Spanish. When she learns that "little" Renita Perez, whom Ricky once danced with in Cuba, is arriving in town, she insists he dance again with her, claiming it will "help the good neighbor policy." What she isn't expecting is that "little" Renita (Rita Convy) has developed into a voluptuous *señorita*. Jealous, Lucy poses with Ethel as charwomen and they invade the Tropicana during rehearsals of the "Lady in Red" number, just to keep an eye on Ricky and Renita. Determined to keep the two apart, Lucy gets Fred to dress as a cabbie and take Renita on a "shortcut through Philadelphia." At the club, when Ricky introduces Renita and her usual dance partner Ramon who will perform the "African Wedding Dance," Lucy appears instead of the sultry Latin. It's a funny few minutes with Lucy trying to escape the clutches of the voodoo-masked Ramon.

(NOTE: In the first scene, Desi Arnaz made a few mistakes while translating Lucy's English into Spanish, but he covered nicely. Watch for it.)

"The Freezer"; #1050/29; April 28, 1952; with Barbara Pepper.

Lucy and Ethel acquire a huge, walk-in meat freezer from Ethel's butcher-uncle (Oscar), provided they pay the $50 moving charge.

Next, the pair order two sides of beef from Johnson's Meat Company, unaware of the immensity of their request. Later that day, Lucy and Ethel watch with growing horror as delivery men unload seven hundred pounds of meat at a cost of sixty-nine cents a pound, or a total of $483. Lucy's first notion is to glue the cow back together, but the delivery man (Frank Sully) insists he can't take it back even if she "taught it how to walk again." Next stop is a local butcher shop where Lucy tries to unload the beef on unsuspecting customers: "Are you tired of paying high prices? Are you interested in a little high-class beef? You want a bargain? . . . I have sirloin, tenderloin, T-bone, rump; pot roast, chuck roast, ox tail, stump. . . . We do everything ourselves. We rope, we brand, we butcher, we market it. We do everything but *eat* it for ya—seventy-nine cents a pound!" They promptly go out of business when the neighborhood butcher gets wise to their competitive tricks. In an effort to move the beef from the basement freezer into the unlit furnace before Ricky finds out about the $483 meat bill, Lucy accidentally gets locked inside, freezing into a "human popsicle." When Fred turns on the furnace to help thaw Lucy, the meat starts cooking, the aroma rising through the heating pipes.

"Lucy Does a TV Commercial"; #1050/30; May 5, 1952; with Ross Elliott, Jerry Hausner, Maurice Thompson.

Lucy connives to appear in a commercial on the "big TV show" Ricky is emceeing. Standing before a backdrop that reads "Join the Parade . . . Buy Vitameatavegamin Today," Lucy rehearses her speech: "Hello, friends. I'm your Vitameatavegamin girl. Are you tired, rundown, listless? Do you poop out at parties? Are you unpopular? The answer to all your problems is in this little bottle: Vitameatavegamin. Vitameatavegamin contains vitamins, meat, vegetables, and minerals. Yes, with Vitameatavegamin, you can *spoon* your way to health. All you do is take a tablespoonful after every meal [Lucy samples product]. It's so tasty, too. Just like candy. So why don't you join the thousands of happy, peppy people and get a great big bottle of Vitameatavegamin tomorrow. That's Vita . . . Meata . . . Vegamin." After repeated rehearsals, Lucy gets bombed because the liquid tonic contains twenty-three-percent alcohol. Further attempts to polish her performance prove hilarious. This is Lucille Ball at her very best. (NOTE: Maury Thompson, the script clerk, played himself.)

"The Publicity Agent"; #1050/31; May 12, 1952; with Peter Leeds, Bennett Green, Dick Reeves, Gil Herman.

To increase business at the Tropicana, Lucy concocts a publicity scheme that is prompted by a newspaper item claiming that the Shah of Persia has all of Benny Goodman's records. Lucy decides to become the Maharincess of Franistan, who travels halfway around the globe to see her singing idol, Ricky Ricardo. She books a suite at the Waldorf-Astoria, calls all the newspaper editors in town, and enthusiastically pursues her plan. Meanwhile, Ricky chides his press agent Kenny for dreaming up such a "cheap" stunt, but Kenny insists he didn't plant the story. It must be for real. Lucy, as the royal princess, is introduced to Ricky and swoons every time he starts singing "I Get Ideas." But when he warbles "Babalu" one hundred times, Ricky deduces it must be Lucy (Who else would sit still so along?). To get even with her, he lines up a few friends who dress up like Arab-type thugs and scare the veils off Lucy and Ethel. Warding them off, Lucy admits, "I'm not a maharincess; I'm a Henna-rinsess!"

"Lucy Gets Ricky on the Radio"; #1050/32; May 19, 1952; with Bobby Ellis, Roy Rowan.

A planned evening of intellectual conversation falls flat, so the Ricardos and Mertzes opt for a night in front of the TV set. When the set breaks down, radio prevails and the four friends listen to the *Mr. and Mrs. Quiz* show, hosted by Freddie Fillmore (Frank Nelson). To everybody's amazement, Ricky knows all the answers, prompting Lucy to register him as a contestant. When Lucy tells Ricky about his up-coming radio stint, he becomes furious and reveals that the only reason he knew the answers was because he happened to be at the radio station while the program was being taped. Ricky: "All I know is that Columbus discovered Ohio in 1776." Lucy beats a hasty retreat to Freddie Fillmore's office to withdraw Ricky's name as a contestant, but Fillmore is so excited about having "a big-name entertainer" on his show, Lucy can't bring herself to break the news. But she does manage to "steal" the answers to the three questions, later committing them to memory. Unfortunately, just before showtime, the questions are switched and Lucy's memorized answers provide the humor. "Question one—What is the name of the animal that attaches itself to you and drains you of your blood? . . . The director of Internal Revenue; question two—What is a senator's term of office? . . . The sap runs every two years; question three—Why did the French people place Marie Antoinette under the sharp blade of the guillotine? . . . To scrape the barnacles off her hull." Much to their collective surprise, the Ricardos answer the bonus $500 query correctly—"What did George Washington say when crossing the Delaware?"—because Ricky happens to blurt out, "Please let me sit down. This is making me sick."

"Lucy's Schedule"; #1050/33; May 26, 1952.

After Lucy louses up a dinner appointment with the new Tropicana boss, Alvin Littlefield (Gale Gordon), and his wife Phoebe, by being late, Ricky promptly puts his wife on a rigid time schedule. Ricardo informs Littlefield of this at a meeting to dismiss the possibility of Ricky being promoted to club manager, adding, "I've got her jumping around like a trained seal!" Seeing is believing, so Ricky invites the

Littlefields to dinner to watch Lucy "perform." When Lucy gets wind of the plot, she schemes with Ethel and Mrs. Littlefield to teach their time-conscious hubbies a well-deserved lesson. The various dinner courses are rushed to the table and then whisked away in seconds, with Lucy finally donning a catcher's mitt to pitch hot biscuits from the kitchen. Littlefield has seen quite enough: "This is no way to run a house . . . but it is the only way to run a nightclub . . . Mr. Manager."

"Lucy Thinks Ricky's Getting Bald"; #1050/34; June 2, 1952.

When Ricky takes to sporting a hat around the apartment, Lucy fears he's worrying needlessly about getting bald. She visits a store that specializes in hair restoration products and devices. Its manager, Mr. Thurlough (Milton Parsons), demonstrates some of the cures, but Lucy feels these are too drastic in Ricky's minor case. Later, she and Ethel dream up a better stunt—they'll invite a group of bald men to the apartment to prove to Ricky how well off he really is. Lucy: "I want this place looking like a sea of honeydew melons." Thurlough arrives with a number of bare-pated men, each demanding $10 for his services and a meal. Lucy pays up just before Ricky phones from work to inform her he won't be home for hours. Lucy dismisses the bald-headed aggregation and opts for the drastic measures previously shunned. When Ricky arrives at home, Lucy warns him, "Your roots won't know what hit 'em" as she proceeds to use vibrators, mustard plasters, a plunger, and heat cap ("you have to bake for twenty minutes"). Hoping he'll dislike the treatment, Lucy says he'll have to "do it every other night for six months." Strangely, Ricky likes the notion, and Lucy sighs, defeated.

"Ricky Asks for a Raise"; #1050/35; June 9, 1952; with Maurice Marsac.

When Ricky's attempts to secure a raise from his boss, Mr. Little-field (Gale Gordon), fail, Lucy decides to fight back. Noticing a news-paper ad announcing the opening of Xaxier Valdez—"King of the Konga"—at the Tropicana, Ethel conjectures: "Wouldn't it be wonder-ful if no one shows up for Xavier's opening?" This prompts the red-head to make bogus reservations (with the idea of canceling them at the last minute) in various names—Mrs. Worthington Proudfoot, Scarlett Culpepper, Lucille MacGillicuddy—and with the help of the Mertzes' old vaudeville friend, quick-change artist Hal King, they set off to invade the Tropicana and prove Ricky's popularity once and for all. In costume, the threesome parades into the club and then, upon hearing that "Ricky Ricardo isn't appearing here anymore," leave abruptly. They pull this trick a few times (including one scene featur-ing William Frawley in drag), until it is clear to Mr. Littlefield that he cannot afford to be without Ricky Ricardo. This speculation goes

directly to Ricky's head: "I guess I didn't realize how popular I was. . . . I can write my own ticket anywhere."
(NOTE: Hal King was Lucille Ball's makeup man.)

1952–1953

"Job Switching"; #1050/39; September 15, 1952; with Amanda Milligan.

In need of money, Lucy writes on the back of a rubber check: "Dear Teller. Be a lamb and don't put this through until next month." Infuriated, Ricky declares: "Well, Lucy, what have you got to say?" Lucy: "Now I know why they call them tellers. They go around babbling everything they know." Disgruntled by Lucy's spendthrift ways, Ricky insists she would feel differently about money if she had to "bring home the bacon." With Ethel's support, Lucy agrees to switch roles for a week—the girls will get jobs if the boys stay home to do the housework and cooking. The females' first stop is the Acme Employment Agency ("People We Place Stay Put") where Mr. Snodgrass (Alan deWitt) interviews them. Fibbing delightfully, Lucy and Ethel land jobs as candy makers at Kramer's Kandy Kitchen. The factory foreman (Elvia Allman) assigns Lucy to the candy-dipping section where disaster soon strikes, ending in a chocolate fight with a co-worker. Ethel fares no better in the boxing department, and soon both girls are transferred to "wrapping," where their task is to wrap each piece of candy as it goes by on a conveyer belt. Unfortunately, they find it impossible to keep up with the swift-moving contraption and, in one of the funniest scenes ever telecast, are forced to stuff the excess candies into their mouths, hats, blouses, etc. As "housewives," Ricky and Fred are doing no better, so the four finally agree to call off the "switch."
(NOTE: This is one of Lucille Ball's favorite *I Love Lucy* episodes and the first segment directed by William Asher.)

"The Saxophone"; #1050/40; September 22, 1952.

When Lucy learns that Ricky and his band will be going out of town on a series of one-nighters, she wants to go along. Finding her old saxophone in the attic, she demonstrates her musical abilities by playing "Glow Worm," the only song she learned to play in high school at Celeron, New York. To be like "one of the boys," Lucy attends Ricky's band auditions dressed in a wild zoot suit, complete with swinging watch chain: "Hey, man. . . . Hiya, cats! . . . Give me some skin." Lucy auditions valiantly for her bandleader husband, but her sad rendition of "Glow Worm" costs her the job. Determined to keep Ricky from going on the road, Lucy plots to make him jealous. Using Fred Mertz's derby and gloves, she leads Ricky to believe that she spent the afternoon with another man. This sends her husband into a proper jealous rage, until Fred happens to ask what his hat and gloves are doing in the Ricardo apartment. To teach Lucy a lesson, Ricky calls a man at the musicians' union (Herb Vigran) and arranges to have three or four guys, posing as Lucy's lovers, take up temporary residence in the Ricardo closet. The "lovers" arrive and the joke works perfectly, until the union man phones Ricky to tell him he couldn't get anyone to help out. Now Ricky is frantic, without realizing Lucy arranged the call.

(NOTE: Lucille Ball went to high school in Celeron, New York.)

"The Anniversary Present"; #1050/36; September 29, 1952.

The Ricardos' eleventh wedding anniversary is approaching and Lucy finds herself dropping some none-too-subtle hints in Ricky's direction. Little does she realize that her husband has already made plans for the anniversary, having arranged to buy at a discount a string of pearls for Lucy through a neighbor, Grace Foster (Gloria Blondell), who happens to work at Joseph's Jewelry company. But Ricky's many surreptitious trips to Grace's apartment (while Mr. Foster is out of town) to inspect the pearls have got Lucy suspecting the worst: Ricky is having an affair with Mrs. Foster. When Lucy and Ethel overhear what's going on in Grace's apartment (#2-A), using the "snooper's friend" (furnace pipes), they decide to don some discarded painters' overalls and make their way up a scaffold to spy on the "lovers." Naturally, havoc follows when Lucy spies Ricky fondling Grace's neck. Finally, before surprising Lucy with the gift, Ricky pretends he *is* having a tryst with the Foster woman, then exclaims: "Grace and I have decided . . . these are the pearls I will give you for our wedding anniversary." Lucy is agog and all is forgiven.

"The Handcuffs"; #1050/37; October 6, 1952; with Paul Dubov.

After Fred demonstrates his magic prowess with a set of trick handcuffs, Lucy snaps a similar pair on Ricky and herself, in an effort to persuade her husband to stay home that night instead of attending a TV show rehearsal. Much to their mutual horror, they discover the manacles date back to Civil War times (Fred got them at a police benefit in 1919) and no keys exist to open them. Ricky is furious when he realizes he will miss the important rehearsal. The pair's efforts to sleep while still cuffed together are a delight. The next morning, a locksmith, Mr. Walters (Will Wright), arrives with an impressive collection of keys, but none will open the contraption. He knows he has the key at home, but that's in Yonkers, over two hour away. Ricky is panicky—his television show, live from Television Center, Studio A, is only a few hours away. He tells the locksmith to meet him at the studio with the promised key. Still shackled to Lucy, Ricky appears on the *Guest Stars* TV show. With Lucy's right arm acting as his own, Ricky manages to answer questions put to him by the show's hostess (Veola Vonn). Lucy's hammy antics are priceless and continue throughout Ricky's song, "In Santiago, Chile." Finally, Mr. Walters arrives and frees the couple just in time for Ricky's bows.

(NOTE: Director Marc Daniels worked out these handcuff routines with his wife (and *I Love Lucy* camera coordinator), Emily, before instructing Lucille and Desi.)

"The Operetta"; #1050/38; October 13, 1952.

After a meeting of the Wednesday Afternoon Fine Arts League, treasurer Lucy admits to Ethel that for the past two years she has secretly balanced her household budget by borrowing from the club's treasury and vice versa, and now there isn't a dime left in either fund to pay the expenses of putting on an operetta to commemorate the group's twenty-fifth anniversary. The scheme: Save the $100-royalty fee by writing the operetta themselves ("Ethel Romberg and Lucy Friml") and rent the sets and costumes (for the eighteen-scene play) with a postdated check. Lucy plays Camille, the snaggle-toothed old queen of the gypsies; Ethel portrays Lily, a neighboring village girl; Fred takes the part of Friar Quinn, owner of the inn on the River Out; and Ricky plays the hero, "good Prince Lancelot." In the midst of the performance, men from the costume and scenery rental company arrive and proceed to repossess the items. Songs in the *Pleasant Peasant* operetta include "We're the Pleasant Peasant Girls," "Lily of the Valley," "I Am the Queen of the Gypsies," "We Are the Troops of the King," etc.

(NOTE: This was director Marc Daniels's last *Lucy* episode and, coincidentally, his favorite. . . . According to *Newsweek* (1/19/53), this was the first episode of her parents' TV series that little Lucie was allowed to stay up and watch.)

"Vacation from Marriage"; #1050/41; October 27, 1952.

The Ricardos and Mertzes have decided that their marriages are in a rut. Lucy: "We've all let ourselves become four big, dull clumps. . . . We are knee-deep in a pool of stagnation." A library book suggests a "week's vacation from marriage" as the solution. Once separated, the girls miss their boys and vice versa. Ricky: "You know . . . I miss Lucy." Fred: "I can top that. I miss Ethel!" Refusing to swallow their pride, the girls dress to the hilt and appear at the Ricardo apartment, hoping to make the boys jealous. Ethel: "We've been to 21 four times this week . . . that's 84." The revelation doesn't sway the husbands, so Lucy and Ethel return to the Mertz apartment defeated. When they later decide to check on their husbands, they find them missing from the Ricardo apartment. Forced to the roof, they get locked outside and their efforts to elicit help from a neighbor (Mrs. Saunders) fail. Finally Ricky and Fred discover the girls shivering on the roof and douse them with water from a handy hose. Lucy says finally: "I want to be in a rut with you," and embraces Ricky.

"The Courtroom"; #1050/42; November 10, 1952; with Harry Bartell.

The Ricardos give the Mertzes a new twenty-inch television set on the occasion of their twenty-fifth wedding anniversary. Ricky's hasty tuning adjustments cause the set to blow up, and Fred retaliates by kicking in the Ricardos' TV tube. A legal battle develops, landing the foursome in court. With Ricky as defense attorney, Lucy describes, in gruesome detail, what happened. Her testimony is like the classic fish story and culminates when Lucy exposes her shapely legs for the judge. When Fred calls Ethel to the witness stand, she tries the same flirtatious ploy until Fred stops her: "What are you trying to do . . . lose the case for us?" Finally, the judge (Moroni Olsen) decides to reenact the drama by dragging in his own TV set from his chambers. By the time the demonstration is completed, the judge's television set is a shambles, too.

"Redecorating"; #1050/43; November 17, 1952.

A visit to the "Home Show" prompts Lucy and Ethel to dream of households with new furniture. A contest, in which they each entered one hundred cards, will award the lucky winner with five rooms of new furnishings. All the wives have to do is wait for a phone call from the "Home Show" the next day; but Ricky has managed to obtain four tickets to the "new Rodgers and Hammerstein musical." Temptation notwithstanding, Lucy opts to wait for the all-important phone call. So he can attend the musical, Ricky asks Fred to make a phony phone call informing Lucy she has won. Naturally, when the call comes through Lucy is elated and immediately summons a secondhand furniture dealer. For $75, she sells dealer Dan Jenkins (Hans Conreid) all her furniture and promptly spends the cash on new paint and wallpaper to brighten the apartment. The scene depicting Lucy and Ethel wallpapering the Ricardo bedroom is priceless. When Ricky arrives at home and learns that Lucy has sold all their furniture, he chases after Jenkins to buy it back. The price—after the dealer deducts for "overhead, electricity, advertising . . ."—$500. Ricky manages to wheedle Jenkins down to $395, but only because "I like the way you sing 'Babalu.'" After viewing the new striped wallpaper in the bedroom, Ricky learns from Fred that he never made the phony "Home Show" phone call, which means that Lucy really did win the furniture. (NOTE: Dan Jenkins was Lucy and Desi's favorite *TV Guide* writer. . . . This episode was prompted by Miss Ball who said of the existing stage furniture, "I just got tired of it.")

"Ricky Loses His Voice"; #1050/44; November 24, 1952; with Barbara Pepper.

When Ricky arrives home with a bad case of laryngitis, Lucy banishes him to bed. However, the Cuban is concerned about the imminent reopening of the Tropicana, and Mr. Chambers, his new boss, is counting on him to stage a good show. Ricky's throat becomes so sore that he resorts to using a blackboard and chalk to communicate. This prompts dutiful wife Lucy to contact Chambers and tell him that Ricky is in no shape to perform his duties, but before she has a chance to break the news, Chambers informs her that he is going out of town for a few days, adding: "I have every confidence [Ricky's] going to turn out a great show!" Deciding not to tell Ricky and stage the show herself, Lucy hires "some talent that has been grossly overlooked in the past"—Fred and Ethel. Mr. Mertz unearths an old vaudeville script, "Flapper Follies of 1927," and even manages to line up all the showgirls from the original production. At the opening, Ricky is aghast when a chorus line of middle-aged double-chinned flappers cavort to his singing of "Sweet and Lovely." Fred and Ethel do "Nothing Could Be Finer Than to Be in Carolina" and "Charleston." Lucy scores with a ukelele number, "Mississippi Mud," and the finale—featuring ex-vaudevillian Mr. Chambers—is "Varsity Drag" with all joining in the twenties' fun.

"Lucy Is Enceinte"; #1050/50; Decebmer 8, 1952; with Dick Reeves, William Hamil.

After eleven years of marriage, the Ricardos are expecting their first child. Lucy has dreamed "a million times" about this event—breaking the news to Ricky. Her first attempt is at lunch, but, alas, Señor Ricardo is in a bad mood: "Sometimes I think I go back to Cuba and work on a sugar plantation." Next, she journeys to the Tropicana, but with all the onlookers present, Lucy finds it impossible to discuss such a personal matter. In the meantime, Fred and Ethel are absolutely overwhelmed with the idea that they'll be the baby's godparents. In fact, Fred already has purchased a baseball bat, glove, cap, and ball for "little Freddie." Lucy, on the other hand, is desperate; she must tell the father-to-be as soon as possible or "wait and let the baby tell him." At the club that night, Lucy slips a note to the headwaiter during Ricky's "Lady in Red" number. Not knowing it was penned by Lucy, Ricky reads it aloud to the audience: "My husband and I are going to have a blessed event and I just found out today. I've heard you sing 'We're Having a Baby.' Would you sing it for us?" He obliges first by singing "Rock-a-Bye Baby" and in the midst of the number—in a wonderfully sentimental scene—discovers that it was Lucy who wrote the note. Thereupon he signs "We're Having a Baby" to Lucy—and the two parents-to-be are awash in tears.

"Pregnant Women"; #1050/51; December 15, 1952.

The Ricardos are trying to agree on a name for the baby: Gregory or Joanne, Gregory or Cynthia, John or Mary? Lucy: "I want the names to be unique and euphonious." Ricky: "Okay. Unique if it's a boy and Euphonious if it's a girl." The following morning, Ricky offers to cook Lucy's favorite breakfast—waffles. After a series of kitchen mishaps, Lucy exclaims, "Do me a favor. Don't cook breakfast for me . . . I'm not strong enough." Suddenly, however, she gets the misguided idea that Ricky is interested only in "little Sharon or Pierpont," not in her. Ethel conveys these thoughts to Ricky who immediately showers Lucy with inappropriate gifts—a rattle, a baby's bonnet, etc. To patch things up, Ricky invites his wife to the Tropicana for dining and dancing. This manages to do the trick, except now Lucy fears Ricky doesn't love the baby. "You haven't even mentioned little Robert or Madelyn," Lucy sobs, after Ricky sings "Dancing Cheek to Cheek."

(NOTE: Robert and Madelyn referred to Robert G. Carroll, Jr., and Madelyn Pugh—the two talented *Lucy* scribes.)

"Lucy's Show Biz Swan Song"; #1050/52; December 22, 1952.

After harmonizing to "Nothing Could Be Finer Than to Be in Carolina," Fred and Ethel are given the nod by Ricky to audition for his new Gay Nineties revue. Lucy, of course, also wants in, despite Ricky's insistence that the approaching stork should have dampened her show biz aspirations. Lucy: "Would you begrudge a particular swan her song?" At auditions the next day, Pepito, the Spanish Clown, performs his world-famous baby-crying act, the lion tamer routine, and rides the world's tiniest bicycle. Next in line, according to agent Jerry (Jerry Hausner) is an act called "MacGillicuddy and Mertz." Lucy and Ethel attempt "By the Light of the Silvery Moon" and are promptly rejected. Lucy: "What a lousy excuse he gave us." Ethel: "You mean telling us we stank?" Ricky finally offers Fred and Ethel a chance to appear in the revue—as one half of a barbershop quartet, along with him and George Watson. Lucy manages to get to Watson first and, hence, becomes the fourth member of the "Sweet Adeline" foursome, with typically chaotic results.

(NOTE: Pepito, the Spanish Clown, was instrumental in devising the vaudeville routines Lucy and Desi performed on their 1950 road tour.)

"Lucy Hires an English Tutor"; #1050/53; December 29, 1952.

Ashamed of her sloppy English and the inevitable effects it could have on the baby, Lucy hires a tutor, after telling Ricky: "Please promise me you won't speak to our child until he's nineteen or twenty." The teacher, Percy Livermore (Hans Conreid), arrives and proceeds to teach the Ricardos and Mertzes lesson number one: "Never use the words 'okay,' 'swell,' and 'lousy.'" The instruction period goes downhill thereafter, finally prompting Lucy to crack, "I would say 'okay.' . . . That's a swell way to get off to a lousy start!" Ricky becomes concerned about the cost of the tutoring until it becomes evident Lucy made a deal with Livermore: In return for free diction lessons Ricky is to allow Livermore to perform his song,

"Tippy-Tippy-Toe," at Ricardo's "nocturnal bistro." To get even with Lucy, Ricky enlists Livermore's aid, promising him an audition with all the record companies if he'll agree to speak English (?) the way Ricky does. Livermore acquiesces; and Lucy, patiently disgusted, gives up the idea of English lessons.

"Ricky Has Labor Pains"; #1050/54; January 5, 1953; with Doris Singleton.

Six months pregnant, Lucy is given a "surprise" baby shower by five members of the Wednesday Afternoon Fine Arts League. It later dawns on Lucy that Ricky has become jealous of the baby because all the attention is concentrated on her and the upcoming blessed event. When Ricky starts complaining of nausea, dizzy spells, and pains in his stomach, Lucy consults Dr. Rabwin (Lou Merrill) who diagnoses the problem as "morning sickness." Assuring Lucy that her husband's ailment is merely psychosomatic, the doc suggests she make him the "center of attention" for a while. Ethel suggests a baby shower for Ricky. Lucy changes the idea to a "daddy shower," whereupon Fred turns it into a stag party. A little apprehensive about the turn of events, Lucy decides to attend the daddy shower/stag party disguised as a newspaper reporter with Ethel posing as her photographer-partner. "Pete" and "Sam"—of the New York *Herald Times Tribune*—arrive at the party that is attended by many of Ricky's friends, including Jerry (Jerry Hausner). It doesn't take long for the guest of honor to realize the intrusion by the girls, and the party comes to an abrupt halt. In the final scene, pregnant Lucy enjoys a snack of pistachio ice cream covered with hot fudge and sardines.

"Lucy Becomes a Sculptress"; #1050/55; January 12, 1953.

No child should grow up without an artistic influence in his life, so Lucy looks into some possibilities at a local art supply shop. Mr. William Abbott (Shepard Menken), who runs the store, leads her to believe she has an incredible sculpting talent and fast-talks her into buying fifty pounds of modeling clay. Ricky and the Mertzes don't think much of Lucy's new leanings and after an ill-fated modeling stint by Fred, they insist she give up the art because it is obvious she has no talent. Better to prove his point, Ricky informs her that he is bringing home an art critic, and if he judges her work to be less than promising, she must give it up entirely. In retaliation, Lucy consults a book that describes how to make a plaster mold of one's head, and hence, a perfect replica. When this method fails, she simply encases her head in a thin layer of clay and becomes her own "bust." Mr. Harvey (Paul Harvey), the critic from the *Times,* arrives and is ecstatic over Lucy's "talent." In fact, he wants to buy the sculptured head for $500. But when he proceeds to remove the bust off the table, Lucy lets out a shriek, and Harvey rushes out mumbling under his breath.

"Lucy Goes to the Hospital"; #1050/56; January 19, 1953; with Barbara Pepper, Peggy Rea, Bennett Green, Ralph Montgomery.

With the baby due momentarily, Lucy is trying to remain cool and calm, despite Ricky's nervous demeanor (Lucy: "He keeps staring at me like I'm going to explode."), so she invites the Mertzes over to act as buffers. Pretty soon, Lucy has to contend with three nervous Nellies, so she retires to the bedroom to rest. Meanwhile, Ricky suggests that the three of them "rehearse" Lucy's trip to the hospital so that when the time comes, it can be carried out with dispatch. Ethel is charged with phoning Lucy's doctor, Joe Harris; Fred promises to take care of the suitcase; and Ricky will see to it that Lucy is prepared for the taxi ride. They rehearse their roles twice and all goes smoothly, until Lucy appears in the doorway and calmly announces: "Ricky, this is it." Despite the careful preliminaries, pandemonium results and it's a minor miracle that Lucy arrives at the hospital at all. While Lucy is taken to her room (354), Ricky retreats to the fathers' waiting area where he encounters Mr. Stanley (Charles Lane), the father of six girls. Realizing he has little time to get to his nightclub job, Ricky asks Fred to bring his makeup kit "for the voodoo number" to the hospital. In full witch-doctor drag, Ricky departs hurriedly for the Tropicana, leaving Fred to do the parental pacing. Lucy delivers a boy (James John Gouzer), and Ricky races back to the hospital for his first look (and fainting spell) at Ricky Ricardo, Jr.

(NOTE: Dr. Joseph Harris was Lucille Ball's physician. . . . This episode—seen by more people than any other TV show of its time—is one of Desi Arnaz's favorites.)

"Sales Resistance"; #1050/45; January 26, 1953.

With Lucy still at the hospital, Ricky sings "There's a Brand New Baby at Our House," as Fred and Ethel look on. The three then recall with amusement Lucy's lack of sales resistance as a flashback carries us to the time Lucy spent $7.98 on a useless Handy Dandy Kitchen Helper. After Ricky insisted she return it for a refund, Lucy buys a Handy Dandy Vacuum Cleaner for $102.60. When the salesman, Harry Martin (Sheldon Leonard), sold it to her, he said it cost only "Eight dollars and ninety-five cents . . . for the works." Unfortunately, that's all Lucy got—the works, and not the electric cord, the metal cover, or any attachments. When Ricky learns of her extravagant purchase, he demands its immediate return. But Lucy's scared stiff that Martin will probably sell her a Handy Dandy Bulldozer. Instead, she decides to unload the contraption on some other unsuspecting soul, starting off with Mrs. Simpson (Verna Felton), a gruff housewife who lives on the next block. Using the Harry Martin sales pitch, Lucy fails to get rid of the machine and returns home a bedraggled wreck. Lucy: "One more hour and they'd have reported the death of another salesman." Even "sales resistant" Ricky is unsuccessful when he tries to return the vacuum to Martin; he winds up buying a Handy Dandy Refrigerator.

"The Inferiority Complex"; #1050/46; February 2, 1953.

When no one laughs at Lucy's jokes or wants her for a bridge partner, she comes to the conclusion she is inferior. The next morning, she oversalts Ricky's fried egg, leaves the pits in his orange juice, and burns his toast. She cries: "I'm a big fat flop!" Depressed, Lucy retreats to bed where she intends to remain for life. Ricky worries and tells Ethel he's going to consult a "physio-chiatrist." Dr. Henry Molin (Gerald Mohr) suggests flattery, by someone other than Ricky, as the answer. He says he'll arrange to have someone—who will call himself Chuck Stewart—arrive at the Ricardo apartment at 8 P.M. Who shows up but the handsome doctor himself who proceeds to sweep Lucy off her feet . . . a little too far. Ricky doesn't take too kindly to the "treatment" and throws the headshrinker out, opting for a less expensive solution. With the Mertzes' help, he bends over backward in praise of Lucy's joke-telling and card-playing . . . even Lucy's singing. Alas, Lucy is cured.

"The Club Election"; #1050/47; February 16, 1953; with Ida Moore.

While Ricky holds his newborn son, Ethel recalls the time she and Lucy ran for president of the Wednesday Afternoon Fine Arts League. The flashback takes us to the nominations meeting where the first order of business is approving a new member, Ruth Knickerbocker. When the current club president (Lurene Tuttle) open the floor for nominations, Marion Strong and Grace Munson get nods, with Ethel's name being offered up as a presidential hopeful. Jealous, Lucy huddles with Appleby (Doris Singleton) and promises her a new cashmere sweater in return for a nomination. Appleby agrees and there begins a battle for the club presidency between friends, Lucy and Ethel. The deciding vote belongs to new member Knickerbocker, so Lucy and Ethel separately entertain her, hoping to corral the needed vote. Ricky sings "Cuban Cabby" in a Tropicana nightclub scene, before Lucy and Ethel break the news that they have both won the election and will share the presidential honors.

"The Black Eye"; #1050/48; March 9, 1953; with Bennett Green.

Lucy is reading a murder mystery to her husband when Fred and Ethel overhear a bit of dialogue: "Hit me—I dare you!" Thinking the Ricardos are having a terrible spat, they phone upstairs, hoping to break up the quarrel. Ethel: "Is there anything I can bring you? Cookies, ice cream . . . iodine?" Moments later, Ricky playfully tosses the book at Lucy, hitting her squarely in the eye. When the Mertzes spy the resulting shiner, they cannot accept the "farfetched" explanation Lucy offers. Taking it upon himself to patch up the Ricardos' "misunderstanding," Fred sends flowers to Lucy, but accidentally signs his own name to the card, not Ricky's. "Darling, I love you, I love you, I love you. Eternally yours, Fred," the message reads. When Lucy opens the box and sees the signature, she can't help but wonder, "Fred who?" Sarcastically, Ethel assures her it isn't Fred MacMurray, just before finding her husband hiding in Lucy's closet. Without asking for an explanation, Ethel belts Fred in the eye. He, in turn, smacks Ricky in the eye for starting the whole mess. After things have cooled down, Fred apologizes, finding the book-in-the-eye story quite plausible, indeed. In fact, he and Ethel have recreated the scene and now she, too, has a shiner. The four, black-eyed friends laugh uproariously, and everything returns to its usual state.

"Lucy Changes Her Mind"; #1050/49; March 30, 1953; with Johnny Hart.

First, Lucy can't decide which dress to wear for dinner, then has trouble choosing a restaurant. But once seated at the Jubilee restaurant, she quickly makes up her mind about what to eat—roast beef. The bespectacled waiter (Frank Nelson) takes her order, then Ethel's—lamb chops. Lucy asks if she can change her order; she'd prefer lamb chops. When Ricky mentions steak ("rare, thick, and juicy"), Lucy changes her mind again. To add insult to injury, Lucy keeps changing tables at the restaurant, finding one too drafty, another viewless. Fred: "Stand by for another troop movement." The waiter becomes so befuddled, he quits. Ricky is properly furious with Lucy, pointing out that she never finishes anything she starts and is guilty of constantly changing her mind. The next day, Lucy happens upon an old, unfinished love letter she once wrote to Tom Henderson who's now a furrier. She decides to finish the letter and leave it around for Ricky to read. But Mr. Ricardo gets tipped off to the scheme by Mr. Mertz and doesn't bat a jealous eye when Lucy flaunts the letter in his face. Determined to make Ricky foam with envy, Lucy travels downtown to Henderson's fur salon where she spies a short, dumpy man (Phil Arnold). This can't be Tom, Lucy reasons, "unless he shrunk." With Ricky and Fred approaching, Lucy hops into the salon window and to make Ricky jealous starts "flirting" with a handsome male mannequin. All goes smoothly until the dummy separates in the middle, which makes for some superior Lucille Ball schtick.

"No Children Allowed"; #1050/57; April 20, 1953; with Peggy Rea, June Whitley, Kay Wiley, Janet Lawrence.

Like all newborn babies, Little Ricky is cranky. The result—sleepless nights not only for Lucy and Ricky, but also for other tenants in the apartment building, most notably Mrs. Trumbull (Elizabeth Patterson). She reads from her lease: "It is expressly understood that at no time will children be allowed to live in said building." Lucy and Ethel's attempts to humor the elderly neighbor fail, and the conversation ends with Mrs. Trumbull warning Mrs. Mertz that she and other tenants may move out. Ethel takes a firm stand: "My friendship with the Ricardos means more to me than all the money on earth." At first, Lucy and Ricky deeply appreciate the Mertzes' loyalty, until it becomes painfully clear Ethel won't let them forget it. She repeats her "friendship-with-the-Ricardos" story ad nauseam to anyone who will listen until Lucy is forced to crack: "That speech has had more performances than *South Pacific!*" This leads to a giant battle during which Little Ricky is left unattended in the apartment. Realizing their stupidity, the foursome races back to the Ricardos', only to discover a not-so-crabby Mrs. Trumbull holding the infant in her arms. (NOTE: This was Elizabeth Patterson's first appearance as Mrs. Mathilda Trumbull.)

"Lucy Hires a Maid"; #1050/58; April 27, 1953.

Lucy's sleepless nights caring for the baby prompt Ricky to hire a maid. Before the woman arrives, Lucy and Ethel discuss how to handle household help. Lucy has even prepared a list of dos and don'ts that she intends to read to her new employee. When Mrs. Porter (Verna Felton) arrives, she has her *own* list of dos and don'ts. The maid's first chore is to fix Lucy's lunch, a pitiful peanut butter sandwich. The maid had already polished off a jar of jelly, half a roast beef, and an entire head of lettuce (Mrs. Porter: "If I didn't have a salad, I'd have starved to death!"). In short, the maid takes over the entire Ricardo household, and Lucy wants to fire her but she can't muster up enough courage to do so. Instead, she transforms the apartment into a pigpen, hoping the maid will leave in disgust. Only after messing up the house does Lucy learn that Ricky already had dismissed the servant.

"The Indian Show"; #1050/59; May 4, 1953; with Dick Reeves, Jerry Hausner.

Ricky believes Lucy's show business aspirations have ended now that she has assumed the role of mother, but it's not so. The moment she hears that Ricky is staging a new Indian show at the Tropicana, she—along with the stagestruck Mertzes—want to be a part of it. Lucy reads up on the subject in a book, *Blood Curdling Indian Tales,* and is despondent when Ricky hires the Mertzes but not her. Nevertheless, Lucy manages to appear in the "Waters of the Minnetonka" number by making a special deal with the regular performer. But who's caring for Little Ricky? Lucy has the infant strapped to her back in a papoose.

"Lucy's Last Birthday"; #1050/60; May 11, 1953; with Byron Foulger, William Hamil, Ransom Sherman, Elizabeth Patterson.

Lucy is feeling sorry for herself because everyone has apparently forgotten her birthday. Mrs. Trumbull's efforts to cheer her with a small cake and some confetti meet with only gloomy enthusiasm. Lucy decides to take a walk, leaving Little Ricky with the elderly neighbor. Ending up on a bench in Central Park, Lucy is confronted by a motley group of musical itinerants known as the "Friends of the Friendless." They learn of her problem and offer a brassy chorus of "Happy Birthday." Her fury rekindled, Lucy decides to teach Ricky and the Mertzes a lesson in "the true meaning of friendship" and enlists the aid of the friendly band. Pounding a bass drum, Lucy marches into the Tropicana with her friends. Standing bravely before the well-dressed aggregation, Lucy offers her tale of woe: "I was just a bit of flotsam in the sea . . . I was a mess." As she looks about the nightclub, she recognizes the faces of her dear friends—the Orsattis, the Sedgwicks, the Morgans—who jump up and yell a happy birthday surprise. Lucy is overwhelmed as Ricky says, "I've got a wonderful present for you. . . . Do you want to hear it?" Ricky sings the *I Love Lucy* theme song while Lucy, tears streaming down her face, is given presents galore. Finally, she drops them all to plant a big kiss on Ricky's glowing face.

(NOTE: This was the only time the theme-song lyrics were heard.)

"The Ricardos Change Apartments"; #1050/61; May 18, 1953.

Lucy thinks the Ricardos need a larger apartment now that they have the baby, so she tries all her tricks to cajole Ricky into agreeing to switch apartments with the Bensons who have recently married off their daughter and don't need the extra bedroom. Lucy fills her apartment with junk, including a sliding pond and teeter-totter, to give it a "cramped" appearance; but Ricky is worried about the additional $20 per month the larger flat will cost until Lucy promises to pay the extra cost out of her household budget. Mrs. Benson (Norma Varden), who is still bemoaning the "loss" of her daughter, finally agrees to exchange apartments. Lucy, Fred, and Ethel perform the moving chores themselves (Lucy is the foreman, much to the Mertzes' consternation), and the Ricardos end up in a new apartment (#3-B) with a window in the living room.

"Lucy Is Matchmaker"; #1050/62; May 25, 1953.

When a friend of the Mertzes, Eddie Grant (Hal March), stops by for an unexpected visit and finds they are not at home, he leaves a message for them with Lucy. When she learns that the lingerie salesman is a bachelor, she immediately begins brewing plans to fix him up with her girlfriend Sylvia Collins. The plan backfires (of course) and, through a clever montage of misunderstandings, Lucy and Ethel wind up in Charlie's hotel room, wearing some very skimpy negligees. The girls have some tall explaining to do when Ricky and Fred arrive on the scene. Ricky: "Lucy! You here . . . dressed like

213

that? You must be out of your mind!" Fred: "Ethel! You here . . . dressed like that? *He* must be out of his mind!" It's all a big mistake—Charlie was merely trying to show his appreciation for the girls' hospitality by selling them some lingerie wholesale.

"Lucy Wants New Furniture"; #1050/63; June 1, 1953.

Without Ricky's permission, Lucy buys a new sofa and coffee table for $299, using the old furniture as a down payment. Until she can find the proper moment to break the news to him, she hides the new pieces in the kitchen—leaving the living room barren. Denied the use of the kitchen, Lucy serves Ricky dinner in the living room. When she forgets the knives, salt, and butter (Lucy: "Butter on bread??? I'll never get used to your Cuban dishes!"), and has to make repeated mad dashes through the Mertz apartment to retrieve the items from her own kitchen, Ricky gets suspicious and finally discovers the new furniture hidden in the kitchen. Now Ricky intends to take the furniture to the club and keep it there until Lucy can pay for it out of her allowance, adding, "Cut down on some of your 'stravaganzas." But Lucy wants desperately to attend the Carroll's party at the Tropicana on Saturday for which she'll need a new dress and have to get her "hair dyed . . . *done!*" She tries earnestly to make her own dress and give herself a home permanent. Unveiling the finished fashion, Lucy says proudly: "I made it with my own two hands." Ethel: "It looks like you made it with your own two feet!" Her hair turns out no better, prompting Fred to exclaim, "Well, if it isn't Little Orphan Annie!" When Lucy sobs, Ricky gives in—he'll buy her a new dress, let her get her hair done, and bring home the furniture.

"The Camping Trip"; #1050/64; June 8, 1953.

When Lucy begins to notice the widening separation of interests between Ricky and herself, she decides to develop an interest in the sports pages in hopes of striking a mutual bond. With unknowing disgust, Lucy comments on an item: "They're racing little girls at Churchill Downs. First race won by a three-year-old." A summer camping trip is in the offing and Lucy itches to tag along. Fred: "If Lucy goes, Ethel will want to go, and I can be miserable at home." The men hatch the perfect scheme: Ricky will take Lucy on a weekend "trial run" and make life in the woods so rough on her, she won't want to join them for the summer sojourn. Ethel overhears the dastardly doings and informs Lucy who puts together her own bag of tricks. On the overnight trip, Lucy manages, with an assist from Ethel, to outfish, outhunt, and outeverything her husband. All goes smoothly until she challenges her outdoorsman husband to a round of duck hunting, even though Ricky insists there are no ducks within a hundred miles of their campsite. According to plan, Ethel—perched high in a nearby tree—throws down a dead "duck" after Lucy fires her rifle. When Ricky retrieves the butcher-shop-acquired pullet, he comments: "Pretty good shooting. Not only did you kill the duck, you knocked off its feathers, and cleaned it too!" Finally, Lucy tells her handsome husband that she really doesn't want to share "everything" with him, just a kiss.

"Ricky and Fred Are TV Fans"; #1050/66; June 22, 1953.

When Lucy and Ethel become TV boxing match widows, they decide to go out for a bite to eat, leaving their husbands in front of the Ricardo TV set. Much to their dismay, the atmosphere at a local café seems no better: All of the customers, a cop (Allen Jenkins), and even the restaurant counterman (Larry Dobkin) are glued to the tube. Unable to get the latter's attention to get some change, Lucy helps herself and is caught with her hand in the cash register. She manages to escape the cop's clutches by yelling, "Look, a knockout!" and, with Ethel, takes refuge on the roof of their apartment building, where she snips the TV antenna wires. Officer Jenkins catches the pair and hauls them down to police headquarters where they are questioned by Sergeant Nelson (Frank Nelson) who recognizes them as "Pickpocket Pearl" and "Sticky Fingers Sal." Lucy insists she's not a notorious criminal, suggesting that the flatfoot call Ricky (MUrray Hill 5-9975) and straighten out the misunderstanding. After a good deal of confusion, due mainly to the Ricardos' phone being off the hook, Lucy and Ethel manage to prove their innocence and they return home just as the fight broadcast is winding up. Ricky and Fred aren't even aware that the girls have been gone.

"Never Do Business with Friends"; #1050/67; June 29, 1953.

After the Ricardos acquire a new washing machine, they sell their old one, despite Ricky's apprehensions, to the Mertzes for $35. The next day, the old machine breaks down, erupting like Vesuvius. Amid soap bubbles and spilled water, Lucy and Ricky offer their sympathy: "Gee, Fred, that's too bad." The Mertzes, however, feel differently ("Good thing we found out in time!") and take the stand that since no money changed hands yet, the deal is invalid. Possession, contends Ricky, is nine-tenths of the law. Seeing red, the Mertzes call the machine "a lemon" and the Ricardos storm out. The following day, Lucy finds the old machine outside her door. This leads to a tug-of-war, which Mrs. Trumbull (Elizabeth Patterson) manages to break up, with the broken-down contraption. She suggests that her nephew Joe (Herb Vigran), who works at an appliance store, have a look at it. He does and is willing to pay $50 for it. Now the Mertzes want to claim possession again, as do the Ricardos. Another mad tug-of-war ensues climaxing with the ancient washer cascading over the porch railing and smashing on the pavement below. This is all too much to take seriously, and the Ricardos and Mertzes laugh over it and make up.

215

1953–1954

"Ricky's Life Story"; #1050/65; October 5, 1953.

When *Life* magazine prints a story about Ricky but only features a picture of Lucy's left elbow, she rebels in typical style: "Just think . . . when Little Ricky goes to school and some of his playmates ask who his parents are, just what is he going to say? 'My father is Ricky Ricardo, the internationally known entertainer . . . and then there's my mother whose name escapes me at the moment.' " Lucy still yearns for a show business career. Fred advises Ricky to teach Lucy a lesson by showing her "how hard show business really is." They concoct a bogus performing job for Lucy—a "challenge dance" routine for which she rehearses six hours a day for three days. Saddled with all the difficult dance steps, Lucy poops out, but on her way home overhears a stagehand mention that they "still need a girl for the balcony scene." Ricky relents after Lucy promises never to ask again, but matters take a turn when Lucy discovers that Ricky has tricked her. To teach *him* a lesson, she decides to "upstage" him during his "Lady of Spain" number. The audience loves Lucy's antics, but Ricky thinks the applause is meant for him. He does an encore, then "The Loveliest Night of the Year" and, finally, after spying Lucy, a rousing rendition of "Babalu" with Lucy as the conga drum.

(NOTE: *Life* magazine of April 6, 1953, featured a cover story about the Arnazes titled "TV's First Family," printing a picture of Lucie and Desi IV.)

"The Girls Go into Business"; #1050/68; October 12, 1953; with Emory Parnell.

Certain they will become millionaires overnight, Lucy and Ethel decide to buy Hansen's Dress Shop. The asking price: $3,000. Lucy talks Mrs. Hansen (Mabel Paige) down to $1,500, just as two women customers (Barbara Pepper and Kay Wiley) snap up $200 in merchandise. Exclaiming, "It's a gold mine," Lucy figures that, at that rate, the store will gross $19,000 a day. They gladly pay Mrs. Hansen the original asking price. The new partners get into an immediate argument over a name for the new business—Ethelu's, Lucyeth's, Lucy and Ethel's Dress Shop, Ethel and Lucy's Dress Shop. The first day they make five sales—to each other. However, their future brightens when a man offers to buy the store for $3,500. Then they find out he sold it for $50,000 to make way for a skyscraper.

"Lucy and Ethel Buy the Same Dress"; #1050/69; October 19, 1953; with Shirley Mitchell, Doris Singleton.

The Wednesday Afternoon Fine Arts League is staging its yearly talent show (just three months after the last one), which is to be televised on Charlie Appleby's TV station at midnight Monday. Lucy promises the girls that Ricky will emcee the show, despite the fact he earlier wanted nothing more to do with the ladies group. Offering that "next to sugar, Cuba's biggest export is ham," Lucy uses a little reverse psychology to get Ricky to appear. She tells him she has the perfect MC—Dan Jenkins, who plays tissue paper and comb. Ricky changes his mind and even helps Lucy and Ethel rehearse their duet, "Friendship." But sparks fly when Lucy brings out the dress she intends to wear—it's identical to the one Ethel bought (Lucy got hers at Gimbel's and Ethel found hers at Macy's). To avoid a fight, both decide to take back their dresses. But later we learn that neither took her dress back, thinking the other would, and while they perform their song on TV, they rip each other's dresses to shreds until Ricky and Fred have to break up the on-camera scuffle.

"Equal Rights"; #1050/70; October 26, 1953.

After a heated argument about equal rights, during which the girls insist they want to be treated exactly as if they were men, the Ricardos and Mertzes go off to an Italian restaurant (on Thirty-ninth Street near Eighth Avenue) for dinner. When Xavier, the waiter, on Ricky's insistence, presents four separate checks, the girls discover they have no money. They are ordered by the management to wash dishes (so many that Lucy suggests, "I think he takes in dirty dishes from other restaurants"), and the girls decide to get back at the boys by phoning them from the restaurant, informing them that they are being robbed and mugged. Ricky subsequently calls the police, then rushes down to the restaurant himself only to find Lucy and Ethel unharmed. To counter the subterfuge, Ricky and Fred disguise themselves as crooks, burst in the kitchen, and surprise the girls. Just then, the cops arrive and arrest Ricky and Fred. At the police station, Lucy and Ethel are uncertain about bailing them out. "Mean-looking, aren't they?" Lucy snarls, before relenting.

"Baby Pictures"; #1050/71; November 2, 1953.

The Mertzes and Ricardos take an oath not to brag about Little Ricky, now thirteen months old, even though Charlie and Caroline Appleby (Hy Averback and Doris Singleton) will no doubt drag out pictures of their son Stevie (born four days before Little Ricky) when they arrive for an evening get-together. Ricky also doesn't want to jeopardize a TV emcee stint Charlie has offered him, so when Caroline asks Lucy to "guess what little Stevie did before we left," Lucy can't resist countering, "Don't tell me he took a picture of *you* for a change." To get even, Lucy dresses Little Ricky in his finest duds and decides to pop in on Caroline the next day, unannounced. The two mothers exchange barbs. Lucy: "When do you expect little Stevie to reach normal size?" Caroline: "He just seems small to you because you are so used to looking at little fatty here." After putting the two boys in a playpen, the women continue their sarcastic exchange.

217

Caroline: "Has Little Ricky ever said, 'Morning, Mommy'?" Lucy: "In English or Spanish?" Caroline: "You mean he speaks Spanish?" Lucy: "Only when he's mad." The session ends when Lucy accuses little Stevie of "scratching himself and peeling bananas with his feet." Certain that her outspokenness will cost Ricky the TV job, Lucy tries to talk him out of it: "[Television's] only a passing fad, like goldfish-swallowing and flagpole-sitting." Naturally, Ricky is furious when Charlie cancels the show, but Lucy insists she can remedy the situation. After singing "Acapulco," Ricky introduces Stevie Appleby as "a beautiful, adorable, and intelligent child."

(NOTE: See Doris Singleton's anecdote about this episode on page 104.)

"Lucy Tells the Truth"; #1050/72; November 9, 1953; with Doris Singleton, Shirley Mitchell.

Fed up with Lucy's constant fibbing, Ricky and the Mertzes bet her $100 that she can't go twenty-four hours without telling a lie. Lucy accepts the challenge before realizing she must attend a bridge game at Caroline Appleby's. Obliged to be candid, she untactfully tells Caroline what she *really* thinks of her new Chinese Modern furniture. Marion Strong gets frank opinions about her new hat and way of laughing (Lucy: "Marion, stop cackling. I've been waiting ten years for you to lay that egg!"). Lucy also finds herself in the untenable position of having to answer truthfully questions about her age (thirty-three), weight (129 pounds), and the original color of her hair ("mousy brown"). At home, she accuses Fred of being a "tightwad," Ethel of "looking tacky," and Ricky of being a "coward" for not letting her have her fling at show business. Lucy: "You're scared to death I'll steal the show!" Ricky takes her to a TV show audition where she is asked by the casting director (Charles Lane) to list her talents: "Lucille MacGillicuddy—singer, dancer, comedienne, monologist, mistress of ceremonies, after-dinner speaker, saxophonist, star, bit player, or extra." When questioned on the matter of experience, Lucy hedges by saying she has just finished an eleven-year run at Ricardos ("a three-ring circus") and has appeared in "3-D" (not third-dimension, but her apartment number). She finally lands the job of assistant to Professor Falconi (Mario Siletti), a knife thrower. Lucy has managed to tell the truth, and the Mertzes and Ricky pay up.

(NOTE: Lucille Ball's age, when she filmed this episode, was forty-two.)

"The French Revue"; #1050/73; November 16, 1953; with Louis A. Nicoletti, Dick Reeves.

Unable to read the menu at a French restaurant, the Ricardos and Mertzes almost order "four orders of closed on Sunday." Because Ricky plans a French revue at the Tropicana, Lucy hires Robert

DuBois, the waiter, to teach Ethel and herself some conversational French. In return for the free lessons, Lucy promises DuBois a part in the revue. The girls become adept at saying pencil, pen, table, and cat in French. At first, Ricky is mad that Lucy has horned in (Ricky: "There's one word that's the same in Spanish, French, and English—no!"), but finally agrees to hire the waiter on the basis of his excellent "Louise" rendition. However, much to Lucy's consternation, Ricky forbids her to "come near the club." She does her best to get into the Tropicana, first disguising herself with a lampshade and then stowing away inside a bass fiddle case. Nothing works until opening night when she appears as a fat matron with pince-nez, then quickly changes into a chorus girl outfit to join four other gals for "Valentine."

"Redecorating the Mertzes' Apartment"; #1050/74; November 23, 1953; with the Mayer twins (Joe and Mike).

Lucy's new mink stole never gets worn after she offers to help the Mertzes paint their apartment and reupholster their twenty-year-old furniture. Ethel, it seems, is too ashamed to hold the next meeting of the Wednesday Afternoon Fine Arts League at her place because of the way it looks. Lucy's so-called painting party turns into a free-for-all when Fred turns on a fan to blow the paint fumes out the window at the same time Lucy is removing feathers from an overstuffed chair. After ruining the Mertzes' furniture, Lucy gives them her living room set, including the two-piece sectional sofa. When Ethel admires Lucy's new one-piece sofa, she asks: "What happened to your mink stole?" Lucy: "You're sitting on it."
(NOTE: Miss Ball made one of her very infrequent mistakes in this show when she said to Ricky, "Let's paint the furniture and reupholster the old furniture," instead of "Let's paint the apartment and reupholster the old furniture." It was Desi who managed to save the exchange of dialogue by ad-libbing. Look for it.)

"Too Many Crooks"; #1050/75; November 30, 1953; with Allen Jenkins, Elizabeth Patterson.

Fred's birthday is approaching and the Ricardos decide to buy him a custom-made tweed suit as a surprise. Lucy sneaks into the Mertz apartment to borrow one of Fred's old suits (to serve as a model), but Mrs. Trumbull, unaware of Lucy's true intentions, sees her and tells Ethel. Because of a robbery scare in the neighborhood involving a "Madame X," Ethel immediately jumps to the conclusion that Lucy is she. But when Lucy spies Ethel, wearing Fred's hat and coat, lingering on her fire escape, she assumes that Ethel is the crook at large. After a funny scene involving fingerprints on Ricky's silver cigarette case, Lucy decides to play a trick on Ethel, hoping to expose her as Madame X. She tells her friend she's going out for the evening, but instead hides behind a chair in the living room, fully expecting Ethel to break in. However, the *real* Madame X appears (although Lucy doesn't know it) and a struggle ensues. The noise summons Ethel, and Lucy suddenly realizes she's made a mistake.

"Changing the Boys' Wardrobe"; #1050/76; December 7, 1953.

Off to see the new Marilyn Monroe movie, Lucy and Ethel are disgusted that the boys insist on wearing their oldest clothes in public. The following day and without the husbands' permission, the girls give the ratty clothing to a secondhand man (at Third Avenue and Thirty-second Street). When shop owner Zeb Allen phones Ricky at the club, asking if he wants to buy back his old clothing, Ricky and Fred start plotting. They get some Brooks Brothers' boxes and put the old clothing in them (including Fred's Golden Gloves of 1909 sweater and Ricky's University of Havana sweat shirt), telling the wives they have bought new outfits. Meanwhile, desperate to drum up some publicity for Ricky, Jerry (Jerry Hausner) arranges to have his star client named "one of the ten best-dressed men," and Fred as his "fashion consultant." Elated, Ricky instructs Lucy to "get dolled up" and join him at the club. Lucy and Ethel, dressed in ragged attire, arrive just as a photographer snaps their pictures for a newspaper layout.

"Lucy Has Her Eyes Examined"; #1050/77; December 14, 1953.

When Ricky brings home Bill Parker (Dayton Lummis), a motion-picture talent scout who happens to be casting *The Professor and the Coed,* Lucy and the Mertzes break into a rip-roaring chorus of "There's No Business Like Show Business," hoping to get parts in the picture. Parker suggests that Lucy practice the jitterbug and he'll be glad to audition her at Ricky's club the next evening. Arthur "King Cat" Walsh teaches Lucy the finer points of jitterbugging to "Stompin' at the Savoy" (a classic Benny Goodman number). When Lucy notices that Ricky has another headache, she insists he see an eye doctor. When the doctor perceives that Lucy's eyes are the ones in need of care, he administers drops that will blur her vision for several hours. Knowing of her imminent jitterbug audition, Lucy tries to knock out the drops from her eyes, but it doesn't work. Nonetheless, Lucy performs her number, and Fred and Ethel, bedecked in raccoon coats, sing "Varsity Drag."
(NOTE: Ethel translates *Variety* headline—"Parker Preps Prod for Pitts Preem" so Lucy can understand: "Parker Prepares Production for Pittsburgh Premiere.")

"Ricky's Old Girl Friend"; #1050/78; December 21, 1953.

A magazine quiz titled "How to Rate Your Marriage, or Is Your Spouse a Louse?" causes problems for the Ricardos. When questioned on the matter of "old lovers," Lucy lists her ex-boyfriends (among them are Billy, Jess, Jerry, Bob, Maury, Argyle, Bud, Wilbur, George,

Phil, Karl, and Martin). To get even, Ricky invents Carlotta Romero, an old Cuban flame. Lucy flies into a jealous rage and refuses to speak to Ricky. By coincidence, a singer by that same name is appearing in New York at the Opal Room, according to a newspaper item in the New York *Gazette*. The next evening, press agent Jerry (Jerry Hausner) arranges for Carlotta Romero (with whom Ricky did work many years ago when she was part of the Five Romero Sisters) to see Ricky again. Much to Lucy's delight, Carlotta is now a heavyset, middle-aged woman whom Lucy describes as "so full of . . . well, so full." (NOTE: The names of Lucy's "boyfriends" were taken from the show's staff, namely Billy [Asher, director], Jess [Oppenheimer, producer/head writer], Jerry [Thorpe, assistant director], Bob [Carroll, writer], Maury [Thompson, camera coordinator], Argyle [Nelson, production manager], Bud [Molin, film editor], Wilbur [Hatch, musical director, Karl [Freund, director of photography], and Martin [Leeds, a Desilu vice-president].)

"The Million-Dollar Idea"; #1050/79; January 11, 1954.

Having spent her allowance until June 12, 1978, Lucy is determined to come up with a "million-dollar idea." She decides to market "Aunt Martha's Old-Fashioned Salad Dressing" by advertising on a three-hour, morning TV show hosted by Dickie Davis (Frank Nelson) that is carried on Charlie Appleby's TV station (located at the corner of Leeds Boulevard and Hickox Avenue). For the commercial, Ethel poses as Mary Margaret McMertz, a home economist who invites "an unbiased opinion from an average housewife . . . picked at random from our audience." The "average housewife" is Lucy, of course, posing as Isabella Klump who raves about the dressing so convincingly, she elicits twenty-three immediate orders. Lucy and Ethel set up their salad dressing plant in the Ricardo kitchen and proceed to fill the first orders (forty cents per jar, three cents of which goes to Caroline Appleby as commission) until Ricky informs them, after a little figuring, that they are losing money. He demands that they fill the existing orders "and get out of business" just as Fred drags in a huge mail sack filled with more orders. To "unsell" the product, the girls go back on TV: This time Lucy is scruffy Lucille MacGillicuddy who feigns food poisoning, exclaiming, "Looks like Aunt Martha had too many old-fashioneds!" But viewers love the "comedy" and the gals rack up a total of 1,153 orders, which they finally fill by purchasing brand-name dressing and pasting an Aunt Martha label on the jars.
(NOTE: Leeds Boulevard and Hickox Avenue referred to two Desilu vice-presidents, Martin Leeds and Andrew Hickox.)

"Ricky Minds the Baby"; #1050/80; January 18, 1954; with twins Joe and Mike Mayer.

Lucy complains that Ricky spends so little time with his son that the boy hardly knows him. Agreeing, Ricky changes his vacation plans so he can spend all his time with Little Ricky. In one brilliant scene that runs nearly five minutes, Ricky recites *Little Red Riding Hood* in Spanish. The child joins his father for breakfast ("a Spanish omelet with green peppers, green onions, and mushrooms"), allowing Lucy a few extra hours of sleep, which is interrupted when she overhears the menu. Bored with nothing to do, Lucy decides to go shopping with Ethel, until she sees Little Ricky wandering around in the hallway by himself. Ricky and Fred have been so involved in a TV football game, they hadn't noticed him wander off. To teach Ricky a lesson, Lucy phones her husband and nonchalantly asks about Little Ricky. Panic sets in when father realizes his son is missing. After a well-timed series of "baby-snatchings," the segment ends with Little Ricky safely in his crib.

(NOTE: Fred and Ethel mention they are married twenty-three years in this show; in "The Courtroom" episode, aired a year *earlier,* they were married twenty-five years.)

"The Charm School"; #1050/81; January 25, 1954.

The Ricardos are playing host to the Mertzes and Bill and Lou Ann Hall, when suddenly another friend, Tom Williams, brings his knockout date, Eve Whitney. A honey, the boys swarm around her, making fools of themselves—much to Lucy and Ethel's disgust. Lucy: "What's Eve Whitney got that we haven't got? Nothing! We've got just as much as she's got, only lots more!" Ethel: "Yeah, but all the lots more is in all the wrong places." They decide to take advantage of an offer for a free analysis at Phoebe Emerson's Charm School. Phoebe (Natalie Schafer) tests Lucy and Ethel who wind up with respective scores of 32 and 30 (out of a possible 100 points). The "uncharming" pair sign up for a full course. Soon Lucy dons a sexy, black sequined gown to surprise Ricky. Even Ethel, wearing a tight-fitting, leopard-design dress, looks great, causing Ricky to ask "Who's that?" Fred: "Who's that? *What's* that?" The girls demand a night out, and the boys hurriedly dress in outlandish garb (Ricky as a cavalier, Fred looking like Mr. Peanut) to show them how "ridiculous" they look. They decide to go back to the way they were before: "four natural, lovable slobs."

"Sentimental Anniversary"; #1050/82; February 1, 1954; with Barbara Pepper, Bennett Green.

For their thirteenth wedding anniversary, Lucy buys Ricky a set of golf clubs and he presents her with Stone Marten furs, but their real wish is spending the anniversary alone at home where Lucy has a candlelit dinner planned. The Mertzes, on the other hand, have arranged a surprise party for them, and when Ethel asks Lucy where they'll be that night, Lucy quickly concocts a dinner meeting with

Rodgers and Hammerstein. As the party guests start arriving, Lucy and Ricky move their champagne dinner into the hall closet. Finally, they manage to divert the guests' attention so they can slip out the front door and make a proper grand entrance, "surprised."

"Fan Magazine Interview"; #1050/83; February 8, 1954; with Elvia Allman.

Agent Jerry (Jerry Hausner) informs Ricky that magazine writer Eleanor Harris (Joan Banks) will arrive at 7 A.M. the following morning to interview the "happily married" Ricardos for an "average-day-in-the-life-of" story. The average day starts out with Lucy, in a lavish lace apron, cooking breakfast for Ricky who enters the kitchen in a smoking jacket, exclaiming, "Oh, I didn't know we had company. I woke refreshed, and with a song on my lips." On the guise of borrowing a cup of sugar, earring-clad Ethel arrives, followed shortly by Fred who sports a suit, tie, and derby "to fix the faucet." The "average day" continues when Jerry informs Ricky he's sent out three thousand invitations to ladies on the Tropicana mailing list, signing Ricky's name to them and inviting each of them for dinner and dancing . . . as Ricky's "date." When Lucy discovers a sample invitation (inscribed to Minnie Finch) in Ricky's jacket pocket, she flies into a rage and takes Ethel with her to search for this Finch woman. Minnie Finch, like her neighbors, is a slovenly dressed old lady. Lucy is properly relieved when she finds out it was just a publicity stunt, and the Ricardos return to their "happily married" state once again. (NOTE: Eleanor Harris was a real magazine writer who often wrote about Lucy and Desi. . . . Jerry Hausner quit the show after filming this episode; see page 102.)

"Oil Wells"; #1050/84; February 15, 1954.

When new tenants (Apt. 4-B) Sam and Nancy Johnson (Harry Cheshire and Sara Jane Gould) of Texas tell the Ricardos and Mertzes about some available oil stock—"a sure thing . . . but only a few shares left"—Ricky and Fred immediately express their disapproval. Lucy complains: "Our one big chance to live on Easy Street, and we're married to a couple of roadblocks." The next day, the Ricardos learn, with some surprise, that the Mertzes bought the remaining oil stock (ten shares for $1,200), despite Fred's previous attitude. An argument ensues, and Lucy accuses the Mertzes of "jumping our claim." The landlords finally soften (and sell them half their shares) when Lucy hints: "We were counting on the extra money for Little Ricky's college education." According to Ricky, the girls "cross their chickens before their bridges are hatched" when they rush out and buy (on approval) a mink coat and fur stole. Of course, level-headed Ricardo is no better—they catch him in the act of pricing a "custom-built periwinkle blue Cadillac with a horn that plays 'Babalu' ($12,000)." But when a detective friend of Fred's (Ken) comes looking for the Johnsons, our shareholding foursome jumps to the conclusion they have been swindled. Using a tape recorder, Lucy confronts the Johnsons, hoping to get evidence. Despite Mr. Johnson's insistence that the "oil stocks are as safe as U.S. government bonds," Lucy demands her money back. Mrs. Johnson: "Oh, give her back her nasty old money." Sam does and Lucy goes off to tell Ricky and the Mertzes that she has saved the day; not quite—moments later, Ken tells Fred about "some dopes who sold their stock back just before a gusher came in."

"Ricky Loses His Temper; #1050/85; February 22, 1954; with Madge Blake.

Ricky throws a terrible temper tantrum when Lucy purchases another new hat. She wagers he will lose his temper before she buys another hat. The bet: $49.50, cost of the hat. But when Lucy returns the headdress to the Jeri Hat Salon, clerk Mrs. Mulford interests her in a new chapeau ("a turquoise cocktail hat with little pearls"), which Lucy promptly purchases. Now she has to get Ricky to blow his Latin top before the new hat is delivered the next day. Lucy tries everything to provoke her husband, but nothing makes the Cuban lose his complacent composure. She even resorts to a "trick" drinking glass, but when Ricky ends up with tomato juice on his white tuxedo, he only comments, "It's a lovely shade of red." Next, agent Morris Williams starts bickering with Ricky over the performing fee of his client Sir Hume, a ventriloquist. The agent requests $500; Ricky calmly offers $200. Suddenly, Ricardo realizes he accomplishes more by remaining calm and calls off the wager with Lucy, generously offering to buy her a new hat. Seconds later, Lucy's jeweled chapeau arrives by messenger, and Ricky realizes he actually won the bet.

"Home Movies"; #1050/86; March 1, 1954.

Ricky's feelings are hurt when the Mertzes walk out and Lucy falls asleep in the middle of his home movies. The next day, Lucy implores her friends to apologize to Ricky. But when Fred eloquently comments, "I'm just dying to see those lousy movies again," Ricky informs the trio that they will never have to see another film of his . . . not even the TV pilot he is making. Taking theatrical matters into their own amateurish hands, Lucy and the Mertzes make their own film—a "western-musical-drama" shot entirely in the Ricardo living room. When TV producer Bennett Green arrives to see Ricky's pilot, *Ricky Ricardo Presents Tropical Rhythms,* he is treated to a spliced-in sampling of Lucy's theatrical travesty. Ricky's on-screen singing of *"Vaya con Dios"* is not-so-professionally intercut with "I'm an Old Cowhand," making for a ridiculously jumbled montage. Ricky is ashamed, but Green loves the "comedy" and calls Ricardo a "genius." Lucy: "How did you ever think of it, dear?" Ricky: "I don't know . . . just came to me."

"Bonus Bucks"; #1050/87; March 8, 1954.

A newspaper is conducting a "Bonus Bucks" contest, and Lucy and Ethel are checking all their dollars in hopes of unearthing a winner. After Ricky discourages them by reminding them of the incredible odds, he discovers in his wallet a winning bill (B78455698), worth $300. He plants the buck in Lucy's purse so she will experience the thrill of discovering it herself. However, the next day Lucy, ignorant of Ricky's thoughtfulness, pays a grocery boy with the prize single who, in turn, passes it to Mrs. Mertz as change. Both gals immediately claim ownership, and a resulting argument ends with the bill being torn in half. To save their friendship, both families intend to split the spoils, so each retains half a bill. Not trusting Lucy, Ricky takes possession of their half, placing it in the pocket of his pajamas before taking a shower. Meanwhile, the Speedy Laundry man arrives and Lucy gives him Ricky's sleepwear. The Ricardos now must retrieve their bill at the commercial laundry, where Lucy gets caught in the starch vat with obvious and amusing results. The pair locates the split single and races by taxi to the newspaper office, arriving moments before the 3 P.M. deadline. They claim the $300 prize, but after paying for damages to the laundry, taxi fare, and a speeding ticket are left with only $1, the same amount they started with.

(NOTE: Such contests proliferated in the 1950s, usually under the name "Lucky Bucks." However, Desilu's contract with sponsor Philip Morris precluded them from ever using the word "lucky," the name of a competing cigarette.)

"Ricky's Hawaiian Vacation"; #1050/88; March 22, 1954.

Lucy is determined to accompany her husband on a concert tour of Hawaii, even though he can't afford to take her. To wangle a free trip, she composes a sob story letter to Freddie Fillmore (Frank Nelson), host of the TV game show *Be a Good Neighbor,* requesting the complimentary passage to the islands for the Mertzes . . . and their old "mother"—Lucy. Fillmore, himself a devilish prankster, contacts Ricky and arranges for him to be present at the taping. While the Cuban sings "I Get the Blues When It Rains," Lucy is doused with gallons of water; when Ricky warbles "I'm in Love with You, Honey," she is sprayed with honey. After being bombarded with eggs, coffee, and pie in the same manner, time runs out on her stunt and Lucy loses . . . in more ways than one.

"Lucy Is Envious"; #1050/89; March 29, 1954; with Dick Elliott.

Cynthia Harcourt (Mary Jane Croft), a wealthy ex-schoolmate of Lucy's, is collecting for charity. Informing Lucy that their mutual friend Anita "gave six," Cynthia is instructed by Lucy to "put me down for five." But when the uppity friend arrives to collect the pledged funds, Lucy is shocked to learn that her "five" meant $500. Not to be outdone by her wealthy friend, proud Lucy intends to earn the necessary cash. Ethel sees an encouraging advertisement in *Billboard* magazine—Al Barton (Herb Vigran) needs someone "brave" for a publicity stunt involving a new movie, *Women from Mars;* the salary, $500. Taking the job despite the evident risks, Lucy and Ethel dress in Martian drag and "invade" the top of the Empire State Building. The stunt makes headlines and, for Lucy, the needed $500.

"Lucy Writes a Novel"; #1050/90; April 5, 1954.

When Lucy learns of a housewife who made a fortune by writing a novel, she decides to do likewise. Much to their dismay, Ricky and the Mertzes discover that Lucy has incorporated in her book bits about them, and they begin a frantic search for the manuscript, finally finding it hidden in a window shade. Entitled *Real Gone with the Wind,* the story boasts such characters as Nicky Nicardo and Fred and Ethel Nurtz, whose characteristics are a little too true to life. The three critics take drastic action by burning the book. When Lucy returns from a shopping jaunt, she notes the fire. Ethel: "Nothing like a good book and a roaring fire." Ricky: "You mean, nothing like a good book *in* a roaring fire!" Ethel suggests a new title— *Forever Ember.* However, Lucy has taken precautions and surprises them by producing three carbon copies. When a $100 advance arrives from a publisher, Dorrance & Company, Lucy wastes no time in beginning a sequel, *Sugar Cane Mutiny.* In the midst of the second effort, she learns that the publisher has made a mistake—they don't want her novel after all. Dramatically, Lucy says: "I can't cry. . . . This is deeper than tears. Sorry, Book-of-the-Month . . . you had your chance, Bennett Cerf." When Mr. Dorrance phones Lucy a few days later, he suggests she contact Mel Eaton (Dayton Lummis) who might be interested in her literary efforts. Eaton is: He wants to include her work in his new book, *How to Write a Novel . . .* in the chapter titled "Don't Let This Happen to You."

(NOTE: Dorrance & Company is a genuine publisher based in Philadelphia.)

"The Club Dance"; #1050/91; April 12, 1954; with Shirley Mitchell, Doris Singleton.

In an effort to replenish its depleted exchequer, the Wednesday Afternoon Fine Arts League decides to form an all-girl orchestra. Saxophonist Lucy is rejected when Ethel comments to the membership, "When Lucy plays . . . it sounds like a moose with a head cold." Lucy plots to gain entry into the female quintet by offering Ricky's professional services, without his permission, of course. After much hemming and hawing, Ricky relents, and the all-girl quintet becomes a sextet with a seasoned bandleader. At the first rehearsal, Ricky is appalled by the girls' meager musical talents when they attempt their big number, "Twelfth Street Rag." They sound pitiful. Things take a turn for the worse, if that's possible, when an item appears in a newspaper hinting that "Ricky Ricardo has formed an all-girl orchestra." To save his reputation, Ricardo plants six members of his own band, dressed as women, in the club orchestra for its dinner-dance engagement.

"The Black Wig"; #1050/93; April 19, 1954.

When Ricky forbids Lucy to get "one of those new Italian haircuts," she rebels by borrowing a wig from her hairdresser Roberta (who insists Lucy looks like a different person with it on) with the intention of testing Ricky's fidelity. The salon manager, Doug, tips off Ricky to the scheme, so when Lucy starts flirting, Ricky flirts back: "I could even teach you to rumba." Lucy returns home fuming mad; a divorce would be the easy way out, she reasons. Ethel: "Yeah, stay married to him. That'll teach him!" Posing as the "other" woman, Lucy makes a date with Ricky, telling him she'll bring along a friend. The friend, of course, is Ethel who enlists the help of "Mother" Carroll, an old vaudeville friend who runs a local costume shop. The girls appear at Tony's Italian Restaurant at the appointed hour. Lucy is dressed in a slinky gown and black wig, while Ethel, unable to rent one complete costume from her friend, wears mismatched portions from three different outfits—Eskimo, Chinese, and American Indian—prompting Lucy to crack: "You look like an ad for a trip around the world!" The waiter (Louis A. Nicoletti), playing along with Ricky and Fred, tell the girls that their "dates" have just left with a blond and a redhead. Lucy now figures her plan has backfired: "I wish I were dead." Ethel: "You know what? I wish you were, too!" As they start to leave, Ricky and Fred sneak out from the kitchen and surprise them. And, as usual, all is forgiven.
(NOTE: Desi Arnaz offered to teach Lucille Ball how to rumba on their first meeting at RKO studios in 1940.)

"The Diner"; #1050/92; April 26, 1954; with Marco Rizo, Nick Escalante, Alberto Calderone, Joe Miller.

When Ricky becomes fed up with the nightclub game, he considers going into business for himself. The Mertzes want in, and the four friends decide on a diner as the perfect enterprise. Lucy and Ricky have the "name"; Fred and Ethel (having worked in a diner in Indianapolis) have the "know-how." For $2,000, they purchase Bill's Place from Mr. Watson (James Burke) who says business is so good, he has "to close once a week to let the seats cool off." After a little bickering, the new partners decide to call their diner A Little

Bit of Cuba. Business is brisk, thanks largely to Ricky's nightclub following. But suddenly the Mertzes feel they have got the short end of the deal—they're doing all the work while the Ricardos stand around, acting as hosts. How about switching duties? Fine, says Lucy before admitting she knows zero about restaurant cooking. Ethel assures her that it's easy: "You just put the meat on the griddle, and when your face gets redder than the meat, it's done!" Heated words are exchanged after which the partners decide to divide the restaurant into two separate eateries, with the Mertzes naming their half A Big Hunk of America. When the only customer of the day—a drunk—shows up, a hamburger price war erupts, then a pie fight. In the midst of it, Mr. Watson wanders in, suggesting that he "misses the old place." The Ricardos and Mertzes gladly sell back the diner to him for $1,000. Watson, it turns out, makes his living by selling the diner to people who want to go into business for themselves, and then buying it back from them at half the purchase price.

"Tennessee Ernie Visits"; #1050/94; May 3, 1954.

A special-delivery letter from Lucy's mother arrives ("Dear Lucy: How are you, and how is Xavier. . . ?"), informing them that "a friend's roommate's cousin's middle boy, Ernest" is coming to New York from Bent Fork, Tennessee, and will Lucy and "Xavier" show him some hospitality? "Cousin" Ernie (Tennessee Ernie Ford) appears and soon disrupts the Ricardo household with his early-morning warbling of "Wabash Cannonball." In an attempt to get rid of the overbearing houseguest, Lucy dresses like a "wicked city woman"— the type Ernest's mother warned him about—and proceeds to seduce him. Unfortunately for Lucy, Ernie likes the "vamping" and decides to extend his visit, commenting: "Ya took me to yer bosom . . . I've got a home."

"Tennessee Ernie Hangs On"; #1050/95; May 19, 1954.

The second segment of a two-parter starring Tennessee Ernie Ford opens with Cousin Ernie finding in the hallway a "planted" one-way bus ticket back to Bent Fork, his hometown. This was the Ricardos infallible scheme to get rid of the unwanted guest. But being a good samaritan, Ernie tries to locate the ticket's rightful owner, which just happens to be the first person he approaches. Lucy's next infallible plan is to pretend that she and Ricky are penniless and can't afford to buy food, something Ernie has a special fondness for. The idea *almost* works, but Ernie learns that his cousin (Dick Reeves) is the host of a variety show, *Millikan's Chicken Mash Hour*, that awards $200 talent prizes. Cousin Ernie rounds up his "cousins," the Ricardos and Mertzes, dresses them like country bumpkins, and goes on the air as "Ernie Ford and His Four Hot Chicken Pickers" singing "Ya'll Come to Meet Us When You Can." With his share of the winnings, Ernie buys a ticket back to Bent Fork, and the Ricardo household returns to "normal."

"The Golf Game"; #1050/96; May 17, 1954; with Louis A. Nicoletti.
When Lucy and Ethel become lonely golf widows, they decide to take up the game, but their husbands do not share their "togetherness" enthusiasm. Ricky: "It's against the law." Fred: "Mamie [Eisenhower] doesn't play." The wives are not swayed, so the boys plot to make their first round incredibly difficult by concocting a cockamamie collection of rules for the new duffers to follow. After playing a few holes, Lucy and Ethel meet golf pro Jimmy Demaret who sets them straight, golf-wise. Lucy: "There's a rotten Cuban in Denmark." They convince Demaret to help teach their husbands a lesson. Since Ricky and Fred are teamed with Demaret in a National Golf Day championship tournament, Lucy and Ethel decide to act as their caddies. When Demaret himself employs some of the "unconventional" golf rules—like asking "May I?" before attempting a shot—Ricky's eyes bug out . . . more so than usual.

"The Sublease"; #1050/97; May 24, 1954.
When Ricky decides to take Lucy and Little Ricky with him on a two-month summer booking in Maine, real-estate saleswoman Mrs. Hammond informs them that she can find a suitable tenant who would be willing to sublet their apartment for $300 per month. At first, landlord Fred doesn't like the idea and reminds his tenants in 3-D that their lease calls for "approval of the sublessee by the lessor." The Mertzes thereafter turn down six prospective tenants, prompting Lucy to crack, "The Mertzes wouldn't even approve Ike and Mamie." Patient Mrs. Hammond suggests that, to be fair, the Ricardos should split the monthly profit of $175 with the Mertzes. Suddenly Fred sees the light and approves the next potential tenant, Mr. Beecher (Jay Novello), a timid man who seeks peace and quiet following a nerve-racking murder trial on which he served as a juror. After the sublessee has been approved, Ricky learns that the Maine engagement is canceled. The Ricardos want their apartment back, but Beecher won't budge. There's nothing left to do but move in with Fred and Ethel—lock, stock, and Little Ricky. Life with the Mertzes is hell, and vice versa, so Lucy and Ethel dream up a scheme to scare Beecher into leaving. Meanwhile, Fred has located and paid two months rent on a temporary apartment for the Ricardos. Just then, Ricky bursts in with the good news—the band has been booked in Del Mar, California, for the summer.
(NOTE: The Arnazes actually spent the summer of 1954 in seaside Del Mar, relaxing from their strenuous *Lucy* chores.)

229

"The Business Manager"; #1050/100; October 4, 1954; with Elizabeth Patterson, Michael and Joseph Mayer.

In thirteen years of marriage, Lucy's household budget has never been in worse shape, prompting Ricky to hire a business manager. After inspecting Mrs. Ricardo's accounts, Mr. Hickox (Charles Lane) congratulates his new client for having "the first set of books that have baffled me in twenty years." When Lucy is presented with only $5 as spending money for the month, she hatches a scheme that will reap plenty of extra cash. She purchases groceries for other tenants in the building and charges them to a credit account Hickox set up, pocketing her neighbors' money. "It's my hobby," Lucy tells one of her grocery customers, Mrs. Trumbull. When Ricky spies the mountainous roll of greenbacks in Lucy's purse and Mrs. Trumbull's latest food order scrawled on a memo pad—"buy can All Pet"—he immediately concludes that Lucy is playing the stock market . . . and winning. Following the "tip," Ricky buys stock in Canadian Allied Petroleum (can All Pet) and fires Hickox who said it was a bad investment. Ricky soon pockets an easy $1,000 from the stock maneuver, splitting it with his "genius" wife. Ricky: "I suppose you are going to put it right back in the market." Aware of her $473 grocery bill, Lucy says, "Yeah, that's what I am going to do with it, all right." (NOTE: The Arnazes' actual business manager was named Andrew Hickox.)

"Mertz and Kurtz"; #1050/102; October 11, 1954.

Fred Mertz wants to impress his ex-vaudeville partner Barney Kurtz (their old act had been billed "Laugh 'til It Hurts with Mertz & Kurtz"), by making him believe he's a big real-estate tycoon. Lucy agrees to help out by posing as the Mertzes' maid Bessie. Barney (Charles Winninger), who says he travels around the world entertaining "crowned heads," is duly impressed with Bessie and the Mertzes' obvious affluence. But when a letter from his daughter arrives, informing him that grandson Barney, Jr., will be coming to New York to see his grandfather perform, he admits he is a "fraud." He isn't a seasoned world traveler; he's a cook in the Bronx. Feeling sorry for the washed-up vaudevillian, Ricky allows him to perform at the Tropicana. As little Barney looks on proudly, the Ricardos, Mertzes, and Barney stage a revue around the theme of Atlantic City with songs that include "I Found a Peach on the Beach in Atlantic City," "By the Sea," "They Go Wild, Simply Wild Over Me," and "On the Boardwalk in Atlantic City."

"Lucy Cries Wolf"; #1050/98; October 18, 1954.

A newspaper account about a woman who was robbed and then ignored by her husband in her dire moment of need prompts Lucy to assume the same will happen to her. Would Ricky rush home from the Tropicana if Lucy phoned in a similar predicament? He assures her he would: "Right between the Baba and the lu." But when Lucy tests Ricky's valor once too often, he decides to teach her a lesson. While Lucy perches on the apartment ledge, feigning being kidnapped, he and the Mertzes have their fun. Fred: "Are you going to call the police?" Ricky: ". . . bad publicity." Knowing full well that Lucy can hear everything he's saying, Ricky offers Ethel his wife's clothes. Ethel: "I will have to have them altered. They're much too big in the hips." For Little Ricky's sake, Ricky admits he'll remarry, but "I'll wait a respectable length of time . . . about ten days." This is more than Lucy can stand, and she reappears upset. Ricky assures her that they knew all along she was just "yelling tiger" (crying wolf). When Lucy really *is* being carried off by a group of thugs, Ricky and the Mertzes think she's bluffing again, much to Lucy's dismay.

"The Matchmaker"; #1050/99; October 25, 1954.

Lucy makes big plans to further a romance between Dorothy Cooke (Sarah Selby) and Sam Carter (Milton Frome) by inviting the wedding-shy pair to dinner so they can observe firsthand an ideal marriage, the Ricardos'. Lucy's scheme—starting off with a nice chicken dinner, then a peek at Little Ricky asleep in his crib, topped off with the telling of romantic tales in front of the fireplace—falls flat on Cupid's bow and arrow. Ricky itches to retire to bed early because of a morning recording session, the baby frets, and the chicken burns beyond consumption. Lucy's matchmaker-meddling sets off a big tiff between the Ricardos, ending with Ricky storming off in a rage. Marital bliss resumes when a telegram arrives shortly thereafter from Mr. and Mrs. Sam Carter, who insist their marriage was inspired by the Ricardos' thirteen years of wedded joy.

"Mr. and Mrs. TV Show"; #1050/101; November 1, 1954.

Over lunch at 21 with Harvey Cromwell of Cromwell, Thatcher, and Waterbury (advertising agency), Lucy discusses Ricky's chances of hosting a new TV show. Ricky is reluctant when he learns that the sponsor, Phipps Department Store, prefers a husband-and-wife format. Nonetheless, Ricky agrees to do the show. But when Lucy learns that he hadn't wanted her to be in the show at all, she decides to get even by sabotaging the *Breakfast with Lucy and Ricky* dress rehearsal being conducted at the Ricardo apartment. What Lucy doesn't know is that the so-called rehearsal is actually being broadcast to the entire City of New York in an effort to achieve that "unrehearsed" look. As the show begins (Ricky: "Why, hello there . . . I didn't see you come in. Won't you have breakfast with us?") Lucy promptly complains of a backache from sleeping on a Phipps mattress; then comments, after savoring the Phipps-prepared breakfast, "Food always tastes different when they fix it. I don't know what they do to it!" She then disappears into the bedroom only to reappear moments later in a potato sack—an example of what Phipps' fashion department can do for a woman. She adds insult to Ricky's injury by singing her own lyrics to the sponsor's theme song—"Phipps is a great big bunch of gyps!"

"Ricky's Movie Offer"; #1050/103; November 8, 1954.

When Hollywood movie scout Ben Benjamin (Frank Nelson) arrives at the Ricardos to discuss a possible screen test for Ricky, he is greeted by Lucy and Ethel, who suspect him of being a burglar and smash a vase over his head. The east-side neighborhood quickly gets wind of the talent scout's presence, and the Ricardo living room soon becomes an audition hall. Mrs. Trumbull (Elizabeth Patterson) enters, offering a weak rendition of a Spanish love song; neighbor Mrs. Sawyer requests a tryout for her poodle; and Pete the grocery boy yearns to be the next Harry James. Lucy can't imagine how the movie news leaked out. Ethel: "I didn't tell a soul, and they all promised to keep it a secret!" On the night Benjamin is to audition Ricky, everyone converges on the Ricardo apartment, hoping to nail down a role. Finding a part in the script for a "Marilyn Monroe-type," Lucy outfits herself in a slinky red gown, blond wig, and oversized beauty mark; Fred and Ethel make an appearance as a matador and *señorita;* and Mrs. Trumbull saunters in clicking her castanets, followed closely by a trumpet-tooting Pete. In the midst of this three-ring circus, Ricky phones from Benjamin's hotel suite with the news that he has already auditioned and been given the nod for a screen test for *Don Juan.* Ricky: "Anything new at home?" Lucy: "Everything here is about as usual."

"Ricky's Screen Test"; #1050/104; November 15, 1954.

Lucy is excited about the possibility of living in California while Ricky makes a movie: "Where do you want to live . . . Hollywood or Beverly Hills? . . . The important thing is to find someone who can build us a swimming pool in the shape of a conga drum." According to a story in *Variety,* Ricky is a "sure thing" to star in *Don Juan,* a $3 million color film. Lucy begins to have certain apprehensions when the story reveals: "Being considered for the female lead are such names as Marilyn Monroe, Ava Gardner, Jane Russell, Yvonne DeCarlo, Arlene Dahl, Betty Grable, and Lana Turner." When Lucy becomes convinced that her minor "part" in Ricky's upcoming screen test will make her a big star, Ricky deflates her hopes by informing her she's only needed to "feed me the lines"; the back of her head is all that will be seen. Ethel: "Lucy, what are you going to do?" Lucy: "I don't know, but the back of my head isn't going to take this lying down." During the screen test, she tries every method and means to get her face on camera, much to the director's (Clinton Sundberg) growing annoyance.

"Lucy's Mother-in-Law"; #1050/105; November 22, 1954.

Ricky's Spanish-speaking mother (Mary Emery) arrives for a visit while Lucy is in the middle of her apartment-cleaning chores. Moments after the unexpected arrival, a cablegram from Mother Ricardo appears. Lucy: "It's in Spanish, but I have a feeling you're arriving today." Lucy tries hard to make the relative feel welcome, but her efforts meet with disaster at every turn. She burns the *arroz con pollo* dinner, loses her in-law on the subway, and scorches one of the woman's dresses. When Ricky makes plans to invite some Cuban friends to the apartment that evening, Lucy realizes she will be unable to converse. Therefore, she employs Professor Bonanova, a mind reader who uses tiny mikes to perform his nightclub act, to translate the *español* for her. At the festive get-together Lucy manages to speak fluent Spanish, much to Ricky's astonishment. Everything goes smoothly until the professor is forced to depart suddenly (his wife has just given birth to a boy), robbing Lucy of her bilingual talents.

"Ethel's Birthday"; #1050/106; November 29, 1954.

With his wife's birthday approaching, Fred entrusts Lucy to select the proper present. Upon seeing the gaudy hostess pants, Ethel whines, "I wanted a toaster!" This sets off a heated argument between the two friends, until Lucy takes the pants, saying, "I'll wear them myself . . . after taking in the seat eight inches!" The boys appear just as Ethel complains: "She called me a hippopotamus." Lucy: "Oh, I did not, Ethel. I called you a little hippy. . . . On second thought, you *do* have the biggest potamus I've ever seen." Lucy storms out of her landlord's apartment, saying, "Happy birthday, Mrs. Mertz, and I hope you live another seventy-five years!" Since the girls now refuse to go to the theater together (Ricky bought four tickets to *Over the Teacups* as Ethel's birthday gift), the men scheme to rekindle the friendship by fooling them into believing the other has exchanged the tickets. Upon arriving in the balcony, Lucy and Ethel realize they will be sitting next to each other as they watch the sentimental production. The play moves them to tears, and the two make up.

(NOTE: The voice of John Emery was featured in the off-camera, *Over the Teacups* scene.)

"Ricky's Contract"; #1050/107; December 6, 1954.

After two weeks of waiting for a phone call from Hollywood concerning his *Don Juan* screen test, Ricky is despondent. His constant companion is the telephone, which he even takes to bed at night. He further forbids Lucy to phone her girl friends for fear Hollywood might be trying to get through. One day while the Ricardos are out, Ethel takes over the phone vigil in case Benjamin calls and comments to Fred: "What a shame there can't be a message saying Hollywood called." With only good intentions in mind, Fred puts pen to paper, scrawling, "Hollywood called. You got the job!" Intending to destroy the fake message, Ethel is distracted by another phone call. When Lucy returns, Ethel hands over the stack of messages, including the "Hollywood" memo. Lucy spies it, after Ethel's departure, and immediately phones Ricky at the club, leaving a message with Marco, the pianist. Enter Ethel who tries to locate the fraudulent note before Lucy sees it, but—alas—it's too late. Now Lucy and the Mertzes try to figure out their next move. Lucy: "We'll just tell him the truth. Of course, I'll be holding Little Ricky at the time. He wouldn't dare hit a woman with child." Just then, Ricky floats in: "Hello, baby. We're on our way to Hollywood." It turned out that Benjamin has phoned Ricky at the club with the good news.

"Getting Ready"; #1050/108; December 13, 1954.

After a little Lucy Ricardo indecisiveness, Ricky lays down an ultimatum: She must make up her mind about the trip to California. Is it to be via plane, train, or bus? Lucy's final decision: car. When the Hollywood-bound pair informs the Mertzes of their plan to travel cross-country by auto, Ethel gets teary-eyed. Lucy: "Even after we win the Oscar, we'll still be the dearest, closest friends." Ethel longs to go with her friends and complains to Fred that they never get to go anywhere. Not so, says Fred who reminds his wife of her visit to Minnesota. Ethel: "I went to Mayo Brothers to have my gallstones taken out!" After a little good-natured haggling, the Mertzes are invited to go along on the trip; Ricky even agrees to pay their expenses. Now all they need is a car, but finding suitable, reasonably priced transportation is not easy. Fred recalls a friend who owns a used-car lot in New Jersey and returns with a Cadillac convertible. The Ricardos are delighted until they see the vehicle—a vintage roadster more than twenty-five years old. Fred defends his $300 purchase: "Two other people wanted to buy this car." Lucy: "Where were they from . . . the Smithsonian Institute?" All their efforts to dispose of the antique auto fail, and it appears Ricky is out some money.

"Lucy Learns to Drive"; #1050/109; January 3, 1955.

To replace the clunker Cadillac, Ricky buys a brand-new, 1955 Pontiac convertible (180 hp, with automatic transmission) for the upcoming trek to Hollywood. Against his better judgment, he agrees to teach his wife how to drive. When they return from the first lesson, they're not on speaking terms. Lucy tells Ethel: "Oh, he makes me so mad! . . . How was I supposed to know we didn't have enough room to make a U-turn in the Holland Tunnel?" Before Ricky departs for the Tropicana, he reminds his ex-student to notify the insurance agent about a policy for the new convertible. Now Ethel itches to learn how to drive, and "experienced" Lucy decides to teach her. Within seconds, Ethel collides with the old Cadillac, locking together the two bumpers. Fearing Ricky's temper, Lucy attempts to take the two cars to be repaired, but meets with an added disaster on a hill—another crack-up. When Ricky sees the tangled mass of steel, he shakes his head in disbelief. Luckily, he's insured . . . or is he? Lucy forgot to call the insurance man; but Ricky, having been married to Lucy for fourteen years, has made the policy arrangements himself.

"California, Here We Come!"; #1050/110; January 10, 1955; with Elizabeth Patterson.

The day before their departure for California, Lucy's mother, Mrs. MacGillicuddy (Kathryn Card), arrives, suitcase in tow, ready to accompany her daughter and son-in-law "Mickey." Ricky won't hear of it and flatly refuses to take her along, lamenting: "Everyone we've ever known is coming with us to California." Overhearing Ricky's comment, the "Tag-along Mertzes" decide not to go, which, in turn, prompts Mrs. MacGillicuddy to cancel. Now Lucy says she isn't going either. Confusion ensues, but everything is straightened out and departure time for the sextet is scheduled for 6 A.M. It takes Fred four hours to pack the car with all the junk the ladies want to take along, and, upon viewing the mad mélange of paraphernalia strapped to the shiny Pontiac, Ethel comments: "I could have loaded it better with a pitchfork!" They decide to send the excess baggage ahead by rail. Mrs. MacGillicuddy then changes her mind about the long auto trip, opting for a plane ride to California with Little Ricky. Twelve hours later, but with all problems solved, the Ricardos and Mertzes are finally on their way west. As they cross the George Washington Bridge, the four excited travelers sing "California, Here I Come!"
(NOTE: This was Kathryn Card's debut as Mrs. MacGillicuddy.)

"First Stop"; #1050/111; January 17, 1955.

Tired and hungry after a long first day on the road, the Ricardos and Mertzes pull up to a rundown café outside Cincinnati. Owner George Skinner (Olin Howlin) greets them cheerily, then serves the "specialty of the house"—stale, cellophane-wrapped cheese sandwiches (he's all out of steak, roast beef, and chicken). Hoping to find something better elsewhere, Ricky pays the check ($4.80) and they leave, only to return several hours later, fooled by some purposely misleading road signs. Ricky: "We're not in the same place, are we?" Lucy: "We are, unless there's a chain of these across the country." Because it is late and they are hopelessly tired, the four decide to rent Skinner's only cabin for $16. As everyone quietly prepares for bed, a freight train passes precariously close, causing the shaky cabin to quake severely. Unable to rest with the noise, the four weary travelers decide to leave without paying for the room. When they get to their car, they discover the steering wheel is missing. By coincidence, Skinner has one just like the one they had, and he'll sell it to them for . . . $16. Reluctantly, Ricky pays, and the Hollywood-bound foursome is on its way west again.

(NOTE: This was the first time the *I Love Lucy* crew ventured out of the studio to film location footage.)

"Tennessee Bound"; #1050/112; January 24, 1955.

The Ricardos and Mertzes are arrested for speeding (40 mph in a 15 mph zone) in Bent Fork, Tennessee (population: 54). Ricky decides to pay the $50 fine and leave, but Lucy feels they have been taken advantage of. When she rebels, the sheriff (Will Wright) imposes a stiff twenty-four-hour sentence. Just then, the travelers realize they have a friend in Bent Fork—"Cousin" Ernie (Tennessee Ernie Ford). Ernie arrives and helps the westward-bound jailbirds in a scheme to escape by sawing through the steel bars with files. While Ernie warbles "Birmingham Jail," the New Yorkers free themselves, but are caught by the sheriff and thrown back into the poky. To clear his friends, Ernie agrees to marry one of the sheriff's chubby daughters, Teensy, the identical twin sister of Weensy (the Bordon Twins). The Ricardos and Mertzes finally manage to make their escape during a square dance/going-away party/hoedown featuring the tubby twins singing "Ricochet Romance."

"Ethel's Home Town"; #1050/113; January 31, 1955; with Dick Reeves.

After a brief stopover in Amarillo, Texas, the foursome arrives in Albuquerque, New Mexico, home of Ethel Mae Potter Mertz. Ethel's father, Will Potter (Irving Bacon), greets them with the news that the entire town "is in an uproar" over the visiting, Hollywood-bound celebrity. Assuming that Potter is speaking of him, Ricky's head starts swelling until he learns the celebrity is Ethel Mae who, apparently, has been telling some white lies in her letters home. Ethel's former boyfriend, *Chronicle* writer Billy Hackett (Chick Chandler), shows up to photograph the "star" for a "Local Girl Makes Good" story. Feeling upstaged, the Ricardos and Fred plot to teach Ethel a lesson. On the night of Ethel's homecoming performance at the Little Theatre (marquee: "Ethel Mae Potter—We Never Forgot Her"), they fiercely upstage her by incorporating some old vaudeville schtick into her serious singing of "My Hero" from *The Chocolate Soldier* and a chorus of "Shortnin' Bread." They manage to make their point, but Mrs. Mertz gets the last laugh when Hackett wants a photo of the foursome to be captioned, "Ethel Mae Potter and Company."

(NOTE: Vivian Vance was raised in Albuquerque, New Mexico, and became the star player in the town's Little Theatre.)

"L.A. at Last"; #1050/114; February 7, 1955; with Harry Bartell, Eve Arden.

Upon their arrival in Hollywood, the Ricardos and Mertzes check into the Beverly Palms Hotel (rooms 315 and 317, respectively) and meet their bubbly bellboy Bobby (Bob Jellison). Ricky goes off to M-G-M, leaving Lucy and the Mertzes to hunt movie stars, Lucy: "I wonder if there's any place where they gather in a herd?" There is— Hollywood's famed Brown Derby restaurant. Seated at a circular booth surrounded by caricatures of celebrities, the three tourists spy movie star William Holden in the adjoining booth. Lucy creates quite a ruckus as she stares at the star who, in turn, teaches her a lesson by staring back. Embarrassed and feeling ill at ease, Lucy hastily leaves the popular bistro, but not before causing an entire tray of desserts to splatter on Holden. Coincidentally, Ricky encounters the star later that day at M-G-M's Culver City studios, in the office of executive Mr. Sherman (Dayton Lummis). Holden offers to drive Ricky to his hotel and, as a favor, meet his wife, Lucy. When Ricky arrives with Holden in tow, Lucy is in the bedroom. Obviously, she is not thrilled when Ricky informs her that "one of the biggest stars in the motion-picture business" is waiting to meet her. Forced into being polite, Lucy disguises herself with frumpy glasses, a kerchief, and a long putty nose to "meet" the famous celebrity. During their encounter, Lucy's pliable nose grows to Pinocchio proportions, prompting her to crack: "This California sun sure makes your skin soft!" When Holden offers to light Lucy's cigarette, he accidentally sets her fake nose ablaze. Lucy nonchalantly extinguishes her flaming proboscis in a nearby cup of coffee, just before Holden recognizes her. Much to Lucy's surprise and delight, Holden turns out to be a good sport— he doesn't let on to Ricky what transpired at the Derby.

(NOTE: William Holden plugged his new movie, *The Country Girl*, which costarred Grace Kelly. . . . The putty nose routine is Lucille Ball's favorite comedy bit. . . . The script got an Emmy nomination the following year.)

"Don Juan and Starlets"; #1050/115; February 14, 1955; with Maggie McGuiness.

Lucy becomes jealous when five gorgeous starlets arrive at the hotel to pose for publicity pictures with Ricky. Naturally, she connives to be included in the shots, but studio representative Ross Elliott (Ross Elliott) explains: "Mrs. Ricardo, if you stand there, you will be in the picture." Why shouldn't Lucy be in the picture? Elliott: "*Don Juan* is all about love; it has nothing to do with marriage." Lucy is further upset when Ricky goes off to his first Hollywood premiere without her . . . and on the arms of the five beautiful gals. She decides to wait up for her gallivanting husband, but instead falls asleep on the sofa, not awakening until late the next morning. When she finds Ricky's bed apparently unused, she jumps to the conclusion that he spent the night out with the starlets. (What really happened is that he did return home, but had to leave early the next morning for a "call" at M-G-M, and the maid made up his bed without Lucy's knowledge.) Trying to be helpful, Fred covers for Ricky, saying he slept in their hotel room, but the fib doesn't hold water. Lucy is ready to ask for a divorce since

Ricky's explanation of the mixup falls on deaf ears. Finally, the hotel chambermaid (Jesslyn Fax) clears up the confusion when she admits to having made up Ricky's bed.

"Lucy Gets in Pictures"; #1050/116; February 21, 1955; with Louis A. Nicoletti.

Lucy is dying to appear in a Hollywood movie, her desire further sparked when she learns the Mertzes have got parts in a picture (through their old vaudeville friend Jimmy O'Connor) and Bobby the bellboy (Bob Jellison) has landed a speaking role in a hospital drama. She decides to take drastic action: "I went to Schwab's today to get discovered. But they won't let you sit at the counter unless you order something. So I sat through four chocolate malteds and three ice cream sodas." Ethel: "And no one did any discovering?" Lucy: "Oh, I did. About an hour ago, I discovered I was turning a light shade of green." Finally, Lucy lands a part in an M-G-M musical in which she is to play a Busby Berkeley-type showgirl who is shot during a nightclub sequence. Much to director Mr. William's (Lou Krugman) chagrin, Lucy has trouble wearing an enormous feathered headdress in the "A Pretty Girl Is Like a Melody" staircase number. After numerous ruined "takes," the director replaces Mrs. Ricardo, giving her "death scene" to another showgirl. "Wouldn't you like to see me die?" Lucy asks the director. "Don't tempt me, Mrs. Ricardo," he responds. Determined to get on camera, Lucy excuses herself from the set after she is offered the part of a girl already dead on a stretcher, only to return with her name emblazoned on the soles of her high-heels.

"The Fashion Show"; #1050/117; February 28, 1955.

While bemoaning the lack of a suntan, Lucy yearns for a Don Loper original so she'll fit into the Beverly Hills life-style. Ricky relents, allowing Lucy to purchase one outfit, provided it costs under $100. At the famed couturier's salon, the saleswoman (Amzie Strickland) shows Lucy and Ethel some outfits, but the price tags—nothing like those at Gimbel's basement—shock them. In the meantime, Sheila MacRae walks in and tells Mr. Loper that Joel McCrea's wife, Frances, will be unable to appear at an upcoming fashion show benefiting the charity Share, Inc. Lucy quickly picks up on their conversation and talks her way into replacing Mrs. McCrea as a celebrity fashion model —the most appealing part of the arrangement being that Lucy gets to keep the dress she models. Ashamed more than ever over her New York pallor, Lucy spends the next day basking in the warm California sun and winds up looking like a Maine lobster. This condition makes wearing a tweed suit at the charity show quite uncomfortable, but Lucy manages. Appearing in the Don Loper showing, besides Sheila MacRae, are the wives of William Holden, Dean Martin, Van Heflin, Forrest Tucker, Alan Ladd, and Richard Carlson.

"The Hedda Hopper Story"; #1050/118; March 14, 1955; with Bob Jellison.

Lucy's mother (Kathryn Card) arrives in Hollywood with Little Ricky (Mayer twins). Mrs. MacGillicuddy: "Long time, no see, Mickey." She describes the wonderful plane trip on which she met a newspaper woman who wants to do a story on Ricky. Interrupting the family chat, Ricky's new press agent Charlie Pomerantz (Hy Averback) enters, exclaiming: "Dad, I'm going to make you the Cuban Liberace!" He concocts a publicity stunt that is sure to land Ricky in Hedda Hopper's gossip column—all he has to do is save a drowning woman at the Beverly Palms Hotel pool during a tea the following day. At poolside, Ricky sings "Cuban Pete," before preparing himself for the rescue act in which Lucy is to be the "victim." When they spy an object that resembles Miss Hopper's hat passing in the background, Lucy makes a mad dash for the pool and falls in. But, alas, it was a false alarm; it wasn't one of Hedda's famous chapeaus—just a bowl of fruit. After a few more fake drownings, the Ricardos give up and return, soaking wet, to their hotel suite where they discover Hedda Hopper, the "newspaper woman" Mrs. MacGillicuddy encountered on her airplane trip. Through clenched teeth, they ask: "Mother dear, why didn't you tell us it was Hedda Hopper?" Mrs. MacGillicuddy: "You didn't ask me."

(NOTE: Charlie Pomerantz was connected with *I Love Lucy* in a public relation's capacity and is now Lucille Ball's personal press representative.)

"Don Juan Is Shelved"; #1050/119; March 21, 1955.

When an item in *Variety,* hinting at the imminent shelving of Ricky's picture *Don Juan,* proves correct, Lucy, the Mertzes, and Mrs. MacGillicuddy take matters into their own hands by penning five hundred fan letters to Ricky and dressing as bobby-soxer members of the Ricky Ricardo Fan Club. To assure Ricky's reinstatement, Lucy hatches another idea—she's going to hire an actor to pose as a famous film producer and have him present when M-G-M Studios chief Dore Schary arrives at the hotel to talk to Ricky. At the Beverly Palms pool, Lucy spots the perfect sap, offering him $7.50 for the acting stint. What she doesn't know is that the man is actually Dore Schary (Phil Ober), who happens to have a good sense of humor. Schary: "I don't usually work this cheap, but things are tough what with television and stuff." Posing as George Spelvin, Schary is quickly coached by Lucy in the proper portrayal of a cinema producer and, with Fred's help, outfits the executive in some outlandish clothing. When Ricky arrives for the meeting with his boss, he obviously recognizes Schary, and Lucy and the Mertzes are horrified. Dore never reveals Lucy's sinister shenanigans, but does inform Ricky that even though *Don Juan* has been canceled, M-G-M wants to pick up his option in the hopes of locating a suitable motion-picture property for him. When Schary departs, Lucy reasons that the fan mail must have done the trick, whereupon Bobby the bellboy (Bob Jellison) enters with a huge bundle of unstamped, unsent mail.

(NOTE: M-G-M's Dore Schary was supposed to play himself in this episode but got cold feet at the last moment. Vivian Vance's then-husband, Phil Ober, stepped in.)

"Bull Fight Dance"; #1050/120; March 28, 1955; with Marco Rizo.

Lucy's been asked by *Photoplay* magazine to write an article entitled "What It's Like to Be Married to Ricky Ricardo." In the midst of her writing, a press agent from M-G-M, Ross Elliott, calls to let Ricky know he will be hosting a coast-to-coast TV benefit for the Heart Fund. Naturally, Lucy wants to appear in the show, but Ricky turns her down. She resorts to a little "friendly" blackmail. Unless he allows her to perform, she is going to rewrite the *Photoplay* article to imply that Ricky Ricardo "is a dirty rat." They rehearse a counterpoint arrangement of "Swannee River" and "Humoresque," but Lucy can't seem to get it right. Next, Ricky offers her a spot in the Spanish dance number—playing the bull to Ricky's matador. Ethel: "For once, the bull will be full of Lucy." Displeased with the turn of events, Lucy transforms the bull's image from that of a snarling beast to a mincing creature resembling Elsie, the Borden cow. The benefit show, broadcast from CBS Television City, features Fred and Ethel singing "Shake Hands with Your Uncle Max, My Boy" and Lucy upstaging Ricky during the bullfight scenes.

"Hollywood Anniversary"; #1050/121; April 4, 1955.

It's anniversary time again and, alas, Ricky has forgotten the exact date. He even goes so far as to wire the hall of records in Greenwich, Connecticut, where he and Lucy were married fifteen years ago. His wife makes a big issue of his forgetfulness, and this tips off an argument. As his only defense, Ricky insists he's already arranged a big party at the Mocambo nightclub, which was supposed to be a surprise. Now, much to his astonishment, an item in a gossip column appears, bearing out his party "plans" and mentioning a long list of invited, celebrity guests. Lucy sees the newspaper piece and forgives Ricky. But when a telegram from the Greenwich county clerk arrives, containing the Ricardos' exact wedding date, Lucy flies into a rage and refuses to speak to Ricky. She'll go to the Mocambo that night, but not with Ricky. She presses Bobby the bellboy (Bob Jellison) into service as her date, but when they arrive at the nightspot, they are seated at a separate table away from the Ricardo anniversary party. Lucy softens when Ricky pays her a compliment and sings "Anniversary Waltz."

(NOTE: This episode was inspired by a true-life incident that happened

240

on November 30, 1953, when Desi surprised Lucille with a thirteenth anniversary party at the Mocambo.)

"The Star Upstairs"; #1050/122; April 18, 1955.

Cornel Wilde becomes the one hundredth movie star Lucy has seen in Hollywood when she learns he is occupying the penthouse directly above the Ricardo suite. Determined to gain a glimpse of the handsome actor, Lucy first disguises herself as Bobby the bellboy (Bob Jellison), then hides under the star's luncheon cart to gain entry into Wilde's suite. Things go smoothly until she's locked out on Cornel's terrace and must make her way down the side of the building using a few blankets as rope. As Ethel looks on horrified, Ricky enters, demanding to know Lucy's whereabouts. Ethel: "She's hanging around the hotel."

"In Palm Springs"; #1050/123; April 25, 1955; with Kathryn Card.

The Ricardos and Mertzes are becoming bored with each other. Each one is fed up with the others' annoying habits—Ricky's constant finger-tapping, Lucy's incessant coffee-stirring, Ethel's noisy eating, and Fred's loose change-jingling (Ethel: "For twenty-five years I felt like I've been married to the Good Humor man!"). The only solution is to split up for a brief vacation. With a flip of a coin (Lucy: "Heads, we win; tails, you lose.") the girls are on their way to sunny Palm Springs. After only a short stay, Lucy laments: "I miss Ricky." Ethel: "I can top that. I miss Fred." Back in Los Angeles, the men are faring no better. The Hollywood Stars baseball game has been rained out, and they're beginning to miss their wives, bad habits and all. When Dore Schary's secretary phones to ask Ricky to meet her movie executive boss in Palm Springs, he and Fred are delighted by the "coincidence," an excuse to be reunited with their spouses. At poolside in Palm Springs, Lucy and Ethel meet handsome Rock Hudson who introduces himself before going into a long-winded story about a script girl he knows, Adele Slip, who had a quarrel with her husband over their annoying habits. The tale hits home, and the girls start whimpering. Just then, Rock summons Ricky and Fred (who asked the star to concoct such a story) into the scene, whereupon the two couples melt into each others' arms. Lucy gets the last laugh when she admits to being the voice of Dore Schary's secretary.

"The Dancing Star"; #1050/125; May 2, 1955; with Wilbur Hatch.

Caroline Appleby (Doris Singleton) arrives in Hollywood en route to Hawaii and decides to visit her dear friends, Lucy and Ethel. Naturally, she wants to meet some of the movie stars whom Lucy has led her to believe are her close personal friends. When Lucy learns of Caroline's stopover, she is left with no alternative but to trick her. While Mrs. Appleby watches from a balcony high above the hotel pool, Lucy flirts with Van Johnson. But what Lucy's friend from New York

241

can't see is that Johnson is fast asleep. When Lucy discovers that Caroline, who suffers from nearsightedness, has lost her glasses on the plane, she compounds her chicanery by mentioning that she and Johnson are partners in a dance act being featured at the hotel nightclub. What a shame that Caroline has no glasses and can't watch a rehearsal. But the airline suddenly returns the missing spectacles and Caroline is dying to see Lucy perform with the famous movie idol. Desperate, Lucy races to Johnson's side and pleads with him for a chance to be his "partner" for just a few minutes. Lucy: "I'll name my next child after you . . . if I have one. If I don't, I'll change the name of the one I have." Johnson reluctantly agrees and, while Marco Rizo accompanies the duo on the piano, Lucy and Van dance to "How About You?" as Ethel and Caroline look on. Caroline is thrilled, envious of Lucy's being able to "rub elbows with the stars." Lucy confirms: "Our elbows are practically raw!" That night, much to Lucy's surprise and delight, Johnson phones and asks her to be his dance partner (Hazel, his usual companion, is ill). After a little initial nervousness, the nightclub number goes well. Caroline rushes backstage to congratulate Lucy and lets her know she has decided to stay an extra day in order to attend the "open house" Lucy plans to throw for all the stars.

(NOTE: Peggy Carroll created the choreography.)

"Harpo Marx"; #1050/124; May 9, 1955.

Lucy is frantic because she has promised Caroline Appleby (Doris Singleton) that there would be real movie stars at an "open house" she envisioned, assuming, of course, that Mrs. Appleby would already be on her way to Hawaii. Remembering that her New York chum is practically blind without her spectacles, Lucy and Ethel scheme to steal the eyeglasses and use movie star masks to fool her. Caroline arrives at the Ricardo suite ("Any stars yet?") whereupon Lucy quickly makes off with Appleby's glasses before excusing herself "to go next door for a cup of sugar." Meanwhile, down by the hotel pool, "sun-worshipers" Ricky and Fred encounter funnyman Harpo Marx (there for a benefit) who kindly agrees to stop by and visit Lucy. Disguised as Gary Cooper, Clark Gable, Jimmy Durante, and others, Lucy manages to fool the nearsighted friend. But suddenly, while Lucy is away changing into another disguise, Harpo Marx appears. Ethel assumes it's Lucy until Lucy herself arrives dressed as Harpo Marx. After an unusual harp rendition of "Take Me Out to the Ball Game," Harpo and Lucy enact a classic mirror bit, recreating the famous pantomime scene from one of the Marx Brothers' movies, *Duck Soup*. The episode concludes with Fred and Ricky, dressed as Chico and Groucho, making an appearance, hoping to help Lucy impress Caroline . . . who has already left for Hawaii to join husband, Charlie.

"Ricky Needs an Agent"; #1050/126; May 16, 1955.

Lucy poses as Ricky's no-nonsense, fast-talking (and nonexistent) talent agent, Lucille MacGillicuddy, when she meets with M-G-M executive ("vice-president in charge of Ricky Ricardo") Walter Reilly (Parley Baer) in an effort to pressure the studio into using Ricky in another film. Employing a well-known bargaining technique, Lucy, the agent, tells Reilly that "Dick and Oscar are just wild about the boy" and want to star the Cuban "in their next Broadway musical." Reilly quickly confers with Dore Schary by phone and then informs a speechless Miss MacGillicuddy: "Metro doesn't want to stand in Ricky's way . . . so we're releasing him from his contract." Shocked, Lucy insists M-G-M reconsider, perhaps by starring Ricardo in remakes of successful films—for instance, *Gone with the Cuban Wind; It Happened One Noche; Seven Brides for Seven Cubans; The Ricardos of Wimpole Street; Andy Hardy Meets a Conga Player; Meet Me in St. Ricky; Ricky, Son of Flicka.* But the executive is a busy man and his secretary, Miss Klein (Helen Kleeb), shows a hesitant Lucy to the door. Heartbroken and dejected, she returns to the hotel and decides to tell Ricky what she has done. As expected, his Cuban temper flairs violently and he storms out, blood in his eye. All ends happily when Lucy manages to convince the studio that "some crazy woman" is going around town impersonating Ricky's agent.

"The Tour"; #1050/127; May 30, 1955; with Barbara Pepper.

While Ricky lunches with Richard Widmark and Fred goes off to a baseball game, Lucy and Ethel embark on a Grayline Bus sightseeing tour. After taking in the local sights—the La Brea Tar Pits, Pacific Palisades, Holmby Hills—the tour winds through the tree-lined streets of Beverly Hills as the driver (Benny Rubin) points out homes owned by various movie stars—Joan Crawford, Alan Ladd, Betty Grable and Harry James, Shirley Temple, Ava Gardner. Lucy becomes obstreperous with the driver when she starts interrupting his patter. As the bus passes Richard Widmark's mansion, Lucy jumps up and addresses the tour entourage: "My husband is having lunch with Richard Widmark right now!" The bus driver is not impressed: "I'll be sure to tell Lana about it at dinner." Spying a grapefruit tree in Widmark's backyard, Lucy yearns for a souvenir to go with the autographed Robert Taylor orange she picked up at the Farmer's Market. Warned by the driver that they will be left behind if they disembark from the bus, Lucy and Ethel decide to take their chances. Getting the souvenir fruit proves more difficult than Lucy imagined—the tree is behind a huge wall that surrounds the Widmark estate. When she reaches for a sample, Lucy loses her balance and falls over the wall, getting trapped in the process. As she sneaks through the house to rejoin Ethel on the street, Widmark and Ricky arrive. Quickly, Lucy takes refuge inside a huge bearskin rug in the movie star's trophy room. When she tries sneaking out on her hands and knees, Widmark's dog Cap stops her and Lucy is exposed. Despite everything, Widmark remains a gentleman and even autographs the infamous grapefruit for Lucy.

(NOTE: Richard Widmark managed to plug his 1955 Columbia film, *A Prize of Gold.*)

"Lucy Visits Grauman's"; #1050/128; October 3, 1955.

With only a week left in Hollywood, Lucy bemoans her lack of souvenirs while Ricky inspects a box full of goodies including a tin can run over by Cary Grant's rear tire, chopsticks from Don the Beachcomber, a Robert Taylor orange and Richard Widmark grapefruit (shriveled to an unrecognizable state), menus from the Brown Derby, and a napkin boasting Lana Turner's lip-prints. Lucy's next souvenir-hunting stop—Grauman's Chinese Theatre where *The Tall Men* with Clark Gable and Jane Russell is playing. There, she and the Mertzes view the many stars' foot and handprints, imbedded in cement slabs located in the famed theater's forecourt. When Lucy notices that John Wayne's concrete prints are loose, she decides to take home a souvenir to end all souvenirs. Later that day, Lucy returns to the theater with a crowbar and pail of fresh cement, much to Ethel's apprehension. Lucy: "If you're going to get scared on a routine souvenir hunt . . ." Fred arrives in the midst of their devious doings, proclaiming the scheme "real Bellevue bait." They manage to steal the slab, but not without Lucy's foot getting stuck in the pail of wet cement. When Ricky discovers the stolen slab at the hotel, he mutters some unprintable Spanish to which Lucy retorts: "I've got a feeling it isn't 'Hot-diggity, just what I always wanted!' " He demands the "souvenir's" immediate return whereupon Lucy and Ethel drop it, causing it to break into a million tiny cement chips.

"Lucy and John Wayne"; #1050/129; October 10, 1955; with Louis A. Nicoletti.

Ricky is reading a newspaper account that describes the recent theft from Grauman's Chinese Theater of John Wayne's footprints by "a dishwater blond and a frowzy redhead." Ricardo calls the theater, explains the situation, and agrees to have the slab back before the premiere that night of *Blood Alley*, Wayne's latest film. While the girls are having their hair done by Irma, the hotel beautician, Ricky calls "the Duke" to explain the predicament. Being a good sport, the actor agrees to come to the Beverly Palms Hotel and plant his footprints in a fresh slab of cement. But when Lucy and Ethel see the replacement, they erase the impressions, assuming they are the work of "Freddie the Forger" who earlier had tried unsuccessfully to duplicate Wayne's prints. Duke is good enough to oblige a second time, but this effort is obliterated by Little Ricky (Mike Mayer) who decides to plant his own prints in the fresh mixture. Next, Lucy and Ethel sneak into Wayne's studio with another slab of wet cement, intending to ask Wayne to oblige yet a third time. Posing as the actor's masseur George, Lucy gains entrance into the star's dressing room, but the deception doesn't work. Finally, Wayne arranges for "a six-month supply" of prints, and the gals are relieved to learn they will not have to face theft charges.

(NOTE: The *I Love Lucy* hairdresser was named Irma Kusely. . . . The September 16, 1955, *Daily Variety* reported that John Wayne "was enjoying his guest stint with Lucille and Desi.")

"Lucy and the Dummy"; #1050/130; October 17, 1955.

When Chip Jackson of M-G-M asks Ricky to perform at a studio party to be attended by the executives, he refuses, preferring to go deep-sea fishing instead. However, Lucy has other ideas and tells Jackson that Ricky will be glad to appear. Using a rubber replica of Ricky's head attached to a stuffed dummy (Lucy calls it "Raggedy Ricky"), Lucy steals the spotlight as she dances to "I Get Ideas." In the middle of the number, Lucy dramatically announces that "Ricky" has taken ill, and she drags the dummy into the wings. Lucy completes the act herself—"The show must go on," she insists—but the dummy gets caught on her Spanish *señorita* outfit, refusing to come loose. The performance is hilarious, and the studio offers her a one-year contract as a comedienne. She dreams of the big career in show business she has wanted for so long, but her allegiance to Ricky and the baby comes first and she decides to turn down the studio offer.

"Ricky Sells the Car"; #1050/131; October 24, 1955.

When Ricky manages to sell the Pontiac convertible to Ralph Berger at M-G-M for more than he originally paid for it, he decides to return east via train, utilizing the economical "family plan." But what about the Mertzes who traveled to California in the car with them? Ethel: "I presume that when he sold the car, the back seat went with it." Lucy assures her friends that Ricky hasn't forgotten them, but when the envelope containing only three Union Pacific Domeliner tickets arrives, it becomes painfully evident that Ricky has. Feelings hurt, Fred and Ethel leave in a huff and prepare to journey cross-country on a $50 antique Harley-Davidson. When Ricky returns from the studio after saying his good-byes and learns of his oversight, he and Lucy rush to the hotel garage where they find their "former" friends ready to depart on the luggage-laden cycle. The Mertzes' trip, however, is short-lived—Fred accidentally backs the vintage contraption into a brick wall. Ricky agrees to buy the Mertzes train tickets, but is unable to secure compartments for them, only a pair of upper berths. Unaware of this situation, Lucy gives the expensive tickets to her friends and now has to figure out a way to switch them. Ricky: "You're vice-president in charge of sneaky switches." After much calculated confusion, including Ethel's mistaken belief that Lucy has the hots for Fred, the easterners are ready to return home.

(NOTE: Desilu's head scenic designer was named Ralph Berger.)

"The Great Train Robbery"; #1050/132; October 31, 1955; with Louis A. Nicoletti, Sam McDaniel.

Having safely boarded the New York-bound train, Lucy realizes she has left her purse containing the tickets on the Union Station platform. With just a few moments before the scheduled departure, Ricky rushes off to retrieve the pocketbook while Lucy pleads with the conductor (Frank Nelson) to hold the train. He flatly refuses, so Lucy is left with no alternative but to pull the emergency brake, causing the train to come to an abrupt halt. Conductor: "Madame, did you stop this train by pulling that handle?" Lucy: "Well, I didn't do it by dragging my foot." A mixup with Mrs. MacGillicuddy's (Kathryn Card) tickets results in Lucy having a run-in with a gun-wielding jewelry salesman (Lou Krugman) when she assumes he is responsible for her "missing" mother and son. Panicked, Lucy pulls the emergency brake again. When questioned by a detective (Joseph Crehan) concerning a jewel thief suspected of being aboard the train, Lucy warns the shamus about the gun-toting man in the next compartment. However, the real jewel thief (Harry Bartell) fools Lucy into believing he's with the FBI and wants her to cooperate with him in locating the salesman with the valuable jewelry collection. When Lucy realizes that she's made a mistake, she again beats a hasty path to the emergency brake. The ensuing chaos permits the criminal to be captured, and Lucy winds up a heroine.

"Homecoming"; #1050/133; November 7, 1955; with Bennett Green.

Upon their return to Gotham, Lucy and the Mertzes are surprised to learn that Ricky has suddenly become a famous celebrity. His many fans clamor for a chance to get a glimpse of the star who Mrs. Trumbull (Elizabeth Patterson) calls "another Valentino." Lucy is a bit plussed by all the attention Ricky is getting, so when reporter Nancy Graham (Elvia Allman) requests an interview with *her*, she is delighted. Graham arrives for "The Lucy Ricardo Story" and Lucy begins her prerehearsed tale: "I was born Lucille MacGillicuddy in the thriving metropolis of Jamestown, New York, in nineteen. . . . Let's just say I was born. I graduated Jamestown High School in. . . . Let's just say I graduated four years after I began. . . ." Lucy soon realizes, much to her ego's chagrin, that Graham only wants to know about . . . him. "Him" is Ricky Ricardo. The reporter convinces Lucy that her movie star husband is "special," that he now "belongs to the world." This prompts Lucy to begin treating Ricky like a king. The overattention is more than Ricky can stand, so he decides to teach his devoted wife a lesson by becoming "the most revolting movie star" she's ever encountered. He has her shining his shoes, typing his song lyrics, cooking his favorite meals, lighting his cigarette, and answering his phone calls—all at the same time. His demands become so insistent, so beleaguering that Lucy finally rebels: "You can shine your own shoes! . . . And if you want another roast pig, you can crawl in the oven yourself, you big ham!" Ricky is happy to have Lucy back as a wife, instead of a fan.

"The Ricardos Are Interviewed"; #1050/134; November 14, 1955.

Lucy and Ricky are scheduled to make a TV appearance on a

Person to Person-type interview program, *Face to Face,* hosted by Ed Warren (Elliott Reid). Since the show is to originate from the Ricardos' meager East Sixty-eighth Street digs, Ricky's new agent Johnny Clark (John Gallaudet) suggests that the pair move to a more fitting abode on swanky Park Avenue. Lucy, of course, does not want to leave the Mertzes, and vice versa. But with only good intentions in mind, Fred and Ethel deliberately pick a fight with the Ricardos, hoping they'll pack up and move to a better address. This ploy eventually results in an all-out fight, culminating in the severing of friendly relations between the two couples. The night of the TV show, the Ricardos and Mertzes try hard to be civil to each other, but another argument breaks out . . . on the air.

(NOTE: John Gallaudet was one of William Frawley's closest friends and a pallbearer at the latter's 1966 funeral.)

"Lucy Goes to a Rodeo"; #1050/135; November 28, 1955.

Fred wants Ricky to perform in his lodge show next Friday, but the Cuban can't oblige—he's scheduled to do a radio show that day. However, Lucy and Ethel offer their talents for the lodge shindig, suggesting *The Pleasant Peasant* operetta that their ladies' club staged a while ago. Fred prefers a Western theme for the lodge show and enlists the services of his old friend Rattlesnake Jones (Dub Taylor) who's in town to see his brother perform in a Madison Square Garden rodeo. Fred and Ethel audition for Jones by singing "Birmingham Jail," and Lucy tries out by yodeling "Home On the Range." Her lousy performance prompts Jones to suggest she try her hand at bell-ringing the melody of "Down By the Old Mill Stream." Suddenly, Ricky learns from his agent Johnny Clark (John Gallaudet) that the radio show date is really a rodeo show engagement. Desperate because he has to put together a Western show in two days, Ricky even hires Lucy and the Mertzes to appear with him at the Garden show. After Ricky's rousing rendition of "Texas Pete" ("Cuban Pete" with a cowboy hat), the rodeo announcer introduces "Lucille Cannonball MacGillicuddy and Her Western Bell-Ringers."

"Nursery School"; #1050/136; December 5, 1955; with the Mayer twins, Jesslyn Fax.

Ricky wants his son to attend nursery school, but Lucy doesn't share his scholarly enthusiasm. After reading from Dr. Spock's book— "Nursery school doesn't take the place of home . . ."—Lucy thinks the subject is closed. Ricky reads on: ". . . it adds to it. It is particularly valuable for the only child, for the child without much chance to play with others, for the child who lives in a small apartment." Ricky believes Spock's baby-care bible. Lucy: "What does he know? He was never a mother!" However, Ricky prevails and the boy is sent off to nursery school. He enjoys the experience, and all the adults seem pleased, until young Ricky develops a cold. Lucy blames the school: It's a hotbed of bacteria!" The child's pediatrician Dr. Gittelman (Olan

Soule) diagnoses the problem as tonsillitis and suggests a tonsilectomy. When Lucy learns she is not permitted to spend the night with Little Ricky in his hospital room (#602), she disguises herself as a nurse and creates untold hospital havoc. Ricky comes looking for his wife and finds her curled up in Little Ricky's hospital crib, fast asleep.

"Ricky's European Booking"; #1050/137; December 12, 1955; with Hazel Pierce, Harry Antrim, Barney Phillips.

See text p. 127.

"The Passports"; #1050/138; December 19, 1955.

Lucy needs her birth certificate if she intends to apply for a passport; and the Jamestown bureau of statistics has no record of her being born. However, passport officials assure Ricky that if Lucy can produce two people willing to sign affidavits swearing that they have known her since birth, they will waive the birth certificate requirement. Consequently, Lucy heads straight for her former baby-sitter Helen Kaiser Erickson (Sheila Bromley) who now lives in Manhattan. Helen is just about to put her signature on the paper when her lawyer-husband, Sidney, arrives. He takes one look at the document and refuses to allow his wife to sign it. It seems that Helen has apparently lied about her age to Sidney and couldn't possibly have been Lucy's baby-sitter. Lucy's frantic and even threatens to stow away in a steamer trunk. Trying one on for size, she promptly gets locked in. When Dr. Peterson, the MacGillicuddy family physician, arrives to identify Lucy for the passport people, he is unable to see her to make a positive identification. But when Lucy recalls a song that she and the old doctor used to sing years ago, "Skip to My Lou," Peterson is certain that the girl inside the trunk is Lucille MacGillicuddy. Lucy later learns she was born in West Jamestown when a special-delivery letter from her mother arrives with the needed certificate.

"Staten Island Ferry"; #1050/139; January 2, 1956.

Fred suddenly remembers he suffers from seasickness. Lucy tries to allay his fears, insisting the problem only exists on small vessels: "We're going on the *Constitution*, one of the best." A visit to the huge liner fails to relieve Fred of his doubts; he gets sick even though the ship is tied to the dock. Lucy suggests some new seasickness pills and a trial run on the Staten Island Ferry as a surefire cure. Before embarking on the ferry trip, Lucy is reminded that the Passport Office closes at 5 P.M.; she must be back before then to file her application. Amid the "high" seas of New York harbor, Fred does fine, thanks to the pills. Lucy, on the other hand, begins to feel queasy, so she swallows a handful of seasickness tablets, unaware of their side effects. After five trips to Staten Island, a ferry attendant awakens the two, fast asleep on a bench. With only six minutes left to apply for their passports, Lucy and Fred burst into the government office where the officious clerk (Charles Lane) tries desperately to get sleepyhead Lucy to sign the application. It's a comedy of errors that ends happily for the four travelers.

"Bon Voyage"; #1050/140; January 16, 1956; with Jack Albertson, Ken Christy.

After a brief bon voyage party in their *Constitution* stateroom, the Ricardos join the Mertzes on the ship's deck to wave their final good-byes to Little Ricky, Mrs. MacGillicuddy (Kathryn Card), and Mrs. Trumbull (Elizabeth Patterson). Lucy can't bear to leave her little son and rushes off the ready-to-sail ship to give the baby one last kiss. While saying her final farewells on the dock, Lucy's skirt gets caught in the chain of a Western Union messenger's bike. She struggles valiantly to free herself, finally slipping out of her skirt completely, but, alas, she misses the boat. Advised to catch the pilot boat that would take her to the *Constitution,* she misses that too, leaping bravely aboard the boat coming in, not the one going out. It is next suggested that she hire a helicopter at Idlewild; high above New York harbor, Lucy begins to have second thoughts about going to Europe at all. The chopper pilot (Frank Gerstle) assures her there is nothing to worry about as he slowly lowers the tardy voyager onto the deck of the London-bound liner.

(NOTE: Goateed *Lucy* writer Bob Carroll, Jr., can be seen standing beside Vivian Vance in the bon voyage scene.)

"Second Honeymoon"; #1050/141; January 23, 1956; with Marco Rizo, Louis A. Nicoletti.

The romantic shipboard atmosphere, coupled with the fresh sea air has rekindled the Mertzes' twenty-five-year-long marriage. Ethel: "The love bug has bitten my Freddie." Lucy is a little jealous; she and Ricky have been unable to spend any time together because of his band commitment. Understanding his wife's loneliness, Ricky suggests she sign up for some tournaments in the hopes of meeting new friends. Lucy asks the ship's social director to find her a Ping-Pong partner, but he has trouble finding someone single "since there are mostly couples." Lucy: "With everyone paired off, I'm surprised the ship isn't called the S.S. *Noah's Ark!*" A partner finally materializes—Kenneth Hamilton (Harvey Grant)—and he is, indeed, single. Unfortunately, he's also only elementary school age. The precocious youngster becomes Lucy's constant companion (they win the Ping-Pong championship) and even dances with her in the Boat 'n' Bottle Bar that night. Desperate for some time to spend alone with Ricky, Lucy plots to "kidnap" her own husband the next evening. While he is dressing for the show, Lucy locks their stateroom door and tosses the key through the porthole to Ethel. But much to Lucy's surprise, Ricky has managed to get the night off, planning an entire evening of dining and dancing. In a frantic effort to locate Ethel, Lucy sticks her head through the porthole and then finds she's unable to free herself. It takes men with acetylene torches to free Lucy, but Ricky still manages a romantic serenade.

"Lucy Meets the Queen"; #1050/142; January 30, 1956.

In London, Ricky tries to explain the confusing British monetary system to Lucy, who has trouble even with dollars and cents. She reacts: "No wonder the people left here to go to America." Sightseeing at Buckingham Palace, Lucy and Ethel encounter a smileless palace guard and decide to get him to break a time-honored tradition by making him laugh. LUCY: "Did you hear about the book the dog psychiatrist wrote? . . . *Is Your Cocker Off His Rocker? . . . Is Your Poodle Off His Noodle? . . . Collie Off His Trolley?*" Nothing works; the guard remains steadfastly stoic. Lucy soon finds out that Ricky is to be presented to the Queen after his London Palladium performance. Knowing that only performers are allowed a royal audience, she desperately wants to be a part of the circus-themed revue. Despite a cramp in her knee, caused by overpracticing her curtsies, Lucy does fine as a dancer, until a big leap in the finale results in a severe charley horse. Unable to effect the required bow, Lucy must pass up her one and only chance to meet the Queen. Suddenly, Ricky rushes backstage and tells her that Her Majesty wants to meet the girl who did the wonderful comedy dance routine.

"The Fox Hunt"; #1050/143; February 6, 1955; with Trevor Ward.

Lucy is jealous after Ricky danced the night away with Angela Randall (Hillary Brooke), a budding British starlet, but he claims he was only trying to be polite. Lucy plots to get Ricky out of London, and away from Miss Randall, by persuading Sir Clive Richardson (Walter Kingsford), an English movie producer, to invite the Ricardos and Mertzes to his Berkshire Manor estate for the weekend. After going to great pains to wangle the invitation, Lucy is shocked to discover that Angela Randall is the stage name of Angela Richardson, Sir Clive's attractive daughter. Lucy attempts to cancel the weekend visit by saying she forgot about the cricket matches, but Sir Clive reminds her that this is not cricket season. Lucy: "Well, these are young crickets." At the Richardsons' country estate, Lucy is introduced to her horse for the hunt, Danny Boy, whose size frightens the New Yorker. Lucy: "Do you have a large lamb?" After a number of false starts, Lucy is off on her first fox hunt. Many hours later, Lucy hobbles into the stable area, *sans* Daddy Boy, covered with brambles. Lucy: "I have a strange feeling I'm not alone." She isn't—she's sharing the tangle of brush with the fox. Lucy has won the hunt!

"Lucy Goes to Scotland"; #1050/144; February 20, 1956.

About to leave Blighty and with no available time to visit the home of her Scottish ancestors, Lucy dreams of the MacGillicuddy clan's village Kildoonan. She returns to the friendly little town, expecting to be welcomed with open arms. The townspeople welcome her joyously in song, "A MacGillicuddy Is Here," but then inform her that she has returned just in time to be fed to a terrible two-headed dragon that appears every thirty years to appease his appetite with a MacGillicuddy and Lucy is the last available member of the clan. Enter Scotty MacTavish MacDougal MacCardo (Ricky Ricardo in kilts), son of Enchilada MacCardo who came to Scotland on the Spanish Armada. Lucy and Scotty quickly fall in love and he promises to defend her against the hungry two-headed beast. He sings "I'm in Love with a Dragon's Dinner." The Dragon (Fred and Ethel) appears and sings "Two Heads Are Better Than One," then listens to Lucille and Scotty trying to talk him out of his high-calorie plans. When the time arrives for Scotty to save Lucille, he loses his courage. Awakened by her nightmare, Lucy pelts Ricky with her pillow, shouting, "You coward!" Other songs by Larry Orenstein, who also portrayed the mayor of Kildoonan, included " 'Tis Nae a Braw Bricht Nicht" and "Dragon Waltz."

(NOTE: Lucille Ball is part Scottish.)

"Paris at Last"; #1050/145; February 27, 1956; with Fritz Feld.

On a sidewalk in gay Paree, Lucy encounters a friendly Frenchman (Lawrence Dobkin) who offers to exchange her American dollars for francs, at a rate of 450f for every buck (a bonus of 100f). The generous guy claims "low overhead" as the reason why he can be so benevolent, so Lucy gladly exchanges $20 for 9,000 francs. Nearby, she admires the work of a Parisian painter (Shepard Menken) and eagerly purchases his "masterpiece" for 1,000f. Fred and Ethel happen along, and Lucy shares her sudden "wealth" with them, exchanging $10 of Fred's money. Next stop for Lucy, while the Mertzes enjoy a conducted tour of the city, is lunch at a typical sidewalk café, *A La Porte Montmartre*. When the waiter (Maurice Marsac) brings her *escargot*, she grimaces: "Waiter, there are snails in this food." She can hardly bring herself to eat them ("I think one of your American cousins ate my geranium."), so asks the waiter for a bottle of ketchup. When the chef (Rolfe Sedan) learns of her gauche request, he creates such a ruckus that Lucy decides to pay the check and leave. Suddenly, she is accosted by a gendarme—and accused of passing counterfeit francs. Hauled off to the Bastille, she summons Ricky from their Hotel Royale suite, lamenting: "Nobody speaks English. They're all foreigners!" Ricardo rushes to her rescue and through a cleverly devised translation method (featuring a German drunk who speaks Spanish and a French cop who speaks German) manages to clear his confused wife of counterfeiting charges.

(NOTE: Bob Carroll, Jr., was featured in the sidewalk café scene. . . . In the same sequence, the *Lucy* prop department made an error by placing a bottle of California wine—Paul Masson—on the table.)

"Lucy Meets Charles Boyer"; #1050/146; March, 5, 1956.

When Lucy and Ethel spy handsome Charles Boyer seated alone at an outdoor café in Paris, they prepare to carry out their usual movie star assault. While the girls powder their noses, Ricky, fearing the worst, approaches Boyer and warns him about his wife—the scourge of Hollywood. Forewarned, Boyer decides to play a little trick on Lucy. When she sits down at his table, he tells her that his name is Maurice DuBois, he's a struggling actor, and he is annoyed that so many people mistake him for Boyer. Satisfied, but disappointed, Lucy departs. Later that day, she reads an item in Art Buchwald's column that Ricky is supposed to meet with Boyer regarding a possible acting assignment on his *Four Star Playhouse* TV series. Naturally, she begs to tag along. Feigning a king's case of jealousy, Ricky forbids it. This prompts Lucy to prove her faithfulness by hiring Charles Boyer-look-alike Maurice DuBois to pose as the famous actor and have him un-successfully flirt with her in Ricky's presence. When Boyer/DuBois arrives at the Ricardos' Hotel Royale suite, he proceeds to make love to Lucy who responds by nonchalantly peeling an orange. But when Ethel tips off Lucy that Ricky is playing a trick on her and that DuBois really *is* Charles Boyer, she nearly chokes on the fruit and becomes totally flustered by the presence of the French star.

(NOTE: The Arnazes' real-life agent, Don Sharpe, was mentioned in this episode.)

"Lucy Gets a Paris Gown"; #1050/147; March 19, 1956.

Lucy decides to go on a hunger strike until Ricky agrees to buy her a Jacques Marcel dress. The plan works perfectly (even though Ethel has been smuggling food to Lucy)—Ricky finally gives in and buys her an expensive outfit. Eager to take a picture of her in the high-fashion gown, Ricky goes looking for their camera, only to find a roast chicken in its place (Lucy: "It's a 3-D picture of a roast chicken?"). Angered by Lucy's deviousness, Ricky returns the dress. Then, he plots with Fred to get even with his wife. He employs a local tailor to put together some crazy outfits made from burlap potato sacks, along with hats improvised from a horse's feedbag and a res-taurant ice bucket, and presents them to the girls with Jacques Marcel labels sewn in. Thrilled, the wives proudly strut down the street with their Paris originals. But Ricky and Fred can't contain their secret any longer, and break down laughing. To punish the husbands, the girls demand *real* Jacques Marcel outfits, at a total cost of $500. Much to their dismay the next day, Lucy and Ethel spot Marcel's gorgeous models wearing the exact copies of their burlap-sack fashions. Un-fortunately, the gals have burned theirs, the originals.

"Lucy in the Swiss Alps"; #1050/148; March 26, 1956.

When band manager Fred fouls up by sending the orchestra to Locarno, Switzerland, instead of Lucerne, Lucy tries to appease Ricky's ruffled nerves by suggesting a healthy hike in the Alps. All goes well until an unexpected snowstorm forces the foursome into a deserted mountaintop cabin. Lucy hints that an avalanche, like the one featured in *Seven Brides for Seven Brothers,* could prove fatal. Moments later, she makes the dreadful mistake of slamming the shack's door, causing a mountain of snow to cover the tiny cabin. After being trapped for five hours, the victims become famished. Suddenly, Lucy remembers a sandwich in her knapsack; she quietly attempts to devour it without the others discovering her treasure. No such luck—the Mertzes and Ricky pounce on her for a portion of the food. After they've polished off the last crumb, Ethel reveals she would prefer dying with a clear conscience—she confesses she wasn't eighteen when she married Fred, but nineteen. Fred: "I've got news for you— you were twenty-four!" Fred clears his soul by telling the Ricardos he's charged them an extra $10 a month in rent; Ethel reveals she gave back the sawbuck every month. When asked if he would like to get something off his chest, Ricky responds: "I'm no fool. . . . We might be saved!" Within seconds, the distant sound of music is heard, and they are rescued by a Bavarian band playing "La Cucaracha."

"Lucy Gets Homesick"; #1050/149; April 9, 1956.

In Florence, Italy, four thousand miles away from Little Ricky on his birthday, Lucy suddenly has the motherly urge to phone New York and speak to her son. Making the transatlantic call is a problem in itself, compounded by the fact that the hotel's only phone is located in the lobby and the Ricardos' "bridal suite" (room 47) is on the fourth floor. To make matters worse, the elevator isn't working. While Lucy is waiting for the long-distance call to go through, a street urchin shoeshine boy, Giuseppe (Bart Bradley), wanders into the lobby, offering to shine Mrs. Ricardo's shoes. While he is several years older than Little Ricky, Lucy can't help but get teary-eyed at the thought of being so far away from her own boy. Finally, the call comes through, and Ricky and the Mertzes descend the many flights of stairs to be beside Lucy during the conversation. Unfortunately, it's 5 A.M. in New York when Mrs. MacGillicuddy (Kathryn Card) answers the phone and Lucy sadly decides not to have her mother wake the child. Lucy tries phoning the next day, but this time Little Ricky is in nursery school. Heartbroken, Lucy decides to hold a birthday party for Little Ricky in absentia with the shoeshine boy as the guest of honor (it's his birthday too—he's eight and a half). Soon the party grows to enormous proportions—eleven Italian bambinos, each claiming a birthday, arrive for the gala affair. In the midst of the festivities, Ricky summons Lucy to the lobby telephone—he's managed to get through to Little Ricky in New York. With tears in her eyes, Lucy wishes her son a happy birthday, and the foreign children sing the birthday song to him in Italian.

"Lucy's Italian Movie"; #1050/150; April 16, 1956.

En route to Rome by train, Lucy is spotted by famous Italian cinema director Vittorio Fellipi (Franco Corsaro) and chosen to play a part in his new movie, *Bitter Grapes*. Assuming the picture concerns the Italian wine industry, Lucy sets out to immerse herself in the role. In an effort to "soak up some local color," she journeys to Turo, a small town on the outskirts of Rome, well known for its traditional winemaking methods. Dressed in typical peasant clothes and carrying a cluster of grapes, Lucy nonchalantly wanders into a vineyard inhabited by a motley conglomeration of Italian-speaking women. When the male supervisor spots Lucy's feet (one of the local women likens them to "big pizzas"), she is quickly dispatched to the winemaking area. Lucy steps into the huge, grape-filled vat along with a local gal, Teresa (Teresa Tirelli), and the two proceed to stomp the grapes into chianti. Lucy finds the work fun and has a great time skipping through the mush and frolicking with her co-worker. When the diversion wears off and Lucy decides to take a short rest, her partner disapproves. This difference of opinion leads to a grape fight as Lucy and Teresa battle it out in the wine vat, scrapping like street urchins. Grape-stained and defeated, Lucy returns to her Rome hotel where filmmaker Fellipi awaits her. He explains, somewhat belatedly, that the film has nothing to do with the grape industry; the title is merely symbolic. Her part was to be that of a typical American tourist. In her present condition, Mrs. Ricardo will be unable to begin filming her scene the next day. Lucy: "Can't I be an American who's so homesick, she's blue?" No, says Vittorio . . . who turns around and hires Ethel for the role.

"Lucy's Bicycle Trip"; #1050/151; April 23, 1956.

After an exhausting day bicycling from Italy toward the French Riviera, the Ricardos and Mertzes decide to look for a place to spend the night. The terrain is rural and the best accommodations are to be found in the barn of a friendly farmer. With fresh hay as mattresses and a cow as a roommate, the four tired travelers bed down for the night. Bright and early the next morning, the peasant host arrives with their breakfast—cheese and a huge loaf of Italian bread. To wash it down—milk. Unfortunately, the milk is still inside the cow and it becomes Lucy's task to coax it into a pail. Rested and satiated, the bikers continue their journey toward Nice, coming to a stop at the Italian and French border. Everyone but Lucy is permitted to cross the guard-patrolled border for her passport is in a purse that was sent ahead to Nice with the rest of the luggage. Reluctantly, Ricky and Fred bicycle on to Nice to retrieve the required passport. Remaining behind at the border, Lucy and Ethel find it impossible to persuade the rule-spouting guards to allow her to pass without the document. When Ricky phones from the Plaza Hotel in Nice, unable to unlock the suitcase containing the pocketbook that holds the passport, Lucy realizes she has the key with her. Ethel is sent to Nice with the key, as Lucy remains behind at the boundary gate. More confusion reigns before the mixup is unraveled, but Lucy finally is on her way to Nice for the next leg of her European trip.

"Lucy Goes to Monte Carlo"; #1050/152; May 7, 1956.

Upon their arrival in Monte Carlo, Ricky forbids Lucy to go near the gambling casino, suggesting instead that she and Ethel have dinner and go to a movie. The women enjoy their dinner at Le Grill restaurant, which just *happens* to be in the casino. Strolling out, Lucy spots a chip on the floor and, being unable to find its owner, places it on the roulette table. Moments later, she is 875,000 francs richer. Frightened by Ricky's possible reaction, Lucy chooses to hide the money in Ethel's lingerie case. When Ricky accidentally opens the valise, looking for Fred's band accounts, he discovers the loot and accuses Mertz of embezzlement. A fierce argument commences, and Fred quits as band manager. To save the fifteen-year friendship, Lucy tells the husbands that the money belongs to Ethel who inherited it from her French aunt, Yvette. Fred: "You mean my little honeybunch is loaded?" Lucy finally confesses the truth and then decides to get rid of the "ill-gotten gains." She rushes down to the casino and proceeds to gamble away the money. Meanwhile, Ricky has learned the truth about the bundle of cash and he's delighted about Lucy's good fortune. But by the time he reaches the gambling palace to tell Lucy she can keep the cash, Lucy has already lost the fortune.
(NOTE: The gambler wearing the fez in the early casino scenes was Bob Carroll, Jr., *Lucy* writer.)

"Return Home from Europe"; #1050/153; May 14, 1956.

The Ricardos and Mertzes are packing for their Pan American Airlines flight (#155) home when Ricky warns his souvenir-crazy wife that any baggage over sixty-six pounds will cost extra to ship. She finds it impossible to leave anything behind, particularly a twenty-five-pound hunk of rare Italian cheese, a gift for her mother. Assuming babies travel free, Lucy disguises the cheese as an infant and smuggles it aboard the aircraft. Seated next to her during the flight is Mrs. Evelyn Bixby (Mary Jane Croft), mother of four-month-old Carolyn. To be friendly, Mrs. Bixby asks Lucy what her baby is named. Lucy: "Cheddar, er . . . *Chester!*" When the stewardess offers to warm the babies' bottles, Lucy tells her she didn't bring any, adding: "He's too fat anyway." Being a good neighbor, Mrs. Bixby offers Lucy one of Carolyn's bottles. When the heated bottle is presented, Lucy gulps its contents: "He doesn't like to drink by himself." One hour into the flight, Lucy learns that babies do not travel free and that passage will cost $30. Ethel and she attempt to solve the problem by devouring the mammoth hunk of cheese. When Lucy returns to her seat minus little Chester and lets Mrs. Bixby in on her gag, the woman screams. In New York, a U.S. Customs official (Frank Nelson) is trying to piece together the details. Meanwhile, a newsreel cameraman (Louis A. Nicoletti) is itching to get footage on Ricky and the band who are about to open at the Roxy Theatre. When the musicians attempt to play "Home Sweet Home," the music they make is silent. Leave it to Lucy—she stuffed the instruments with the cheese ("the trombone was easy, but that piccolo . . .").

1956–1957

"Lucy and Bob Hope"; #1050/154; October 1, 1956; with Phil Leeds, Lou Krugman, Henry Kulky, Dick Elliott, Bennett Green.

Lucy, the Mertzes, and Little Ricky (Richard Keith) are attending a Cleveland Indians–New York Yankees baseball game at Yankee Stadium when Bob Hope shows up. This is the perfect opportunity for Lucy to talk to Hope about appearing at Ricky's new night spot, the Club Babalu. Disguising herself as a moustachioed hot dog vendor, Lucy gains admittance to the box section where the comedian is seated. Matters take a dark turn as Lucy's distracting antics cause a foul ball to strike Hope on the head. Summoned to the ballpark to confer with Bob about the opening night material, Ricky finds the funnyman treating the bump on his head in the Indians' locker room. Enter Lucy, dressed as a ballplayer, making a second stab at persuading Hope to appear at Ricky's club. When she sees her husband, Lucy attempts to escape, but Ricky pulls her back. The two performers discuss a possible bit for the show, and naturally Lucy wants in. Ricky naturally says no. But Lucy later makes a plea to Mr. Hope: "You have no idea how talented I am." He believes her and demands that she be a part of the baseball song trio. At the nightclub's grand opening, Bob Hope and the Ricardos sing "Nobody Loves the Ump," and Hope does a special-material version of his theme song, "Thanks for the Memories." (NOTE: Ten years prior to this filming, Desi Arnaz was the orchestra leader on Hope's NBC radio show. . . . Jack Baker choreographed the baseball number. . . . This was Richard Keith's debut as Little Ricky.)

"Little Ricky Learns to Play the Drums"; #1050/157; October 8, 1956.

Even though the Ricardos made a solemn promise not to influence their son's future, Lucy buys the boy a doctor's kit and Ricky gets him a little snare drum. The five-year-old opts for the shiny new drum from Schirmer's Music Store, and there begins a four-day nonstop concert consisting of a monotonous but rhythmic beat. The sound becomes so unbearable that Lucy and Ricky find themselves functioning to the unending beat. When Lucy squeezes oranges for Ricky's juice, she does it to the rhythm of Little Ricky's drumming. When she scrapes his toast, a similar situation prevails. Even the Mertzes, godparents of the little musician, are ready for straitjackets. The landlords

256

decide to politely ask the Ricardos to have the child "limit" his playing. Ethel: "Just to give his little hands a rest." But the Mertzes' true feelings are exposed when the youngster pauses momentarily. Fred: "What a relief! I thought he'd never quit!" Ethel tries to soften Fred's statement: "He's just amazed at the child's stamina. He didn't think anybody could keep up that *racket* for four whole days!" Naturally, an argument ensues, and Fred threatens eviction, despite the Ricardos' ninety-nine-year lease. To force their departure, Fred turns off the tenant's water, gas, and electricity. As Lucy and Ricky are about to retaliate by subjecting their landlords to a rousing drum version of the "Nurtz to the Mertz Mambo," another verbal battle begins. Mrs. Trumbull (Elizabeth Patterson) halts World War III when she becomes concerned about Little Ricky who has apparently disappeared. After a frantic search, they find him curled up on the Mertzes' sofa fast asleep—the noise was too much for him.

"Lucy Meets Orson Welles"; #1050/155; October 15, 1956; with Lou Krugman, Jack Rice.

Lucy is denied a vacation to Florida, until Ricky learns that Orson Welles has agreed to appear in a benefit at the club. To keep his meddling spouse away from the actor, Ricky changes his mind and gladly gives Lucy enough money for her Florida trip. While trying on skin-diving equipment at Macy's, she and Ethel encounter Mr. Welles who is autographing copies of his latest record album. Dressed in a wet suit and flippers, Lucy hobbles over to Orson and immediately starts bragging to the Shakespearean expert about her wonderful performance as Juliet in a Jamestown High School production. When Welles learns Lucy's name, he offers her the part of his assistant in the act he plans to do at Ricky's Club Babalu. Lucy, of course, assumes the act is a scene from Shakespeare and proudly informs her high school drama teacher, Miss Hanna (Ellen Corby). On the night of the benefit, Miss Hanna and a group of aspiring student-actors arrive to witness Lucy's stellar Shakespearean performance. What they are treated to is a little bit of the Bard and a whole lot of prestidigitation. During Welles's brilliant levitation trick, Lucy says: "Romeo, Romeo, where for art thou, Romeo? . . . Get me down from here, Romeo."

"Little Ricky Gets Stage Fright"; #1050/156; October 22, 1956.

Just prior to his first music school recital, Little Ricky is gripped by a full-blown case of stage fright, touched off by the nervous attentions of his parents and the Mertzes. The little drummer's teacher, Mr. Crawford (Howard McNear), urges Lucy and Ricky to treat the problem like the classic falling-off-a-horse syndrome. Little Ricky must get right back on the horse, or, in this case, play the drums in public. When Lucy suggests that her son play at the Club Babalu, Ricky agrees. Now the tough part—convincing Little Ricky to do it. Ethel employs reverse psychology: "Little Ricky, you don't want to play those nasty old drums, do you?" Her attempt, like Lucy's, fails. Using a tiny windup toy, Ricky manages to persuade his son to display his musical talents at the club. The night of the performance, the ukelele player, Earl Robey, comes down with the measles, which sends Little Ricky into another nervous spin; he refuses to play without his strumming cohort. It's Lucy to the rescue as she dons a striped blazer and joins "Ricky, Jr., and His Dixieland Band" as they perform an upbeat version of "Has Anybody Seen My Gal?"

"Visitor from Italy"; #1050/158; October 29, 1956; with Aldo Formica, Louis A. Nicoletti.

The Ricardos and Mertzes are surprised when the Venetian gondolier they met during their European travels, Mario Orsatti (Jay Novello), arrives in New York to visit his brother Dominic (Peter Brocco). When Mario discovers a note on his brother's door explaining that he's at Sam Francesco, Lucy helps by translating the message to mean that Dominic is in San Francisco, three thousand miles away. But with only $10 to his name, Mario cannot afford the bus fare to California. Club Babalu owner Ricky obliges by giving the gondolier a job as a busboy. Disaster strikes, and Mario soon finds another job at Mr. Martinelli's (Eduardo Ciannelli) pizza parlor. A visit by an Immigration official (James Flavin) reveals that Mario is working illegally since he has no work permit and is in the United States on a tourist visa. Realizing that he may be deported if he returns to work at the pizza place, Lucy substitutes for her foreign friend by donning the apron of a pizza chef and setting about to fashion her first pie. Lucy makes pizza like she does everything else—hilariously—and is fired after the fiasco. Ricky ends up paying for Mario's bus fare to San Francisco and the $210.33 in damages to the pizza restaurant, just before learning from Mario's brother Dominic that he is not in San Francisco, but was visiting his sick friend, Sam Francesco.

"Off to Florida"; #1050/159; November 12, 1956.

When Lucy misplaces two train tickets to Florida, she and Ethel consult the classified section, hoping to "share a ride" with someone who's driving south. They team up with a peculiar middle-aged woman, Mrs. Grundy (Elsa Lanchester), who's bent on getting to Florida in record time. The health-food fanatic even refuses to stop for meals, preferring to dine on watercress sandwiches while she drives. Lucy and Ethel are famished, and the prospect of one of Grundy's gastronomical delights does not overwhelm the two tag-along travelers. Lucy: "Very tasty, if you like buttered grass." While traversing the back roads of South Carolina, Mrs. Grundy's convertible develops a flat tire, and Lucy and Ethel are called upon to fix it. Grundy: "You'll find everything you need in the trunk." Ethel: "I hope we find a mechanic in there." Exhausted after their tire-changing travails, the girls fall asleep, only to be awakened by a radio broadcast:

"Evelyn Holmby, the famed hatchet murderess, has escaped from a New York State prison and is believed to be heading south in a cream-colored convertible." The gals panic—they're riding in a similar car and they found a hatchet in the trunk while searching for the jack. Before they have time to escape, the lady driver, having slept a few hours in a sleeping bag, reappears and continues driving toward Miami. While the girls are dozing, Mrs. Grundy hears a radio report that leads her to believe that Lucy and Ethel are the wanted criminals. The trio finally stops at a roadside café, hoping to get help. Instead, Grundy slips out and quickly drives off, leaving the New Yorkers stranded. The café owner (Strother Martin) then informs Lucy and Ethel that the hatchet murderess has already been captured in Kentucky. Defeated, tired, and broke, they hitch a ride on a poultry truck and arrive at the North Miami train station in order to make it appear they came by rail. When they are met by Ricky and Fred, who have been enjoying a fishing vacation, the girls try to explain how they arrived two hours before the train . . . and without tickets, which were safely tucked away in Little Ricky's wallet.

"Deep Sea Fishing"; #1050/160; November 19, 1956.

When Lucy and Ethel return from a shopping spree after spending $140 (plus tax), the husbands decide to take them on their next fishing trip to keep them out of the Eden Roc Hotel boutiques. It will be men versus women as to who will catch the largest fish; the wager—$150. To nail down their victory, Lucy and Ethel buy a one-hundred-pound tuna at a local fish market and plan to hide it in the Ricardos' (room 919) bathtub. Unbeknown to the scheming females, Ricky and Fred also have purchased a tuna of equal size to assure their conquest. At the end of a madcap routine, which finds each team trying to hide its "catch," the nefarious doings are exposed. With the bet still in force, the Ricardos (including Little Ricky) and Mertzes embark on a day of deep-sea fishing in the Atlantic. After a long, exhausting afternoon, the only one who's caught anything is Little Ricky. Suddenly, Lucy gets a nibble . . . followed closely by a bite on Ricky's hook. Ricky's pole goes overboard and he dives in after it, only to be reeled in by his wife. When the five fishermen discover that there is a fish lodged in Ricky's jacket, Lucy claims she won the wager because she "caught" Ricky and, hence, the fish.

"Desert Island"; #1050/161; November 26, 1956.

When Lucy and Ethel learn that their husbands have been chosen to judge a Miami Beach bathing beauty contest, they devise a scheme to keep them from officiating. Lucy instructs the dock attendant to fill the gas tank on their boat only halfway so that their precontest cruise will abort in the middle of the ocean. Then, when it's too late for the husbands to attend the contest, Lucy will "discover" a Thermos of gasoline, just enough to get them back to shore. But while the gals are stocking up on suntan oil, Fred discovers the dangerous, gas-filled Thermos and leaves it on the dock. Sure enough, when the time comes to turn back for the beauty contest, the motor sputters and stops. The boat eventually drifts ashore on a seemingly deserted island. Lucy and Ethel go off to explore one part of the terrain, and the husbands and Little Ricky take off in the opposite direction. The men encounter actor Claude Akins who's dressed as a fierce, war-painted Indian, and two bathing beauties (Joi Lansing and Jil Jarmyn) who are filming a documentary about Florida. To teach Lucy a lesson after the gasoline incident, Ricky enlists Akins in a plot to scare the bejesus out of the girls. While Lucy and Ethel are lamenting over their state, along comes ferocious Akins, pretending to be an uncivilized native warrior. When the wives have been sufficiently frightened, Ricky and Fred appear and explain the truth about Akins and the island. Lucy is deflated further when she later learns that the beauty contest has been postponed until the next day.

"The Ricardos Visit Cuba"; #1050/162; December 3, 1956; with Mary Emery, Betty LeBaron, Barbara Logan.

The Ricardos and Mertzes fly to Cuba for a visit with Ricky's relatives and for the bandleader's two-day engagement at the Hotel National's Casino Parisien. Lucy is wary of meeting her in-laws, especially the formidable head of the Ricardo clan, Uncle Alberto. Ricky assures her that all will go well: "Make sure you say *muchas gracias* to Uncle Alberto all the time. He likes that." Lucy is a nervous wreck at the reunion where nothing seems to go right for her. When Uncle Alberto (George Trevino) asks her where she got her beautiful red hair, Lucy replies: "Oh, I get it about every two weeks." She then proceeds to spill punch on his white jacket, rip his straw hat to shreds, and destroy a pocketful of rare Cuban cigars. But when she mispronounces *muchas gracias,* calling the patriarchal uncle "a fat pig" instead, Lucy feels like a doomed woman. Lamenting the next day, she says: "After what I did last night, Cuba might cut off America's sugar supply!" To take her mind off family relations, she goes souvenir-shopping while her husband and son rehearse for their nightclub appearance. Determined to make up for the Uncle Alberto fiasco, Lucy buys him a box of his favorite cigars, Corona Grandos. Finding herself short of cash, she promises the tobacco store owner (Nacho Galindo) that she will return with the extra funds later. An argument develops, made worse by the entrance of Alberto Ricardo himself. To avoid him, Lucy dons a big hat and apron, and proceeds to roll cigars like her co-worker (Angelo Didio). After completing a foot-long stogie, Lucy retreats. The night of the big performance, Ricky sings "A Lucky Guy," then introduces Little Ricky and together they perform "Babalu." Proud Uncle Alberto leans over to Lucy and comments: "Anyone who is the mother of a boy like that is all right with me."

"Little Ricky's School Pageant"; #1050/163; December 17, 1956.

Little Ricky's kindergarten class runs short of cast members for its annual play, and the Ricardos and Mertzes are drafted. Although Ricky expected to be chosen as the play's producer and director (Clifford Terry, who runs an orange juice stand, got that job), he is given the part of a hollow tree. Lucy is to portray the wicked old witch of the forest, Fred will essay the role of Hippity-Hoppity, the friendly frog, and Ethel is lucky enough to cop the coveted Fairy Princess part (only because she fits the costume worn last year by Jimmy Wilson's mother). The Ricardos become concerned when Little Ricky is chosen to play the boy lead; they don't know whether he can handle the responsibility and pressure. But certain that they and the Mertzes will be close-by, Lucy and Ricky cease worrying. The pageant opens with young Suzy (Candy Rogers) reading to Billy—Little Ricky—from a storybook entitled *The Enchanted Forest*. The mini-production goes well, despite Little Ricky forgetting some of his lines, and all are glad when the finale featuring over thirty little children comes to a close.

"Lucy and the Loving Cup"; #1050/164; January 7, 1957; with Hazel Longden, Jesslyn Fax, Sandra Gould, Phil Tead.

After Ricky pokes fun at Lucy's new hat, she jokingly puts on a loving cup he had planned to present to jockey Johnny Longden at a National Turf Association dinner. The problem is that Lucy can't get the trophy off her head. Ethel suggests a silversmith, but the man refuses to make a house call. Wearing a veil over the loving cup in an effort to disguise it, Lucy and Ethel board a Lexington Avenue IRT subway train and, of course, elicit more than their share of stares from the rush-hour crowds. When the pair prepares to transfer at the Bleecker Street station, Lucy gets caught in the pushing melee and is shoved back into the car. Assuming that she, like Ethel, has got off the train, Lucy asks a stranger: "Pardon me, sir, can you tell me where the stairs are?" New Yorker: "You have to get off the train first." Lucy: "I *am* off." New Yorker: "You're telling me!" Lucy's veil accidentally comes loose and she tries to act nonchalant with the loving cup still stuck on her head. The scenes depicting Lucy "reading" a newspaper, hoping to look inconspicuous, are hilarious. She finally manages to exit at Flatbush Avenue (the end of the line) whereupon a crowd gathers. Lucy explains her plight to a cop (Robert Foulk) who, dismissing his urge to take her straight to Bellevue, is nice enough to accompany her to the Johnny Longden banquet where Ricky has been waiting patiently for the arrival of the loving cup. Finally, Ricky presents the award to the champion jockey with Lucy still attached to it.

(NOTE: During the summer of 1955, Desi Arnaz optioned Johnny Longden's life story for a possible motion picture, which was never made.)

261

"Lucy and Superman"; #1050/166; January 14, 1957; with Madge Blake, Ralph Dumke, George O'Hanlon.

Lucy is planning Little Ricky's fifth birthday party for Saturday, the same day that Caroline Appleby (Doris Singleton) has arranged a birthday shindig for her son Stevie. Each affair has the same guest list and neither mother wants to change the day of her affair. Caroline has hired a clown and magician, and even plans to stage a puppet show —hard acts for Lucy to top. Suddenly, however, Mrs. Ricardo remembers that Superman (George Reeves) is in town, and she asks Ricky to invite him to Little Ricky's party. Without waiting for a confirmation, Lucy phones Appleby and announces that Superman is coming to her gathering. Firmly defeated, Caroline cancels her party plans. When Ricky is unable to corral the "Man of Steel," Lucy laments: "If I don't produce Superman, my name will be Supermud." She is left with no choice but to impersonate the comic strip hero. Donning a football helmet, ill-fitting tights, and a flowing cape, she climbs out on the ledge while Little Ricky's party is in full swing. When she is about to make her grand entrance through the living room window, who should show up but the "real" Superman who makes a dashing leap into the room through the louver windows of the kitchen. The party guests are thrilled, and so is Lucy. But much to her chagrin, she finds she has been locked out on the ledge just when a rain storm commences. Who comes to her rescue? Superman, of course, who comments to Ricky: "You mean to say that you've been married to her for fifteen years? . . . And they call *me* Superman!"

"Little Ricky Gets a Dog"; #1050/165; January 21, 1957.

Animal lover Little Ricky has turned the Ricardo apartment into a miniature zoo with frogs, turtles, goldfish, a parakeet, lizard, and now a puppy, thanks to the generosity of little Billy Palmer. Lucy says the puppy must go, but her feelings quickly change when the doggie showers her with friendly kisses. When Daddy arrives home from the club and learns of the recent addition to his family, he heads straight for Little Ricky's room intending to evict the dog. Moments later, Ricky returns from the boy's room. Lucy: "Where are you going, dear?" Ricky: "To the basement to get a box." Landlord Mertz appers and demands: "That pooch has got to go!" But when he learns that Little Ricky has named the new pet Fred, he heads for the basement to prepare a proper throne for his namesake. After a sleepless night caused by Fred's yelping, a grouchy new tenant, Mr. Stewart (John Emery), confronts Lucy, demanding to see for himself whether or not there is a dog being harbored on the no-pets-allowed premises. She denies the presence of any canine, so when Stewart spies some dog biscuits, Lucy claims they belong to her and proceeds to munch one. The disagreeable tenant makes life miserable for everyone, until Fred Mertz puts his foot down: "I'd rather live with a little dog than a big grouch!" Stewart storms out with plans to move. When Ethel reminds her loyal husband that he has just kissed away $250, Fred promptly faints.

"Lucy Wants to Move to the Country"; #1050/167; January 28, 1957.

Fed up with the dirty city, Lucy wants the fresh air and sunshine of suburban life for her family. To exaggerate her case, she moves all the living room furniture together to give the apartment a cramped appearance and sprinkles talcum powder on the mantel to simulate dust. She even powders her face to accentuate her city pallor. Ricky takes the Mertzes into his confidence and breaks the news that he has already put down a deposit of $500 on a house in Connecticut, as a sixteenth wedding anniversary surprise for his wife. When Lucy sees Ethel's eyes filling with tears, the news is spilled. Now Lucy never wants to move away from the Mertzes. Amid the tears and turmoil, Ricky attempts to get back his deposit, but the money will only be returned if the owners find the buyers unsuitable. Lucy and the Mertzes hatch a scheme, guaranteed to yield the $500. They arrive at the Westport, Connecticut, home of Joe and Eleanor Spaulding (Frank Wilcox and Eleanor Audley) dressed as gangsters. Lucy plays a brash, gum-chewing, purse-slinging gun-moll type; Fred looks like a fugitive from the senior citizens' chapter of the Hell's Angels; and Ethel resembles the madam at a discount bordello. Just then, Ricky enters, unaware of the goings-on. He tries to explain to the Spauldings that his wife and friends have only good intentions in mind. Reluctantly, the homeowners return Ricky's deposit. But as Lucy takes a closer look at the warm, homey surroundings, she changes her mind about staying in the city, and the Ricardos become the proud owners of a home in the suburbs.

"Lucy Hates to Leave"; #1050/168; February 4, 1957.

Ricky is losing sleep over the prospect of being a homeowner. He laments: "Do you realize how many times I'm going to have to sing 'Babalu' to pay for that house?" Lucy tries to reassure her husband by calling his paranoia "a bad case of homeowner's heebie-jeebies." A twenty-year mortgage and the thought of buying a houseful of new furniture enters his mind: "Maybe I can get a hit record or something." Fred tears up the Ricardos' ninety-nine-year lease, then asks permission to show their 3-D apartment to some prospective tenants, a young married couple, the Taylors. The couple agrees to rent the flat with the stipulation that they be permitted to move in immediately. The Ricardos kindly agree to vacate four days early and move in with the Mertzes. Since Lucy and Ricky have decided to sell their old furniture to the young couple, there won't be much stuff cluttering Fred and Ethel's apartment before the move to Connecticut. However, when Lucy finds out that the Taylors have plans to cut off the legs on the coffee table, she gets sentimental about her belongings and refuses to part with them. Suddenly, the Mertz abode looks like a warehouse and living under such cramped conditions becomes unbearable for the five friends. To make matters worse, the Spauldings phone with the news that their move has been delayed two weeks. The Ricardos will be unable to take possession of their new home in Connecticut until then.

"Lucy Misses the Mertzes"; #1050/169; February 11, 1957.

After fifteen years of being together, the Ricardos and Mertzes must finally part. They exchange keys and tearful good-byes. After Ricky carries his wife over the threshold of the Conecticut house, a big basket of fruit—a housewarming gift from the Mertzes—arrives. Lucy contends that they must have been really upset and sad. Ricky: "For Fred to spend ten dollars on a basket of fruit, he must have been hysterical!" That night, with Little Ricky spending the night with his new friend Billy, the Ricardos become lonely. Suddenly, they get the idea to take the train into Manhattan and surprise the Mertzes. At the same time, the Mertzes decide to take the train to Westport to surprise the Ricardos. But when Ricky arrives at the railroad station and tries to contact Fred and Ethel by phone, he naturally doesn't find them at home. Disappointed, the new suburbanites return home and go to bed. The Mertzes make it to Connecticut, but Fred refuses to spend any more money (he's already forked out $8.16) on taxis and he insists they walk to the Ricardos'. When they find the house dark, they open the front door with the key Lucy gave them and make themselves at home. The Ricardos are awakened by the noise downstairs and suspect a burglar. After some confusion, the four friends are reunited and enjoying the basket of fruit . . . especially Fred.

"Lucy Gets Chummy with the Neighbors"; #1050/170; February 18, 1957; with Ray Ferrell.

When Lucy determines that her old furniture doesn't quite fit into its new setting, she asks Ricky if she can replace it. He says she can, but allows her to spend only $500. New neighbor Betty Ramsey (Mary Jane Croft) informs Lucy that she can get a forty percent discount at Mr. Perry's (Parley Baer) furniture store. There, Lucy buys new sofas, new chairs, new lamps, new tables, new everything . . . to the shocking tune of $3,272.75. Lucy is so afraid of Ricky's Cuban temper that she phones the Mertzes in New York and pleads with them to take the first train to Westport to protect her from the flak. Sure enough, when Ricky returns from New York and sees the overabundance of new furniture, he hits the ceiling, then demands that she return all but $500 worth. When Lucy tries to make an excuse for not wanting the new items (she says she'd prefer Chinese Modern), Betty Ramsey, who selected them, becomes insulted. Ricky decides to solve the problem himself by having a man-to-man talk with Betty's husband, Ralph (Frank Nelson). At first, Ralph flatters Ricky by offering him a TV gig. This, of course, makes Ricky's task a little more difficult. When he winds up giving Ramsey the impression that Mrs.

Ramsey's taste in furniture leaves something to be desired, the new neighbor is ruffled. Ramsey: "Forget about the TV show. We'll get Cugat!" Enter the Mertzes who break up the unneighborly feud by explaining to the Ramseys that the Ricardos simply cannot afford the new furnishings. The Ramseys understand, and Ralph offers Ricky that TV job again that will pay $3,500 . . . just enough to pay for Lucy's extravagance.

"Lucy Raises Chickens"; #1050/171; March 4, 1957.

Betty Ramsey (Mary Jane Croft) has good news—*House and Garden* magazine wants to do a picture layout on the Ricardos' home; Ricky has bad news—the bills are piling up and he's slowly going broke. Lucy suggests they raise chickens to bring in a little extra money. Very little investment is required, Lucy reasons: "What can a little grain cost . . . fifty cents? That's chicken feed." Ricky advertises for an experienced couple who can care for the chickens in return for a percentage of the profits, and who should answer the ad—the Mertzes. Fred's poultry experience: "For the past twenty-five years, I've been henpecked!" Counting their chickens before they're hatched (literally), Lucy and Ethel buy five hundred baby chicks before Fred has a chance to finish the required chicken coup. In the meantime, it is imperative that the chicks be kept warm, so they place the creatures in the den and turn up the heat to ninety degrees. When they return from the kitchen after a well-deserved snack, they find that Little Ricky has accidentally left open the den door, and the baby chicks are crawling all over the house. While everyone is frantically corralling the birds, the *House and Garden* editors arrive. Unimpressed, they depart. The Ricardos don't mind—maybe next month they'll make the *Chicken Breeders' Gazette.*

"Lucy Does the Tango"; #1050/172; March 11, 1957.

Discouraged by the baby chicks' rate of growth, the Ricardos and Mertzes exchange their five hundred little birds for two hundred laying hens, guaranteed to produce salable eggs. After the first two weeks, the hens have laid exactly six eggs and, by calculation, that's $18 per egg. Ricky is disgusted with the whole enterprise and gives the hens one more day to shape up. Ricky: "I should have raised something I knew about, like sugar cane." Deciding to improve on Mother Nature, the gals buy five-dozen eggs at the market, intending to place them in the nests. On their way to the henhouse with the bogus yolks, they spot Fred. In an attempt to hide the sixty eggs, Lucy and Ethel quickly stuff them in their blouses, pockets, and shirts. When they've crammed the last one out of sight, Ricky comes home, wanting to rehearse with Lucy the tango routine for the upcoming PTA show. All goes smoothly until the final spin lands Lucy in Ricky's arms, eggs first. When he learns of the deception, he intends to get out of the egg business immediately. However, Little Ricky (Richard Keith) and his friend Bruce

Ramsey (Ray Ferrell) have grown so fond of the hens, they decide to hide them so Mr. Ricardo can't get rid of them. The next day when Ricky is about to round up his lazy brood, the chickens are nowhere in sight. Finding a,few in the Mertzes' closet, Ricky accuses Fred of being a chicken thief. A battle results and continues until Betty Ramsey phones, informing the feuding foursome that she has found chickens all over her house. Little Ricky confesses just as Bruce arrives with a basket brimming with freshly laid eggs. The Ricardos and Mertzes are back in the egg business.

(NOTE: The tango/eggs routine resulted in the longest laugh ever recorded on *I Love Lucy*—sixty-five seconds.)

"Ragtime Band"; #1050/173; March 18, 1957.

After Lucy volunteers Ricky's musical services for a Westport Historical Society benefit without consulting him first, he refuses to participate. But Lucy's promised an appearance by Ricky Ricardo and she intends to carry through. Ricky Ricardo, Jr., will be the stellar attraction. She decides to organize her own little orchestra with her son on the drums, Ethel at the piano, Lucy tooting her saxophone, and Fred playing his fiddle. Ethel: "The last time he played was three chins ago." Their first rehearsal is a disaster—Ethel knows only one song, "She'll Be Comin' 'Round the Mountain," and Lucy knows only one, "Sweet Sue" [What happened to "Glow Worm"?]. When Ricky agrees to listen to the ensemble and give his honest opinion of their talents, he decides to save his reputation as an orchestra leader by lending the combo some of his own musicians. At the benefit, Ricky sings "The Woman Is Smarter" while the others support him with calypso-flavored sounds.

"Lucy's Night in Town"; #1050/174; March 25, 1957; with Louis A. Nicoletti, Joseph Kearns, Jody Warner, Robert G. Carroll, Jr.

In Manhattan for the evening, the Ricardos and Mertzes are enjoying dinner before their theater date to see Frank Loesser's musical, *The Most Happy Fella*. When Lucy checks her purse for the tickets (sixth row center, orchestra, row F, seats 104, 105, 106, and 107), she makes the horrifying discovery that they were for the matinee. Lucy tells a distraught Ethel: "Well, at least I didn't forget them. You have to admit that." The gals try their darndest to eat slowly in hopes of being so late to the Imperial Theatre that they miss the show. Lucy insists on chewing each mouthful of food twenty-five times and even intends to peel every lima bean. When Lucy's mistake is exposed, Ricky tries to buy four new tickets, but is able to obtain only two box seats. To be fair, the women will get to see the first act, and the men will see the second act. At intermission, Lucy and Ethel inform their husbands that the two seats behind them were unoccupied during the first act; therefore, all four of them can enjoy the remaining half. As luck would have it, the two ticket-holders arrive, and the girls must relinquish the seats to them, before squeezing in next to their husbands. This causes so much confusion that Ethel's purse containing $500 in cash (apartment house rent receipts) flies off the balcony and lands in the orchestra section. By the time the donnybrook is unraveled, the musical has ended.

(NOTE: Several songs from the original cast album of *The Most Happy Fella* were heard, including "Standing On the Corner.")

"Housewarming"; #1050/175; April 1, 1957; with Frank Nelson.

The Mertzes feel left out when the Ricardos invite only the Munsens, Baileys, and Ramseys to a dinner party. Ethel, in particular, has become envious of Lucy's friendship with Betty Ramsey (Mary Jane Croft). Sensing her friend's hurt feelings, Lucy sets up a nice luncheon for the three gals. Still jealous, Ethel barely opens her mouth during the tête-à-tête. But when Betty casually mentions that she was born in Albuquerque, New Mexico—Ethel's hometown—the two women become inseparable. Now Lucy is jealous of the Betty-Ethel alliance: "Ever since they had lunch here, they've been as thick as thieves. What's so hot all of a sudden about being born in Albuquerque? I could have been born there myself if my parents didn't live in Jamestown!" When Lucy happens to overhear the tag end of a conversation between Betty and Ethel through the newly installed intercom system (connecting the main house with the Mertzes' cottage), she jumps to the conclusion that the pair is planning a surprise housewarming party for the Ricardos and that's why they've been so preoccupied lately. That night, Lucy convinces Ricky to dress to the nines and to expect a barrage of friends to burst through the door any moment. After hours of waiting, no one shows up. Lucy must have been mistaken, and she whimpers to Ricky that they have no friends. Through the same intercom, Ethel hears Lucy crying and, realizing the problem, quickly organizes a surprise housewarming party.

"Building a Bar-B-Q"; #1050/176; April 8, 1957; with Richard Keith.

Ricky's on vacation and he's driving Lucy crazy just hanging around the house. She suggests: "Honey, why don't you call up little Freddie Mertz and ask him to come over and play?" Discussing his idleness with Ethel, Lucy realizes that her husband needs a project to keep him busy. How about that brick barbecue he's been promising to build on the patio? Ethel: "Why don't you do what I do with Fred when I want him to do something? I start it, and when he sees I'm doing it all wrong, he takes over." Ethel's suggestion works like a charm—when Ricky and Fred see the gals slinging bricks and cement everywhere, they agree to do the job. In the midst of the project, Ricky discovers Lucy's wedding ring precariously near the bucket of cement. To teach her a lesson, he decides not to tell her he found it. It doesn't take Mrs. Ricardo long to realize the ring is missing from her finger and when she traces her steps back to the fireplace project, she immediately assumes the ring is in the cement mixture holding together the barbecue bricks. Late that night, she and Ethel converge on the patio and proceed to tear the new structure apart brick by brick. Ethel: "It's times like these when I wish I kept a diary so I could write, 'Dear diary, Tonight I went out to the backyard and felt through wet cement.' " When Ricky sees the travesty the next morning, he hits the ceiling. When Lucy explains the truth, Ricky accepts the blame, telling Lucy that her wedding ring can be found in the pocket of his old work shirt. But Lucy gave the old duds to Ethel for a rag, who in turn gave it to Fred, who gave it to Little Ricky to use as a tail for his kite . . . which just flew away. Heartbroken, Lucy can't enjoy the first hamburger cooked on the new grill: "How can I eat when my wedding ring is somewhere over the Long Island Sound?" As she takes a reluctant bite of her burger, she discovers the ring inside. It had fallen from Ricky's pocket the day before when he bent over to pick up the platter of meat.

"Country Club Dance"; #1050/177; April 22, 1957.

At a club dance, Ricky, Fred, and Ralph Ramsey (Frank Nelson) are smitten with Harry and Grace Munsen's cousin Diana Jordan (Barbara Eden), a sultry blond, much to their wives' collective disgust. The next day Lucy, Ethel, and Betty Ramsey (Mary Jane Croft) are discussing the "spectacle." It seems that Ricky danced with Diana nine times, Ralph eight, and Fred thirteen. They all have been invited to a party the Munsens are giving in Diana's honor, but this time the gals are going to doll themselves up so that their husbands will not even notice the Jordan girl. Lucy will wear her tightest dress, Betty will sport her most exotic perfume, and Ethel will do her hair up like Grace Kelly. Noticing something strange, the husbands decide to play along with the wives that evening. At the gathering, the guys bend over backward trying to be nice to their wives. Ricky's "strange" behavior prompts Lucy to crack: "When you're this sweet, there's something rotten in Cuba." She gathers up her female cohorts and departs. Later that night, the husbands confess that Pat Boone-crazy Diana is too young for them, and they return to their understanding wives.

"Lucy Raises Tulips"; #1050/178; April 29, 1957; with Richard Keith.

Lucy is itching to cop first prize for the "Best Looking Garden" in Westport, Connecticut, and spends every waking moment tending to her beautiful patch of tulips. She is determined to dethrone Betty Ramsey (Mary Jane Croft) who has won the coveted Garden Club award three years in a row. Much to her dismay, Ricky has mowed only half the lawn before taking off for a Yankee ball game. This means she must complete the job if her garden is to look just right. Seating herself on the bulky machine, Lucy takes off . . . and is unable to stop. After upsetting downtown Westport, she manages somehow to mow down Betty Ramsey's tulip beds. Lucy: "I feel just rotten about it." Ethel: "Well, you could give her your tulips." Lucy: "Ethel, I feel rotten, but not *that* rotten!" Lucy replaces the mowed-down flowers with wax tulips she bought at the Village Gift Shop. When the Garden Club judges disqualify Betty's fake flowers, they proceed next door to evaluate Lucy's collection. It seems that Lucy's tulips are wax, too—the result of Ricky mowing the lawn in the dark —and they're slowly melting in the warm New England sun.

"The Ricardos Dedicate a Statue"; #1050/179; May 6, 1957.

It's Yankee Doodle Day in Westport, Connecticut, and the patriotic townspeople are about to unveil a monument to their Revolutionary War ancestors. For the accompanying pageant, Fred has been tapped as the town crier and Ricky has been chosen to give the dedication speech at the unveiling ceremony. Lucy is showing Ethel the beautiful stone sculpture of a patriot kneeling with a musket, when suddenly Little Ricky announces that his dog Fred has run away again. Lucy jumps in the family station wagon (Ford) and, forgetting about the attached trailer holding the statue, takes off. A few moments later we hear a terrible crash; the one-of-a-kind statue is in pieces. Desperate, Lucy contacts Mr. Sylvestri, the sculptor, who wonders why Lucy wants a second statue. Lucy: "Why? . . . Well, Westport is growing and may become twin cities like Minnepaul and St. Apolis." A replacement will take two weeks to prepare. Lucy has a better idea. At the ceremony, after Ricky gives his speech, the statue is unveiled. Dressed as a Minuteman, impersonating the sculpture, is Lucy. She goes undetected until Fred the dog decides to lick the patriot's face. Stone figures don't laugh.

(NOTE: The ceremony crowd scene featured the real-life Arnaz children—Lucie, five and a half and Desi IV, four—the only time they appeared on *I Love Lucy*.)

269

Index

Page numbers in italics indicate photographs